To Sue with all my love, J

A Dean's Diary

D0539775

A Dean's Diary

Winchester 1987–1996

Trevor Beeson

SCM PRESS LTD

All rights reserved. No part of this publication may be
reproduced, stored in a retrieval system, or transmitted,
in any form or by any means, electronic, mechanical,
photocopying or otherwise, without the prior permission
of the publisher, SCM Press Ltd.

© Copyright Trevor Beeson 1997

0 334 02754 3

First published 1997 by
SCM Press Ltd
9–17 St Albans Place London N1 0NX

First paperback edition 1998

Typeset at The Spartan Press Ltd,
Lymington, Hants
Printed in Great Britain by
Biddles Ltd, Guildford and King's Lynn

Contents

Preface

During the last thirty years the English cathedrals, uniquely in Europe, have been transformed from Barchester-like places of ease into lively centres of Christian mission. Today they flourish as never before and, surprisingly perhaps in an era of general decline in church-going, offer a wide variety of expressions of religious faith and practice to the multitudes who converge on them from near and far.

My own appointment to Winchester in 1987 coincided with the emergence in that great cathedral of a number of problems and opportunities. Money as well as mission provided an urgent imperative for change and the following selections from my diary are offered as evidence of how a nine-year period of considerable change and development was experienced by its Dean. I cannot pretend that my record of those hectic years is infallibly accurate, but I do say, 'This is how it seemed to me at the time'.

Cathedrals and their closes offer fertile ground to the novelist, but often enough the facts about contemporary life in these ancient institutions are stranger than the fiction. This is due partly to the rich variety of personality and talent attracted to them, but chiefly to the fact that the statutes by which they are governed belong to the world of the sixteenth and seventeenth centuries and are administratively inappropriate to the needs of the present time. Space for individualism and eccentricity must always be found in any civilized community and certainly in a Christian church. But the price of this can be too high and a cathedral is not exempt from the managerial requirements of any large organization. Reform is urgently needed.

The How? and Why? of appointments to cathedral deaneries – still in the patronage of the Crown – belongs to the realm of unnatural knowledge. On the day following my involvement in the wedding of the Duke and Duchess of York in Westminster Abbey, when I was nursing a painful back caused by long hours of standing in heavy robes, I answered my door bell in the Little Cloister at about 5.00 pm and was handed a long white envelope marked 'Personal' and stamped 'First Lord of the Treasury'. Inside were two smaller envelopes – one marked 'Prime

Minister' and containing a letter topped and tailed by the Iron Lady:

10 Downing Street

My dear Canon Beeson,

As you will be aware, the Very Reverend Michael Stancliffe is resigning from the Deanery of Winchester on 1 October 1986, and it is my duty to nominate a successor to Her Majesty The Queen.

After taking appropriate advice and having considered the needs of Winchester with great care, it would give me great pleasure to put forward your name for this appointment if you are agreeable that I should do so. My Appointments Secretary will be in touch with you on procedural matters.

I very much hope that you will accept my proposal which I would ask you to regard as being in the strictest confidence.

Yours sincerely,
Margaret Thatcher

The other letter was from the Appointments Secretary, Robin (now Sir Robin) Catford, offering any help I might need in considering the Prime Minister's suggestion. Until this moment I was totally unaware that my name had been under consideration.

Back in 1951 when I was ordained in Durham Cathedral by Bishop Alwyn Williams, himself a former Headmaster of Winchester College and destined soon to return to Winchester as its Bishop, any suggestion that I might one day be invited to go to England's ancient capital as Dean would have been regarded as absurd. The Dean at that time was E.G.Selwyn, a New Testament scholar of international repute, and he was succeeded by Norman Sykes, an equally distinguished church historian.

My own non-Oxbridge background, training and inclination pointed clearly to ministries in tough, working-class parishes in the North of England. Which is where I spent the next fourteen years, first in a coal-mining village near Consett, then in a large new council-housing estate in Stockton-on-Tees. These suited me well and in them I discerned the urgency of Christian mission in post-war Britain and of the need for radical change in the churches to facilitate such a mission.

Unexpectedly, a decade of writing and broadcasting followed and, when the demands of this proved to be incompatible with the pastoral needs of the Hertfordshire country-town parish which I was also serving, the then Prime Minister, Harold Wilson, was prevailed upon to appoint me to a canonry at Westminster Abbey. These canonries had often provided convenient bases from which priests could serve the wider church.

I arrived at Westminster just too late to take advantage of such a sinecure. The Abbey had started to respond to the opportunities created by the growth in mass tourism and was also trying to deal with acute financial problems arising from the first Middle East oil crisis. Within a year I had, for want of another candidate, been appointed Treasurer and in 1982 I exchanged this office for the even more demanding role of Rector of St Margaret's Church and Chaplain to the Speaker of the House of Commons.

Margaret Thatcher's letter put me in a dilemma. On the one hand, my ministries in the Abbey, St Margaret's and the House of Commons had some national significance and were, so I was told, deeply appreciated and not to be compared with anything I might accomplish in a cathedral in deepest Hampshire. On the other hand, I was well nigh exhausted by the struggle to combine three very demanding jobs and could hardly expect to survive the stress for much longer.

So after careful thought and consultation with a few trusted friends, virtually all of whom thought I should stay in Westminster, I took the plunge and went to Winchester. And I never – or at least only rarely – regretted this decision. The task turned out to be quite unlike anything I had anticipated. The possibility that it might be a 'put out to grass' appointment in which an exhausted priest could recover his breath and even begin to write again was quickly dispelled. A previously obscured financial crisis soon emerged to demand speedy remedial action and the large number of laity associated with the Cathedral were looking to the new Dean to stir their sleeping giant into life.

All of which accorded closely with my own inner inclination and missionary vision, and this diary tells the rest of the story. There is a danger, however, that, like the television 'highlights' of a Test Match and a Cup Final, the picture here presented may be misleading inasmuch as it concentrates on unusual and decisive action at the expense of the normal, routine background from which the action springs.

This background includes three or more acts of worship every day of every year. Most of these involve the Cathedral community and visitors, but a significant number relate to the life of the church in the Diocese and to the needs and aspirations of the whole Hampshire community. A staff of 70 and over 600 volunteers are involved in an accompanying ministry of welcome and pastoral care and in a programme of conservation and care of one of Europe's finest buildings. Only rarely do any of these people and their activities merit a diary entry, but they form the essence of the Cathedral's life and witness.

Another substantial omission, dictated by the need to keep this volume to a manageable size, relates to my activities beyond the bounds of the Cathedral. The Dean has responsibilities and opportunities in the wider church and community which are an important element in his ministry. The Diocese – of which the Cathedral is the mother church – has an obvious claim, and a good deal of time was spent in meetings of various sorts, as well as in preaching and lecturing in the parishes. I was thankful never to be elected to the General Synod – a necessary part of the Church of England's life but one in which talk has priority over action.

Chairmanship of the governing body of The Pilgrims' School, where the choristers and 150 other boys are educated, and of the King's College, London Theological Trust were enterprises that demanded a certain amount of time, as did involvement in the civic life of the City and the County. Winchester's deep historical roots still give the Dean a place in the life of Hampshire which I believed it to be important to accept and use.

The Presidency of the Trinity Centre, which undertakes vital work among social misfits and drop-outs, kept me aware that not all of Winchester's citizens are highly privileged, and the Chairmanship of Christian Action, founded in 1947 by John Collins, Stafford Cripps and others to express Christian values in the social and poltical life of the nation, also ensured regular contact with aspects of the Christian mission which have always been important to me and which might otherwise have been submerged by the incessant demands of the Cathedral.

Nothing of any of this can be published here, but space must be found for the contribution made by my wife, Jo, who for our first five years greatly enjoyed her role as mistress of one of England's most splendid deaneries. But then came the dehumanizing Alzheimer's disease. Initially the changes in her outlook and behaviour were perceptible only to me and to our two married daughters, but gradually the pace of decline accelerated until she could remember nothing from the immediate past, was incapable of dressing herself, and found it impossible to cope with the geography of a large house. Conversation was reduced to the simplest of subjects and concepts, though she continued happily to attend the Cathedral services and many other events in the Close and City.

Inevitably the pattern of my own life changed as I sought to care both for Jo and for the Cathedral, and I cannot say that this was easy. But there were, as always, some good and ameliorating elements in this experience. Most important was Jo's own unawareness of the horror of her condition.

Loss of memory and lack of full perception provided her with a high degree of protection from stress and, as far as I could ever tell, any significant suffering.

Once the facts concerning her condition became known, the Cathedral community offered a measure of practical, psychological and spiritual support so generous that I was able to continue in office until the scheduled day of my retirement. Almost one year later death came to her as a friend and liberator and in a crowded Cathedral we thanked God for one who had made a great impact for good on others simply by being her own humble, loving, unpretentious self – a necessary complement and corrective to the ministry of an ever hyper-active Dean.

To have been Dean of Winchester for nine years was a great privilege as well as a heavy responsibility and I never fully believed that I was holding this historic office. Yet the mission of a cathedral, however great and glorious, is not essentially different from that of the church in a coal-mining village or a council-house estate. Everywhere the call is to worship God, to proclaim the greatness of God's love, and to mediate God's love to others through compassion and care. That is the only yardstick of Christian success.

My deepest gratitude is due to all those who accepted and responded to my leadership and my best thanks go to Esmé Parker, my former secretary, who typed the manuscript with her customary efficiency and good-humoured forbearance.

TB

1987

At last the move into the Deanery is completed. It has been a mammoth, exhausting business extending over five days, and carried out in the heaviest snow for some years. At the Westminster end everything had to be carried quite a long distance from the Little Cloister to the Poets' Corner entrance, opposite Parliament – the nearest access point for removal vans – and here at Winchester the impossibility of getting the vans through the low mediaeval gateway to the Close meant that all the furniture had to be transferred to the house in a small van. The performance of the contractors has, I must say, been exemplary and I suspect they have used the job for prestige publicity purposes because two photographers were in attendance throughout the move.

The Deanery is extraordinary. It dates back to about 1250 and until 1538 was the Lodging of the Prior of the Benedictine monastery; in fact the last Prior, William Kingsmill, stayed on as the first Dean, so he did not move out. The fine dining hall was modified in the 1660s to provide an upper storey for bedrooms and these now have the benefit of the magnificent timber roof constructed in 1359.

The study is a beautiful long gallery built in 1673 for the use of Charles II and said to be the scene of a confrontation between the King and the then Dean, William Clarke, who returned unexpectedly from a long stay in London and ordered Nell Gwynn out of the Deanery. When the house underwent certain modifications in the late 1960s what was known as the King's bedroom became the kitchen, to the great distress of some local historians who protested to my predecessor. Michael Stancliffe pointed out to them, however, that since it was no longer possible to employ servants the kitchen needed to be in a convenient place, and in any case he felt the memory of Charles II's bedroom ought not to be preserved in a Christian deanery.

Although the house is magnificent and of considerable historical importance, it is obviously going to present some problems. Already it has absorbed a great deal of money, for it has few 'official' furnishings; the

Treasurer says the Dean and Chapter has no funds available for the purpose and the maximum grant payable by the Church Commissioners is no more than about £1,500. Since the main bedroom alone has required 75 square yards of carpet this will not go very far, and it is fortunate that Jo recently had a legacy of £7,000 which she is prepared to use on the house.

Another urgent problem concerns the telephone. Michael Stancliffe, who was really a contemplative, would not have the external line linked to the study. So whenever the telephone rings I must sprint about thirty yards to the receiver in the kitchen, by which time the caller has rung off, naturally believing that I am not at home. I must do something about this, but the telephone engineers are now on strike and it looks as if it will be some time before a settlement is reached. Meanwhile, I will introduce television into the house and get an aerial erected – something that looks as if it may be rather expensive because of the environmental factor.

These, and the intense cold, are minor irritations that will pass. Having been given the privilege of living in such a wonderful house we had better enjoy it, rather than grumble about it. I hope it may be possible to turn all the space to good use.

Thursday 22 January 1987

Although I am not yet the Dean, I made my first public appearance in the Cathedral today – drawn there by the demands of television. Harry Secombe, a well known actor and penetrating tenor, is presenting an edition of *Highway*, a popular Sunday evening hymn-singing programme, from Winchester and wished to interview the Dean.

It was all quite straightforward. I remarked to the gathering of Cathedral staff and voluntary workers, assembled to form a congregation, that it was probably the only occasion on which a Dean had made his first appearance wearing make-up. I was intrigued to find that the great performer, although standing among the Choir, sang not a single note, being content to mime the words of the hymns in preparation for the insertion of the real thing at a studio recording. Unfortunately, I had quite forgotten that some years ago he was knighted and I consistently referred to him as Mr Secombe. But he didn't seem to mind and very kindly offered his services if I ever organized a fund-raising concert.

Sunday 8 February 1987

Yesterday afternoon saw me installed as Dean at an impressive service over which much trouble had obviously been taken. During the morning I telephoned my predecessor, now confined to his bed in Pickering, Yorkshire by cancer of the liver. It seems that he has not much longer to live and he was grateful that I had thought to speak to him on the day of my installation.

Before the service Colin and Sally James gave a lunch at Wolvesey for the VIPs: a County gathering. I found myself seated between the wife of the Lord Lieutenant and the wife of the High Sheriff, and midway through the meal the latter asked me if I had met the new Dean yet. A tricky question this and a challenge to minimize the lady's embarrassment. I confided, confidentially, that I had known him for many years and chanced to be he. It worked. We both laughed and she was eager to relate her *faux pas* to the rest of the table. A good start.

The Cathedral was packed and one of the Canons, apparently prompted by the Bishop, broke with precedent by welcoming the congregation. After I struggled through much Latin before being placed in my stall, I preached on one of my favourite texts II Samuel 24.24: 'I will not offer unto the Lord my God of that which doth cost me nothing', and I related this to the costliness of worship truly offered, of the gospel honestly proclaimed and of community life fully shared. I promised that in my preaching I would never try to dodge the hard questions of life or try to substitute bogus certainty for mystery and faith. I also took the opportunity to respond to the proposal of a House of Commons Select Committee made last Wednesday that government aid for cathedral restoration should be conditional on deans and chapters charging visitors £1 a head for admission. I said, 'A cathedral is neither a monument nor a museum: it is a place of encounter with the living God and anything that turned it into what seemed to be a commercial enterprise would be self-defeating.'

After the service there was a reception in the Guildhall, where I met for the first time the Lord Lieutenant, wearing a sword and spurs, and the Mayor, an attractive woman Social Democrat. Later a crowd of people from the Abbey and St Margaret's, together with a lot of other friends, came to the Deanery for further, somewhat stronger, refreshment.

Towards the end of the party Kenneth Slack took me aside in the study and told me that on Thursday he had been told by a hospital consultant that he had motor-neuron disease and might have no more than a year to live. Grim news indeed for him, for Millicent and for me. Kenneth and I have been close friends since 1965 when I became Editor of *New Christian* and he served as Chairman of the editorial board.

He is the last of the Free Church 'primates' who in the quarter of a century from the end of World War II contributed a great deal to English church life and especially the ecumenical movement. He was General

Secretary of the British Council of Churches in the late 1950s and early 1960s, then Minister of the City Temple, Director of Christian Aid and Moderator of the United Reformed Church.

During the last few years, as a retirement job, he has been Minister of Kensington Chapel and has seen two members of that church die of motor-neuron disease, so he is only too well aware of the horrors of what has always seemed to me to be one of the cruellest afflictions. In the circumstances it was wonderfully good of him to travel down to Winchester to support me, but I find it difficult to cope with the coincidence of my new beginning and his death sentence. There was little I could say to him last evening but I hope he picked up how much I care.

Monday 9 February 1987

I spent most of this morning and this afternoon at Wolvesey at the Bishop's Senior Staff Meeting. Also present were the suffragan Bishops of Southampton and Basingstoke, the Archdeacons of Winchester and Basingstoke and the Diocesan Secretary. We began with Mattins and Holy Communion in the palace chapel – a large and lofty edifice, the white-painted panels of which create the appearance of an ice-cream parlour. Then we repaired to the fine dining room to tackle a very long business agenda, most of which was taken up by the deployment and problems of the parish clergy. Naturally, I knew nothing about the people under discussion, or their whereabouts. Had we been discussing the Diocese of the Arctic my ignorance would not have been more comprehensive.

I turned therefore to consider the portraits of earlier Bishops of Winchester adorning the oak-panelled walls. About them I was better informed. Lancelot Andrewes, the greatest of Winchester's bishops after St Swithun, is portrayed as the holy man he undoubtedly was, with a pointed beard. I wonder if he really looked like that? There is much of a muchness about portraits of seventeenth-century churchmen. Stephen Gardiner, who changed sides after the death of King Henry VIII and officiated at the ill-fated wedding in the Cathedral of Mary Tudor and King Philip of Spain, has a weak face, adorned but not improved by a moustache.

Thus the greater part of the day passed, with barely a word spoken by me. But there was an excellent lunch prepared by Sally James, described to me by George Reindorp as 'the best of the bishops' wives'. He could be right.

My first Chapter meeting was uneventful enough. We met in the Deanery breakfast room – originally the ante-room for the Long Gallery when Charles II was in residence – and the Vice-Dean extended to me a courteous welcome. My appointment was, I suspect, something of a relief to the Canons for they were fearing worse.

I responded by assuring the Vice-Dean, Alex Wedderspoon; the Precentor, Roger Job; the Treasurer, Paul Britton; the Bishop of Basingstoke, Michael Manktelow (who is also a Canon Residentiary); the Administrator, John Lamplugh; and the Chapter Clerk, Richard Alexander that I had no preconceived ideas about the future. Indeed, I intended to spend my first twelve months absorbing the life and ethos of the Cathedral so that I could be aware of its traditions and needs before making any proposals for change, should these be needed.

I would give the highest priority to attendance at the daily worship and also intended to walk about the Cathedral sometime every day in my cassock in order to discover what was going on and also be available to staff, voluntary helpers and visitors. I had, I told them, made a private vow never to refer to the methods of Westminster Abbey because I knew this could be tiresome, and possibly irrelevant anyway.

The main items on the agenda were the possibility of having the Cathedral floodlit and problems related to the Choir's overseas tour. Most of the ancient cathedrals are floodlit these days, but not Winchester – the reason for this being lack of money. The Treasurer, Paul Britton – a man of sombre mien and speech – informed us that there is no Dean and Chapter money available for this purpose, the estimated cost being about £8,000, so it was decided to see if the City Council might foot the bill. Probably not, because there is no desire to promote the City's tourist potential – 'We don't want Winchester to become like Stratford-upon-Avon', a complacent Councillor told me last week. The problem over the Choir tours is that the Organist, Martin Neary, has not consulted fully the Headmaster of the Pilgrims' School, Michael Kefford, over the dates of tours involving absences from school. Although Pilgrims' is the Cathedral's school, it has a high degree of autonomy and this is jealously guarded by its present Headmaster. In this instance one understands his point of view because he is responsible for the boys' education, but some degree of flexibility is necessary if the Choir is to do its job properly.

Before we got to these two items a great deal of time was spent on the minutes of the previous meeting, using them as a kind of check-list to determine whether or not decisions had been carried out. We also had to deal with the minutes of two Chapter Committee meetings, one with the Organist and the other with the Architect, and this seemed to me to involve unnecessary repetition of discussion and decision-making, created partly because the Bishop of Basingstoke, Michael Manktelow, had not been able to attend the committees.

Sunday 8 March 1987

I am preaching every Sunday morning in Lent on St John's understanding of the significance of Christ's life and death. The Vice-Dean made the suggestion that I should do a Lent course in order to make a personal impact from the pulpit and get myself established as Dean in the minds of the Cathedral congregation. This was a good idea and no great hardship for me since for the last five years I have preached virtually every Sunday in Westminster Abbey or St Margaret's – sometimes in both.

The Statutes here decree that the Dean may preach on twelve occasions in the year, including Christmas Day and Easter Day. The original idea of this was not to keep the Dean out of the pulpit but to give him freedom to be away from the Cathedral for long periods, which the seventeenth- and eighteenth-century Deans often were.

My predecessor apparently preached only six times a year, making his appearances in the pulpit something of an event and certainly his sermons, a collection of which has recently been published, were worth waiting for. I intend to use my full quota of twelve, partly because I like preaching but also because I believe a dean ought to be heard fairly frequently in his cathedral.

Monday 9 March 1987

Thank goodness the British Telecom engineers' strike has been settled and I can now look forward to having an external telephone line in this study. It is, I guess, the best – certainly the most beautiful – study in the Church of England. I am told it was the last long gallery to be attached to a private house in Hampshire, as they went out of fashion after the Restoration. Measuring seventy feet by twelve feet, it would accommodate an indoor cricket net, but only for slow bowlers, and the batsmen would have a problem on the leg side, for the floor slopes quite sharply where the pillars supporting the gallery have slipped.

This is the only study that has accommodated all my books – still waiting to be sorted – and the windows which extend over the entire length of the room make it wonderfully light. Obviously, the very large window where I sit is in the style of the fifteenth, rather than the seventeenth, century. I have been given two explanations of this. One is that it was originally located in the gable of the Prior's Hall and was transferred here when the Hall was modified. The other is that in the 1670s there was still a feeling that a church property ought to include some Gothic, so the window was quite deliberately designed that way.

There is some interesting stained glass, including the arms of Charles I and Henrietta Maria, doubtless rescued from the Cathedral at the time of the Commonwealth. Among a trio of delicately painted Flemish windows overlooking the three-and-a-half-acre garden there is a bedroom scene illustrating a story in the apocryphal book of Tobit. Tobit decides to marry Sarah, in spite of the fact that her previous seven husbands all died in the bridechamber. A grave is dug ready for the eighth but not required; the demon who possessed Sarah is defeated by gallant Tobit. A macabre story and a pretty picture.

My secretarial arrangements are primitive. Christine, the Cathedral Secretary who inhabits the main office about 150 yards away, comes at 9.30 am to deliver internal mail and to collect any letters I may have dictated since the previous day. These are returned for signature at 4.00 pm. She also does filing once a week and is available at the end of an internal telephone line if I need help. This is working reasonably well and I don't like secretaries around all the time, but there are many occasions when it would be useful to have more assistance. I can see that if the volume of my work increases significantly, which I suppose it will, some other arrangement will be needed. Finances permitting.

Thursday 12 March 1987

I have now been here for just over a month and am beginning to get the feel of the building. My daily round of the Cathedral seems to be greatly appreciated by the volunteer helpers, of whom there are in total over 500, and also by the staff, though I am not sure if the Virgers like the Dean prowling about observing their activities, or lack of them. If one had the time, useful work could be done among the visitors – about 400,000 come in the course of the year – but I cannot cope with such a potential pastoral load. So it is good to know that during the summer tourist season clergy from the parishes of the Diocese and many retired priests will be on duty and available to visitors.

I must say the interior of the Cathedral is awe-inspiring. To stand at the West door and gaze upon William of Wykeham's majestic nave is for me, and surely for most people, a deeply spiritual experience – infinity made visible. The building is also a great treasure-house of mediaeval art, with the eleventh- and early twelfth-century wall paintings in the Holy Sepulchre Chapel and the Winchester Bible, of the same period, pre-eminent.

Winchester is of course much less cluttered with monuments than Westminster Abbey, though I always valued their visual reminders of the varied character of human life. It is also quite a lot larger. I am conscious too of the fact that its known history, inseparable from Winchester's place as England's ancient capital, goes back much further. I must do some work on Saxon history, of which I am woefully ignorant, if I am fully to understand and appreciate this place.

For me the most mind-boggling items in the Cathedral are the mortuary chests, raised high on the presbytery screens by Bishop Fox in 1525. These chests contain the bones of Saxon kings and bishops excavated by Bishop Henry de Blois in the twelfth century. They include those of King Canute and his wife, Queen Emma; King Kynegils, the founder of the Saxon Cathedral, who died in 641; Egbert, who is generally regarded as the first King of England and died in 837; and Stigand, the last of the Saxon bishops who helped to crown William the Conqueror in Westminster Abbey on Christmas Day 1066 and had what must be the unique distinction of being excommunicated by five different Popes.

Mixed in with these and others are said, on one of the chests, to be the remains of William Rufus, but there seems to be some confusion about this, since a plain tomb in the centre of the Quire is alleged to be that wicked king's resting place. I think he must originally have been buried somewhere near that spot, for when the central tower collapsed in the twelfth century the builders attributed this to divine displeasure at the king's presence rather than to their own limited skill.

Hearing this from one of the guides the other day I remembered the occasion, in 1941 or 1942, when I was taken around Lincoln Cathedral by the learned Canon Herbert Srawley. He advised me: 'If you want to appear knowledgeable about mediaeval cathedrals always ask when you enter one, "When did the central tower collapse?" They all did.'

Wednesday 8 April 1987

Last evening Jo and I were entertained by the Mayor at Abbey House – a rather pleasant dwelling next to the Guildhall used by the Mayor as an office and for official functions. We were summoned for supper, but the meal turned out to be a splendid dinner, with eight other guests, including a brigadier from the Royal Army Pay Corps at Worthy Down and a naval captain from Portsmouth.

I caused some wry amusement by telling the Mayor how relieved I was to find that oysters were not on the menu, for only recently I had learned of the grim fate of one of my predecessors. Shortly before Christmas 1902 Dean William Wood Stephens and some other City notables were served Emsworth oysters at a mayoral dinner and within a few days the Dean and the Coroner were dead. Not surprisingly, this became national news and the infected Emsworth oyster beds were immediately closed down. Compensation was paid for many years to the families of the victims.

I have never tasted an oyster and something tells me that Winchester is not the place to break such a fast.

Saturday 11 April 1987

The funeral of Michael Stancliffe was a very moving occasion and one which he himself would, I think, have appreciated. The Cathedral was packed, for although he was a very private person and in recent years became more and more withdrawn, he was greatly loved. Today's Requiem was an expression of affection for him and also of sadness that death had come less than six months after his retirement.

The Requiem itself was celebrated, very bravely in the circumstances, by his son David, who is the Provost of Portsmouth. How long is it since father and son were at the same time at the head of two English cathedrals? But there the likeness ends, for David Stancliffe is a dynamic, go-getting priest who is turning his cathedral upside down and is obviously destined for much higher office in the church. His style borders on the arrogant, which I don't much care for, but he has quite a lot to be arrogant about.

The address, given by John Taylor, the former Bishop, was memorable and we had better get it printed in the Cathedral Newsletter. Very conscious of the role of the Dean, the family kindly invited me to conduct the committal of Michael's body to the grave freshly dug in the beautiful space beyond the East end of the Cathedral, often called Paradise.

For some reason I don't quite understand – possibly because it is not an official burial ground – we had to get an Order in Council through the Home Office permitting us to excavate. As I stood by its side I noted nearby the memorial stones for two other former Deans – Gordon Selwyn and Oswin Gibbs-Smith – and couldn't help thinking 'I suppose I shall be the next'.

More amusing to me was an incident that occurred at a meeting of the Cathedral guides in the Deanery a few days after Michael's death. When I entered the Prior's Hall I found two of the guides complaining about the obituary which had appeared in that morning's *Daily Telegraph*. They were offended by the reference to Michael as 'perhaps the last of the Church of England's "gentlemen" Deans', believing this to be an insult to his successor. I did not have the heart to tell them that I had written the obituary.

Monday 11 May 1987

The Duchess of York has made her first visit to the Cathedral as Patron of our fund-raising Trust. It has been no easy task getting her on board for, although she belongs to Hampshire, having been brought up in Dummer, she declined our first invitation. This was something of a shock as well as a disappointment, and a few weeks ago Jim Scott, the Lord Lieutenant, who is Chairman of the Trust, chanced to meet her father, Major Ronald Ferguson, on Waterloo Station and told him so.

Shortly after this encounter the Duchess's secretary wrote to say that the earlier decision had been reconsidered and Her Royal Highness was now in a position to become Patron of the Trust. So we invited her down to meet a few people and see something of the restoration work that needs to be financed.

First, lunch at the Deanery. This was preceded by a minor crisis when we discovered that we needed two additional, matching plates to provide for the twelve guests. Telephone calls to Harrods indicated a three to four week delay, but when told that they were needed for entertaining the Duchess of York the manager of the china department undertook to dispatch them immediately by post. Which he did.

The Duchess arrived at the Deanery in an impressive-looking sports car, herself at the wheel and a detective at her side, hopefully to encourage her to keep within the speed limits. I like her. We met a few times before her wedding in Westminster Abbey last July and I find her bright and breezy style refreshing.

It turned out, soon after lunch had started, that she is on a diet of some sort, so Jane Wright, a royal devotee and an excellent cook, chased off to find an apple to replace the calorie-filled pudding she had prepared. Otherwise, it was a straightforward enough occasion and in a brief welcome I was able to call attention to the ADY monogram over the dining room fireplace, this relating to an earlier Duchess of York, Anne Hyde, mother of Queen Anne, who contributed a lot of money for the building of a new Cathedral organ in 1665.

The tour of the Cathedral after lunch was a rather hurried affair as the Duchess had to return to London for another engagement in the late afternoon, but she met many members of the staff and was patient with explanations of stone and timber conservation needs. She will be most useful to us in attending fund-raising events but we have been warned not to expect more than one, or maybe two, such appearances a year. I hope we can negotiate more, and the Trustees hope to get her to the Channel Islands to facilitate the opening of wallets there.

Thursday 11 June 1987

General Election day has for me been marked also by anxiety over our fund-raising Trust. Set up in 1983 with the aim of raising £300,000 a year for ten years, it has had a chequered history and shortly before my arrival sought to make a fresh start. The retired brigadier who had been Director for the last couple of years was replaced by John Thorn, recently-retired Headmaster of Winchester College. He has the assistance of Brian Hoadley, a marketing man, and both work under the chairmanship of Ronnie Taylor, who until his retirement held a number of City direct-orships, while retaining the manner of the Guards Major he used to be.

The basic problem is that none of them really knows how to raise money – at least not on the scale required. Taylor and Thorn believe that a mass-mailing of all Hampshire's rich people will bring in a lot of money. Hoadley believes that good publicity and the buying and selling of souvenirs and so forth will help to do the trick. Shopkeepers in the city have recently been given a Cathedral supporter window-sticker in exchange for a modest donation of £50.

The only result so far of the extensive local publicity has been to get the backs up of the committee of the Friends of the Cathedral who feel that their contribution to the financial well-being of the Cathedral, which goes back to 1931, is being ignored. All rather petty, of course, and trying to keep the peace between the Trust and the Friends has already taken up too much of my time.

More important, and potentially dangerous, is a letter today from John Thorn full of complaints about the Dean and Chapter. He is, he says, very frustrated because we move so slowly and don't discuss matters of common concern with him. He cites the delayed formation of a trading company and the failure of the Cathedral Architect to provide information about the restoration of the tower. He has yet to see my paper on Cathedral publicity and concludes, 'I am seriously considering whether I wish to continue in the job. I am used to a job in which what one did from day to day mattered and had purpose. But the mood in the Close so often seem to be – next month will do, or next year.'

I have quite a lot of sympathy with John, whom I like and admire, but, as I have told him in my reply (the prelude to a personal meeting), 'Capitular bodies are always much slower than most other organizations, for the simple reason that there is no single locus of authority. A Dean can do hardly anything without reference to his colleagues through the formal structures of the Chapter, and I suppose the whole set-up is designed to inhibit impetuous action – which it does most successfully at the price of reducing overall efficiency.' I have also reminded him that the recent interregnum, and some at least of the years that preceded it, have created an enormous backlog of work for the Dean and Chapter to tackle under new leadership. He should be able to read between the lines of my letter.

But the worrying thing is that, while the criticisms have some justification, the points at issue are not germane to the business of serious fund-raising. The tardiness of the Dean and Chapter, which also frustrates me, should not inhibit the Trust from making and executing its own plans. And here, it seems to me, is the nub of the problem and the conflict.

About £650,000 has been raised over the last two years, most of it when the Brigadier was in command, and this has exhausted the most immediate sources of funding. I don't think the new regime has any clear idea where the next £300,000 will come from, or the £300,000 after that, and this is causing them to turn on the Dean and Chapter as an excuse for their likely failure.

My experience of the appeals at Westminster Abbey and St Margaret's convinces me that large-scale fund-raising needs professional skill and experience if it is to succeed. Although it may not seem so to the amateur, a £3 million appeal spread over ten years is much more difficult than a 'blitz' over one or two years. This is partly because the impact is less dramatic – no one can say the Cathedral is about to fall down – and also because busy, moneyed people have only a limited amount of time to give.

But although I know all this, I cannot as the new Dean call into question the whole basis on which the Trust is operating. In any case, I have other, more urgent, matters to attend to at the moment. But this problem isn't going to go away.

Friday 19 June 1987

Keith Walker, who is to join the Chapter, came for lunch. He is to replace Alex Wedderspoon, who leaves us next week, and I have some qualms about this succession. The Bishop raised the matter with me back in March when I told him of the need for a Canon to develop the Cathedral's educational work. There is enormous scope for this as Winchester, and the surrounding area is full of highly educated people who need intelligent answers to their questions about the truth of Christianity and related issues.

The Bishop agreed and wondered if I had anyone in mind, but I was too new in the job to have any names immediately. I thought we might undertake a search for the right man, using our various contacts. The Bishop had, however, a candidate of his own – Keith Walker, a Team Vicar at Basingstoke in the north of the Diocese.

Education is, apparently, very much his forte. He has a PhD and some years ago taught at Wells Theological College. Before going to Basingstoke he was a Canon of Chichester Cathedral and now wishes to return to cathedral work. The Bishop has made great efforts to secure him an appropriate appointment elsewhere but none has come off, and now that a cathedral post has come up here it seems natural he should be offered it.

On paper, anyway. Until today I had never met Keith Walker, but his qualifications are ideal and it turns out that he is also knowledgeable about the visual arts – another area of our life ripe for development. There is just one snag: everyone who knows him says that although he is a highly-gifted priest and teacher, he finds it very difficult to work in a team alongside colleagues of equal status.

This is a common enough problem in the Church of England. Over the course of the centuries our parochial system has attracted individualists – men who wish to be kings of their own castles – and the more gifted they are, the more they seem to be loners. Hence the conflicts that are endemic in cathedral closes and constantly arise in the new team ministries. Having had some very painful experience of this at Westminster Abbey, I am desperately keen to avoid something similar in Winchester.

All this I expressed to the Bishop back in March and asked for other names to be sought and considered. But his mind was pretty well made up, and after I had expressed my hesitation he sent his Lay Assistant, Colin Peterson, across to twist my arm. Which, being a former Whitehall man – indeed he was for some years the Secretary for Appointments at Downing Street – he did without too much difficulty. I agreed that the Canonry should be offered to Keith Walker and that he should meet me to see how we got on. Hence today's lunch.

In fact we got on famously, which is just as well, because half-way through lunch I discovered that he had already accepted the Bishop's offer. He simply wanted to meet me and settle when he might move in. He is a likeable man and we seem to agree about the role of cathedrals and so on.

But that is not my chief concern: the real issue is, will he work collaboratively in the Chapter?

Only time will now tell and I must do everything I can to encourage him. It is, I suppose, unrealistic of me to suppose that hordes of men of a self-effacing, co-operative sort are just waiting to be appointed to cathedral canonries, but when storm cones are hoisted so early in the day I am bound to be apprehensive.

Wednesday 24 June 1987

Immediately after Evensong we said goodbye, with speeches and a presentation, to the Vice-Dean, Alex Wedderspoon, who is to be installed as Dean of Guildford on Sunday. We have got on very well during the last four months, though he hasn't been much in evidence for most of this time, evidently being greatly preoccupied with his move.

I suspect that he would rather have stayed here, but found himself forced by circumstances to go. He followed Michael Stancliffe from St Margaret's, Westminster in 1970, having held the fort there during a long interregnum. The son of a Church of Scotland minister, he is a quiet, rather shy man of scholarly disposition and a very fine preacher.

Like some other Scots, Alex is also canny about money. When the Dean and Chapter were beset by a serious financial crisis in 1970 he was the Treasurer and had the bright idea of posting volunteer welcoming stewards at the Cathedral's main entrance, in close proximity to a large collecting box bearing an invitation to visitors to donate £1. Officially, the stewards were to exercise 'a ministry of welcome' unrelated to money, but their presence nonetheless led to a substantial increase in donations and saved the day.

The success of this enterprise encouraged several other cathedrals to follow suit, and Alex's expertise in these matters took him to the chairmanship of the Cathedral Treasurers' Conference. He was also offered a deanery – the poisoned chalice of Peterborough, I think – but declined. Now with the passage of more years and my appointment to Winchester the powers that be in Downing Street obviously wanted him to move in order to clear the way for other changes in the Chapter here.

But Guildford isn't really the place for him – he would be much happier in an ancient cathedral – yet it is the only vacant deanery at the moment and there is the perk of a good law school nearby where Judy, his bright and attractive and much younger Canadian wife, can complete her training as a solicitor.

He was driven therefore to accept the offer and seems to have been so greatly agitated by the decision that he has withdrawn into himself, and right up to the last moment it was far from certain that he would turn up to the Farewell. I was mightily relieved when he did and the whole ceremony went off well, so perhaps everything will be all right now.

Guildford will certainly notice a change of style at its deanery. The outgoing dean, Antony Bridge, is one of those highly talented men – formerly a professional painter and still an artist with words – who simply cannot cope with the demands of an institution such as a cathedral. His mind fairly sizzles with ideas and he is by no means averse to swearing in the pulpit. In marked contrast, Alex has been likened to a high-class funeral director – silver-grey hair, quietly spoken, courteous, helpful and always immaculately turned out. I hope Guildford will appreciate him.

Monday 13 July 1987

I have attended my first meeting of the St Cross Trustees – properly the Hospital of St Cross and the Almshouse of Noble Poverty. This is said to be Britain's oldest charitable institution, having been founded in 1136 by Henry de Blois, a grandson of William the Conqueror, who became Bishop of Winchester when he was only twenty-eight.

The original foundation was for seventeen old men – the poorest of the poor – but in 1446 Cardinal Beaufort, who was Bishop at that time, made provision for eight noblemen who had lost their wealth. Today the almsmen are recruited without discrimination, though those on the St Cross foundation still wear black gowns and cap, while the Noble Poverty men are clad in claret cloth.

The composition of buildings on the banks of the river Itchen about one mile from the Cathedral is extraordinarily beautiful and not unlike an Oxford or Cambridge college. The lofty, cruciform chapel was begun mainly in the twelfth century and is pure Norman in its architecture, while the apartments for the almsmen, which occupy two sides of the quadrangle, date from the fifteenth century. A sequence of tall chimneys suggests sentries.

Provision was also made for 100 poor men to be given a free dinner every day and, although this has now been reduced to a symbolic 'Wayfarers' dole' (a piece of bread and a horn of ale available at the gateway on request), the fine Hundred-men's Hall remains and houses the Master's car.

The Trustees now devote their time to administrative as well as financial matters but their number includes a number of people of 'worth' to guarantee the integrity of the charity. There was a scandal in the nineteenth century. The Dean, the Mayor of Winchester and the Warden of Winchester College are ex-officio and among the other Trustees are Lord Northbrook, Viscount Fitzharris and Sir James Scott, the Lord Lieutenant.

The style of the meeting was new to me. The Trustees sit around a circular table, with the chairman, Major The Hon. R.J.Palmer, seated on a somewhat higher chair that enables him to look down on his fellows. The Clerk sits with the Trustees, but the other officers, the Receiver and the Architect, occupy another table and are required to stand when they make a report or even answer a question.

I soon perceived that this arrangement creates problems. For one thing, the chairman, who is very ancient, is also very deaf and from his lofty perch fails to hear much of the discussion. The two officers seem very competent but are also very articulate and, having risen to their feet to address the Trustees, appear to be somewhat reluctant to resume their places. Thus the length of the meeting was out of proportion to the quantity and the quality of the business being transacted.

We discussed the possible removal of gravestones in the churchyard, the threat of the M3 motorway passing nearby (strongly opposed), the heating of the chapel, the funding of a new lavatory block and the arranging of a Gaudy Lunch on Holy Cross Day.

The Master – a high-calibre priest who came here apparently after suffering a heart attack in his busy Bournemouth city centre parish – reported that Brother Gillard, aged 98, had been to hospital after a slight stroke but was fully recovered; Brother Ray, aged 87, has also been in hospital very ill with pneumonia and he has recovered; Brother Cowdray suffers from back trouble but does not complain; Brother Stevens will be 101 years of age in August. He added, unnecessarily perhaps, that the Brothers do not like change and were disturbed by the departure of Mrs Parfitt, the Sister.

I was back home just in time for Evensong.

Sunday 26 July 1987

The Southern Cathedrals' Festival, just concluded, has been an exhilarating five days, blessed by good weather and attended by very large numbers, mainly from the regions of the participating cathedrals (Chichester, Salisbury and Winchester) but also from much further afield. There was quite a contingent from the USA and I met a former Winchester chorister who was here during the First World War and had come all the way from Australia.

The Festival moves around the three cathedrals and the host choral foundation is responsible for the choice of the music, the other choirs happily falling in with what is proposed. Sometimes new works are commissioned but the programme consists mainly of standard items from the English cathedral tradition. This has led the recently appointed Dean of Salisbury (The Hon Hugh Dickinson) to protest that the Festival is elitist. It would, he thinks, have a wider appeal if good brass bands and pop music groups were introduced, but he has few supporters. Winchester has special links with the contemporary composers Jonathan Harvey and John Tavener, so we had some of their latest offerings, those of the former being uncompromisingly avant garde. John Tavener's music is obviously influenced by that of the Orthodox churches.

In between the services and concerts I spent a good deal of time wandering in and out of marquees, being generally matey, and as the new Dean it was my turn to preach the sermon at the Festival Eucharist on Friday morning. I tried to tackle the difficult question of whether or not music is anything other than a form of escapism – the opium of the middle classes? In other words, does art, including worship, have a moral as well as an aesthetic content?

My conclusion was that music at its best can be a model for human life, as well as an expression of human feeling and aspiration – harmony and challenge – and I also made the point that beauty, truth and goodness are inseparably intertwined. Therefore good music is, or ought to be, a stimulus to good conduct – personal and social. I don't know how helpful the huge congregation found this, but the former Bishop of Winchester, John V. Taylor, whose judgment I respect, took the trouble to thank me for it. He is, however, a notably kind and generous man.

Wednesday 26 August 1987

I have had to discipline two of the Virgers. Last Sunday morning they were spotted, not for the first time apparently, seated on a bench in the Close smoking while Mattins was going on in the Cathedral. Having led the Choir and the clergy solemnly into the service and got us placed in our stalls, they sloped off through the South Transept door for a quiet smoke, doubtless keeping an eye on their watches so they could return to their posts by the end of the sermon.

We had a similar experience once at Westminster Abbey when every Sunday morning the Queen's Almsmen, gorgeously arrayed in scarlet, escorted the Dean to his stall in the sanctuary, then moved to the Poets' Corner door, depositing their robes in St Faith's Chapel on the way. An ever-vigilant Bishop Edward Knapp-Fisher, on his way back from a confirmation in South London, noticed Almsmen drinking coffee in Grandma Lee's – a cafe opposite Big Ben. Thus ended what was on the way to becoming a long-established practice.

Our Virgers were contrite, for no conceivable excuse was possible, though one said he had been led astray by the other. I tried, without much success, to be tough – pointing out that they needed to be present during the whole of the services to deal with any emergency that might arise, that they should never smoke while wearing their robe, and that smoking was bad for their health, anyway. They agreed and I moved on to discuss with them their work generally.

Virgers are a problem in most cathedrals. The job has become a key one, for not only are they responsible for the custody of the building and the detailed preparation for the worship, ranging from a weekday 8.00 am Holy Communion attended by a handful of people to a great County occasion at which the Queen or some other member of the Royal Family may be present, they are also in daily contact with the multitude of visitors.

A visitor to a cathedral is unlikely to bump into the Dean or one of the Canons. But there is a good chance, or at least there ought to be, that he will encounter one or more of the Virgers, sometimes mistaking them for the clergy. The attitude of Virgers to the visitors is therefore of critical importance. As I have sometimes pointed out to them and to others on duty in the Cathedral, it is no use our preaching from the pulpit about the love of God if visitors are to be insulted at the door.

Thursday 1 October 1987

Just back from Jersey after a three-day official visit. It is Toytown – most of the external apparatus of a great nation-state expressed in miniature on an island of no more than fifty square miles and a resident population of about 65,000. On the one hand it is delightful, on the other it seems a fair bit of nonsense.

Since we were VIPs – itself a clear sign of the scale of the place – we were taken off the aircraft first and transported from the airport to the Deanery in an official car, kindly sent by the Lieutenant-Governor, who is the Queen's representative on the island.

The Dean, Basil O'Ferrall, I knew from Westminster days when he was Chaplain of the Fleet. Since the war the Dean, who is appointed by the Crown, has always been a former senior services chaplain and Basil fills the bill admirably. The gifts of personality, pastoral skill and leadership that took him to the top in the Royal Navy are well deployed in the Jersey community. He treats the island as if it were a large aircraft-carrier and is 'a friend to all on board'.

The social and political role of the Anglican clergy is interesting. Until 1939 the twelve Rectors, of whom the Dean was one, had seats in the States – the equivalent of the Westminster Parliament – and exercised considerable power. This arrangement did not survive the war, but the Dean still has a seat (non-voting) in the States and serves on a number of its committees – transport, health and so on. The Rectors have retained a similar role on their parish councils.

Dinner with the Lieutenant-Governor at Government House was enjoyable and instructive. The services take it in turn to provide a retired senior officer to do a five-year stint in this office and the present incumbent is an Admiral – one of the first engineering officers to reach flag rank, he told me. The office has a large ceremonial element, for the chief locus of power on the island lies with the Bailiff who, in effect, combines the offices of Prime Minister, Lord Chancellor and Speaker, but the Lieutenant-Governor is the link with the mainland.

It was thanks to the Admiral that Basil became the Dean in 1985. When he left the Navy in 1980 no senior job in the church was offered him – how prodigal we are in the use of resources – so he became Vicar of Ranworth, in Norfolk, and the Bishop of Norwich's Chaplain to people holidaying in the Broads. No doubt he was doing this very well when the Deanery of Jersey fell vacant and the Lieutenant-Governor, remembering Basil from naval times, got him appointed.

A hectic programme was arranged for us. I met the Anglican clergy of the island, addressed the Deanery Synod (taking the greatest care never to confuse Jersey with Guernsey, which is a major offence), had a meeting with the Bailiff, called on the Chief Executive of the main town, St Helier, who gave me a tie bearing the town's arms, went to see the Roman Catholic priest, and visited the very impressive ecumenical Communicare Centre on a new housing estate at St Brelade. This incorporates a surprisingly small chapel which serves as the church of the area. In general, church attendance in Jersey is much higher than on the mainland.

In between times we were taken on tours of the island, with its wonderful coastline, not unlike Cornwall, and exceedingly crowded interior. There must be a traffic crisis before long and I wondered why they did not adopt the Bermudan policy of one car per household. It was not, I think, a welcome question.

At various times we talked about closer links between the church in Jersey and the Cathedral, but of course distance is a serious problem and so also is the insular mentality that life on an island inevitably breeds. Nonetheless, we must try to do more and the Dean is keen that we should.

Monday 5 October 1987

The Creation Harvest Festival yesterday turned out, somewhat to my surprise, to be extraordinarily impressive and I think important. There is a large picture of it in progress on the front page of today's *Independent*.

It all began back in February, not long after my arrival, when I was approached by Martin Palmer, a young lay theologian who works on a consultancy basis for the World Wildlife Fund. Following up a meeting of world religious leaders in Assisi last year, the WWF is trying to get the various religious faiths in this country more conservation-minded and Martin Palmer has advised them to start with the Christian Harvest Festival.

I am not sure why Winchester Cathedral was chosen for the big national service, but I could see what they were after and readily agreed to collaborate. Fortunately the Chapter, perhaps wishing to humour the new Dean, raised no objection, though they did not know precisely what they were letting themselves in for. Neither did I, for that matter.

In fact it involved a very great deal of preparatory work, but Martin Palmer and his colleagues did most of this and also recruited a number of Winchester people to lend a hand. My own contribution was to give the best part of two days to the corporate planning of the content of the service and to make the facilities of the Cathedral available for the event. It also turned out that I was to occupy a critical, central place in the service itself.

Thanks to first-class publicity, the Cathedral was absolutely full. Some hundreds of pilgrims walked from Salisbury and Petersfield, and the Cathedral was a most colourful sight – pilgrims' banners, our own Creation banners which came very much into their own, huge Chinese emblems (dragons and so forth) carried in procession on poles, the saffron robes of Buddhist monks, and of course the traditional harvest decorations. Besides the Buddhists there were groups of Jews, Muslims and Bahai's and lots of people from WWF and other conservation bodies.

The content of the service was entirely Christian, though it was devised specially for the occasion and was quite different from any of the official rites of any church, with strong emphasis on thanksgiving for Creation and penitence for our misuse of Creation. The most dramatic moment came near the beginning: a traditional procession of harvest offerings made its way from the West end of the building only to be stopped by me as it approached the altar. I said in my loudest voice:

'No! Come no further. Your offering is not acceptable in the sight of God's Creation from whom you have taken it. Jesus said: "If you are bringing your offering to the altar and there remember that your brother has something against you, leave your offering there before the altar, go and be reconciled with your brother first, and then come back and present your offering." So leave your gifts there. St Francis has taught us to see all creation in terms of brothers and sisters under God. We who have destroyed so much of Sister Earth, wasted so much of God's gifts, slain so many of our brothers and sisters in creation, have no right to bring these gifts to the altar. There is a time for rejoicing and for offerings, but there is also a time for our repenting of our destruction of God's creation. Listen now to the voices of creation telling the nature of their grievance against us – the voices of our brothers and sisters in creation.'

Then came a series of statements, e.g. one apple in five is contaminated by pesticides; every year we are destroying about 4,000 miles of hedgerow in England and Wales; in the North Atlantic, cod populations were so damaged in the 1960s that they are now a third of what they might have been. This part of the proceedings proved to be somewhat ineffective, partly because it was too long and partly because the statements were read from points high in the roof and were heard only with difficulty.

An act of repentance followed, then came intercessions and the eucharistic climax. During the Communion, members of the non-Christian faiths were invited to reflect on a number of readings from their own religious literature printed in the order of service. After the Communion came 'The Rainbow Covenant'. This was based on the biblical story of God's covenant with Noah, after the Flood, never to destroy the earth again – a covenant sealed by the appearance of a rainbow. After reminding the congregation of this story, we all undertook 'not to destroy wantonly any living creature or damage the life on earth to the point of extinction'. Then we took a rainbow-coloured thread (supplied at the beginning of the service) and tied it on to the wrist of the person standing next to us. Apparently the tying of coloured threads to the wrists of others is a Hindu religious custom and I must say that in the context of our Creation Harvest it made a powerful ending. As we left the Cathedral the whole of the West Front was transformed into a gigantic rainbow, using brilliantly coloured sari material donated by Hindu communities.

What next? Martin Palmer and WWF very much hope that what we did yesterday will become a model – scaled down of course – for Harvest Festivals in churches all over Britain. They want – and this must surely be right – the proper element of thanksgiving to be tempered by an awareness that all is not well in the realm of nature and that there needs to be an expression of penitence for the destruction caused by much human activity. They would also like to see the Rainbow Covenant ceremony widely adopted as an annual pledge of better horticultural practice.

I share their hopes, but it is going to need a massive educational programme to get anything like yesterday's service on to the agendas of local churches. Fortunately, WWF realizes this and is using Martin Palmer to plan the next steps.

Saturday 17 October 1987

I was awakened in the night by a rushing, mighty wind, but was not greatly disturbed and quickly went to sleep again. The window shutters protect us against overmuch sound and, hopefully, the perils and dangers of the night.

It turns out to have been 'The Storm of the Century', concentrated on the South of England and with gusts reaching 120 mph. The news broadcasts report seventeen people killed and widespread havoc – houses and other buildings severely damaged and hundred of thousands of trees felled. Winchester did not escape, but there was hardly any damage in the Close – a few small panes of glass dislodged in the Cathedral and one minor tree, that was in any case due to be replaced, blown over.

The Met Office, in which I served during the war, is looking a bit sick, for not only did it fail to forecast the storm, it actually denied there was going to be one. 'There is no need to worry', said the Weatherman after the television news last evening. This stands comparison with a wartime 'Wayside Pulpit' posted on a Liverpool church notice board: 'Don't worry, it may never happen' was its cheerful message, but sadly the church behind it had been completely destroyed by a bomb.

Tuesday 20 October 1987

The meeting with representatives of English Heritage and the City Council turned out to be much more agreeable than I thought it might be. I went to a special meeting convened by the Mayor at the beginning of August, when I found myself very much on the defensive over the question of public access to the Close. Councillors and officials argued that, since the City has made substantial grants towards the cost of repairing our historic houses, ratepayers and others ought to be allowed to see how their money is being spent and to enjoy more of the beauty of the Close. I took the line, which has been Chapter policy for some time, that while the public is perfectly free to walk through the Close and also to enjoy the amenities of the Outer Close, which it does in large numbers, the Inner Close is intended to be a place of peace and tranquillity.

Today's meeting was a follow-up to the August encounter and, with English Heritage joining the fray, I anticipated even greater pressure. And they have a point: £100,000 is being spent on the Deanery at the moment and a great deal of this has come from English Heritage and City grants. We could not maintain our houses without this help and in these days some sort of tangible benefit is expected from all outlay of public money.

I began the meeting by explaining that we understood this point and were now seriously considering ways in which the public might see more of our houses and gardens. I said I was perfectly happy to open the Deanery to the public on certain occasions. This was well received and we were assured that no one wished to be unduly intrusive. Whereupon the discussion turned to the matter of future grants, and the English Heritage people said they hoped to make more money available to us and to do this in such a way that we could plan the restoration work, both to the houses and to the Close walls, more efficiently.

Would that all my meetings were so cordial and so constructive.

Friday 23 October 1987

The Princess of Wales, who is Colonel-in-Chief of the Royal Hampshire Regiment, came for the Laying-up of the Regiment's Colours. The Hampshires have a strong association with the Cathedral going back to their formation in the eighteenth century and, besides the memorial books recording the names of those who were killed in the two world wars, the South wall of the Nave has many memorials to individuals who served in the Regiment. There are also a few Colours from the past, now joined by the latest which was presented by Earl Mountbatten on behalf of the Queen about a quarter of a century ago.

I preached on the theme of remembrance, gratitude and commitment, which was a fairly obvious thing to do and seemed to be well received. But of course the star of the occasion was the Princess. I must say that she carries out these public engagements exceedingly well. It must help to be one of the most beautiful women in the country, attired in the most expensive clothes that an unlimited purse can buy.

23

But there is more to it than her appearance. She has that rare combination of dignity and warmth, and the military people obviously enjoy her company as well as her patronage. She is also quite shrewd: I recall an occasion, not long after her marriage to Prince Charles, when I had to escort her from an evening service in Westminster Abbey to her car at the gate. The Press were there in full force and amidst all the clicking and flashing of cameras I asked her if this bothered her. 'Not at all,' she replied, 'I would be much more worried if they were not interested.'

Saturday 21 November 1987

The Voice Trial for the choirs of the Cathedral and of Winchester College was a gruelling business – for me, and especially for the candidates. Some academic weeding out took place this morning and the task this afternoon was to hear twenty or so boys in the hope of recruiting three or four of them for each of the choirs.

When I enquired some time ago if I really needed to be present, since I would have no contribution to make to the assessment of musical ability, I was told it was most important that I should be there because sometimes there are disputes between the Cathedral and the College musicians over claims on particular candidates and it needs the Dean and the Headmaster of the College to sort things out.

In the event the place of testing in the Pilgrims' School was packed with musicians and schoolmasters, and the boys, who were required to sing a prepared piece, identify notes played on a piano, and beat time with their hands, faced what must have seemed a formidable audience. Fortunately, there were just about enough of sufficient quality to meet the needs of the two choirs, so there was no dispute.

The ordeal was by no means ended, however. The candidates and their parents were assembled in the mediaeval Pilgrims' Hall to await the arrival on its stage of myself, the Headmaster of the College and the Headmaster of Pilgrims'. The latter then read out in a most solemn voice the names of those who had been selected – each of them winning in effect a half-fee scholarship worth just over £2,000 per annum for the next five years. A word of sympathy for the unsuccessful was added, but this did not prevent a flood of tears. Mothers comforted sons, fathers comforted mothers, and the rest of us tried, not very successfully, to be pastoral.

This procedure must not happen again. If it does, I certainly shall not be there. A better, less emotionally charged, way of doing things has to be found. At Westminster telephone calls were made to the homes of the candidates during the evening of Voice Trial day, and this is surely a more humane way of communicating the verdicts. At least it enables the tears to be shed in private and in the security of the home.

Tuesday 24 November 1987

I remain pessimistic about the ability of the Trust, under its present management, to raise the large amount of money needed for the Cathedral's restoration and I told the Chapter so this morning. No one was inclined to disagree. During the last three and a half years just over £750,000 has been raised, which is somewhat below the target, and there is still no sign that the Development Committee has a clue about laying hold of serious money.

The Summer Ball held in Winchester College was a pleasant enough affair, even though the the Licensing laws would not permit alcohol to be served after midnight, but the return on a vast amount of effort was only £10,000. The bickering between the Trust and the Friends has continued and the fact that the Friends have held a Fine Arts Auction is said to have inhibited the Trust from approaching individuals for money over the last eighteen months. The latest bogey is the Church Urban Fund, which is asking the Diocese to raise about £500,000 for projects in urban priority areas, but I cannot see how this will conflict with a very much more wide-ranging effort to get money from the county for its own cathedral.

The Friends, having let it be known that they are thinking of computerizing their records, have been descended upon by the Trust with the suggestion that this should be a joint enterprise, with the Trust playing the major part since it will want to feed into the computer up to 50,000 names of rich people who will be asked to support the continuing appeal. There is talk of using the rateable values of houses as a guide to wealth.

All of which is irritating the Friends no end, at the same time revealing the bankruptcy of thought within the Trust. The prospect of sending mail-shots to a vast army of unknown people fills me with alarm. It is well known that postal appeals are rarely successful, since it is the easiest thing in the world to throw into a wastepaper basket a request for money. The cost of such an operation in time and money is not inconsiderable and, most dangerous of all, it could well get in the way of a more professional approach later.

We spent some time discussing the situation and the not unreasonable suggestion that the Dean and Chapter might do more to raise money within the Cathedral, but there was general agreement that this is not the right moment to tackle the Trust head on. We must wait to see what success or failure attends its plans.

Martin Neary was given a memorable send-off after Evensong, and deservedly so, for he has been an outstandingly good Organist and Master of the Music. He will complete the Christmas services here and start at Westminster Abbey in the New Year, succeeding that most brilliant and most unmanageable of musicians, Simon Preston, who – I gather – has quarrelled with the Dean and Chapter.

When Michael Stancliffe brought Martin Neary here from St Margaret's, Westminster in 1972 quite a number of eyebrows were raised in the church music world and he was taking a risk. Martin had not come up through any of the major Oxbridge choral foundations, nor had he any cathedral experience. No doubt there were other cathedral organists hoping for this senior job.

But he has made Winchester one of the foremost English cathedral choirs. He is an extrovert character and a great enthusiast who can identify good musicians and get the best out of them. My first real awareness of this was when the Winchester choir came to Westminster Abbey to give the first performance of Andrew Lloyd-Webber's Requiem. This, by common consent, was not a great work, and Simon Preston had haughtily refused to let the Abbey choir touch it. So Martin Neary seized the opportunity and opened the eyes, I suppose I mean the ears, of many of us at Westminster to the fact that there was high quality church music being performed outside London.

In my Thank you/Goodbye speech I mentioned this and also applauded the careful attention he always paid to the daily services, especially to the singing of the Psalms, and the great contribution he had made to the musical life of Hampshire because he has encouraged the making of music in many quarters and has been very generous in his readiness to give organ recitals and conduct other choirs.

He was very nearly appointed to Westminster Abbey last time round. When Douglas Guest retired in 1981 we took advice from the church music establishment, drew up a short list, conducted interviews and were about to make a final choice between Martin Neary of Winchester and Christopher Robinson of Windsor – with the odds heavily in favour of Martin Neary. But then as if from nowhere, but in fact from Christ Church, Oxford, appeared Simon Preston as a candidate. Why he had not applied before and what made him show up at the last minute was never made clear. I suspect that one of the Dean's sons, who was a Christ Church man and a friend of Simon Preston, got him on board.

We all recognized him as the top organist and the top choir trainer in the country, so he was immediately given the job. In next to no time he had transformed the Westminster Abbey choir out of all recognition. We soon realized we had a genius in our midst and before long we were discovering the price that has to be paid for such gifts. At the musical level Martin Neary will find Simon Preston's act a horrendously difficult one to follow; Douglas Guest's would have been much easier.

1988

The new year has begun stormily. I am the subject of a fierce, lengthy attack in the correspondence columns in today's *Hampshire Chronicle* by Sir Bryan Thwaites. He has taken the gravest exception to my latest editorial piece in the Cathedral Newsletter.

In this I sought to offer some explanation of why the Church of England is consistently treated roughly by most sections of the national Press, even though church life today is in many respects more vigorous and more on the ball than it has been for many years past. I said that Tory newspapers tend to share the Government's unhappiness with bishops and commissions over their often critical comments on current policies. Also that the Evangelical and Anglo-Catholic groups in the General Synod are, by their constant barking and snapping at the church's leadership, providing the Press with an unceasing flow of damaging material.

Sir Bryan says in his letter that he agrees entirely with the conservative views expressed in the recent *Crockford's* Preface and, having identified me as a man of the church's liberal centre, he accuses me of resorting to 'the standard debating trick of misrepresenting and exaggerating the alleged positions of perceived adversaries'. My language he believes to be 'rather unbridled for a spiritual leader from whom may be expected gifts of understanding and reconciliation'.

Two points seem specially to have annoyed him. First, my suggestion that a recent General Synod debate on homosexuality 'is a good example of a tiny minority whipping up a very small problem into something that sounded like a national scandal'. Secondly, my analysis of government/church conflicts and their consequences, which he regards as 'ridiculous'. He concludes:

'The Dean's article is yet another symptom of the malaise which afflicts the Church of England's hierarchy and which in turn undermines the confidence and faith of those who have spent a lifetime struggling to perceive the truths on which alone the church can be sustained.'

My first reaction, naturally, was 'Who is Sir Bryan Thwaites?' His name was quite unknown to me. *Who's Who* provided part of the answer in a four-inch entry: a Wykehamist and a Cambridge Wrangler; Lecturer, Imperial College, London; Assistant Master, Winchester College; Professor of Theoretical Mechanics, Southampton University; Principal, Westfield College, London; innumerable committees and at the moment Chairman (Government appointed, of course) of the Wessex Regional Health Authority. Knighted in 1986. Club: Institute of Directors.

Noting the Winchester College connection, I asked John Thorn, who came to see me about Trust matters, for further information. He was highly amused and told me the letter was quite typical of Bryan Thwaites, a brilliant mathematician and strongly conservative in all his views. He is married to a devout Roman Catholic of the pre-Vatican II breed, yet they have provided the Cathedral with four Choristers - probably a record for any family. And John assured me that when the two of us meet, as apparently we are sure to do sooner rather than later, we shall get on very well.

A happy new year after all?

Sunday 7 February 1988

I have now completed my first year as Dean and with characteristic thoughtfulness Colin James, the Bishop, has sent me a letter of thanks and encouragement. It has been a much more hectic year than I ever envisaged and the demands on me have been so diverse that it is difficult to take stock and see things whole.

There is, I think, a general feeling that the Cathedral is on the move and I have been warmly welcomed by many of the laypeople associated with our life. They are looking for changes, or at least additional activity, and there are plenty of ideas floating about.

In my reply to Colin I said I was very pleased to be here, but it is rather like driving a large Rolls Royce with its brakes jammed on. As always in major cathedrals, the Chapter is the problem. Not that we are at daggers drawn. Far from it: we get on well, we sometimes have lunch together at a pub in Alresford, the Chapter dinners are always convivial affairs, attendance at the daily services is probably as high, if not higher, than at any other cathedral in the country. All this is very healthy and I am grateful for it.

The basic problem is that my predecessor's 'gentleman-Dean' style inevitably influenced the atmosphere of the place, making the whole set-up very relaxed, even leisurely. This suits Michael Manktelow, who as Bishop of Basingstoke has his hands more than full with diocesan and other responsibilites. Roger Job is probably the best precentor in the country, with a beautiful voice and a meticulous regard for the ordering of worship. Sadly, he does not have a strong constitution and when put under pressure succumbs to disabling migraine attacks. Paul Britton, the Treasurer, was a great admirer of Michael Stancliffe and sees himself in the role of a cathedral canon of a former age – attending the services, reading some good books, tending a fine house and garden, keeping one eye on the finances and fabric and, in his case, becoming one of the finest judges of wine in Hampshire. Keith Walker, the Librarian, is in contrast hyper-active but he is not well organized; his projects tend not to be thought through and thus create a lot of work without always delivering the hoped-for results. The office is also much less efficient than it needs to be.

Thus Chapter meetings are tending to generate conflict – not of the constructive sort, arising from legitimate differences of opinion, but something rather unpleasant created by totally different understandings of what the Cathedral is, or ought to be, about. At the moment I don't see how this fundamental issue is going to be resolved, so any progress we make is going to be costly in terms of patience and charity.

Thursday 18 February 1988

An alarming telephone call the other day from a Sunday newspaper: Was I aware that the excavations required for the making of an underground car park at the new City shopping centre may affect the water-table and therefore the stability of the Cathedral? Shades of the Edwardian crisis, solved by the employment of a diver, and the prospect of the Cathedral floating down the River Itchen to the sea at Southampton.

I had to confess that I was totally unaware of this problem and promised to look into the matter. The Cathedral Administrator, John Lamplugh, immediately got on to the City Council's Planning Department and was told that the excavation, while substantial, was not believed to pose any threat to the Cathedral or to any other large buildings in the vicinity.

The difficulty over a situation such as this is that, while there appears to be no real risk, if anything does go badly wrong and we have not taken appropriate steps to protect the Cathedral, we shall be blamed for the disaster. Our consultant engineer cannot help us because, as it happens, he is advising the developers of the shopping centre.

He believes there is no risk but has today recommended to us a Professor of Engineering at Cambridge who will come down to size up the situation. This must cost us money, as indeed will any protective measures he prescribes. It will be interesting to see if the developers will lend a hand with this. They ought to.

Friday 11 March 1988

David Begbie's stark representation of the Crucifixion, which is being exhibited at the West end of the Nave throughout Lent, is unusual and it is certainly making a powerful impact. But not all of it favourable.

It is made of scrap metal, wire net and barbed wire, and a spotlight projects it enlarged on to a big white screen. The shadows of those who approach the sculpture also appear on the screen, creating the impression that they are present at the Crucifixion. I find it very moving, and it has been praised by the art critic of *The Times*.

The complaints focus on the fact that the figure is without arms and has no feet. This is intended to emphasize the helplessness of the Crucified and the horror of the event. But one of our Honorary Chaplains, a highly-regarded retired priest, doesn't see it that way. He wrote to me soon after it had been installed:

'You are, I feel, playing with fire in sinking to this depth and presenting a mutilated Christ. You are touching upon the nerve of the most deeply treasured imagery most of us preserve in our deep unconscious as well as conscious minds. And I must be perfectly frank with you – I am furiously angry, and had better say so, that you can trample with your feet on my own deepest feelings. (Perhaps others could say the same.) So much do I feel angry that I can now understand why men throw bricks through their enemies' windows. And the cause of this anger lies with you. What we are presented with is a gimmick. There is much else I could say, its theological inaccuracy and so on. But I will content myself by using the word Vulgarity. What is Vulgar by definition is what is offensive to good taste. And perhaps more than that when we think of the Christ we met yesterday at the altar in the Cathedral.'

A cathedral guide, herself an artist of some talent, says, 'I am affronted and utterly dismayed', and goes on with expressions like 'an appeal to instant cheap sentiment', 'vulgar sensationalism', 'deliberate emotional blackmail', 'an insult to the Body of Christ', 'gimmick' and 'vandalism'.

Clearly some raw nerves have been touched, though many people are saying how helpful they are finding this particular representation of the Crucifixion. Some of the problem, I am sure, is a certain fundamentalism about the representation of sacred events. A mediaeval image of the Suffering Christ holds sway in the minds of many, but, as I have tried to

31

explain to those who are complaining about David Begbie's work, this is no more than an icon of the event; it is not an exact reproduction of what actually happened on the first Good Friday.

Other icons are permissible, and this reminds me of the great fuss there was when the Great Screen was restored in the late 1880s and early 1890s. The question arose as to what form of crucifix was to occupy the central position on the Screen. Some thought a plain cross would be best, most wanted a mediaeval-style Suffering Christ, but George Kitchin, the erudite Dean of the time who was largely responsible for the whole project, favoured a Christ Crowned and Reigning from the Cross.

A model of such a figure was displayed in the Cathedral on Easter Day 1894, but public opinion was so strongly against it that the idea was almost immediately dropped. In the following year Kitchin left to become Dean of Durham.

I don't quite see myself being driven away from Winchester by a controversy of this sort, but it is obvious that the introduction of unusual examples of religious art is going to divide the camp somewhat. As long as the items are of high quality I don't think this matters, though we must be sensitive about the feelings of those who worship in the Cathedral regularly. Yet even they are likely to have differing views about these things.

Saturday 26 March 1988

We opened the Deanery to the public as a contribution to a City scheme designed to make available for one day places not normally accessible to local inhabitants. It was hugely successful. Over 250 came and Jo and I took them in groups on tours of the house, while some Cathedral helpers served tea and coffee and generally lent a hand.

I missed lunch as I had to take a wedding at noon, and by the end of the afternoon we were both absolutely exhausted. From one end of the building to the other is quite a hike and the stairs seemed to get increasingly numerous.

But it was good fun and enormously appreciated. Although this is one of the historic houses of Hampshire none of the visitors had ever seen its interior before and they were intrigued by its scale and history.

We must do this again, not only to meet the demands of the City and English Heritage but also to create goodwill and raise some cash for the maintenance of the house.

Invited to give an address at the annual general meeting of the Winchester Citizen's Advice Bureau, I took the opportunity to say some things about the church's involvement in social work and to comment on certain aspects of the government's approach to social problems.

Dealing with the common assertion, often emanating from government circles, that the Church of England is more concerned with social work than with preaching the gospel, I made two points. First, love of neighbour has a social as well as a personal dimension and if the church is to be faithful to the gospel it must speak and act in all areas of human need. Second, far from being too involved in social work, the church is not sufficiently involved. Most local churches are concerned almost exclusively with maintaining their own buildings and life. This compares ill with the practice of the eighteenth and nineteenth centuries when the parson was a little welfare state in himself, undertaking many of the functions now carried out by the social services.

I deplored the now fashionable denigration of the welfare state and quoted William Temple's comment on the Beveridge Report in 1942: 'This is the first occasion an attempt has been made to embody the whole spirit of the Christian ethic in an Act of Parliament.' The need therefore is to improve the welfare state, not to destroy it.

The new Social Fund, I said, represents a return to the pre-welfare state mentality, with its shift of emphasis from statutory to charitable provision for those in need. The church does not have the resources to compensate for the withdrawal of state aid for the poor. In any case, it is doubtful if the church should prop up a system that is fundamentally unjust.

All this went down pretty well, for those involved in CAB work are often at the sharp end of failures in social policy and have much first-hand knowledge of the consequences of the withdrawal of state benefits. The journalists present asked for copies of my address, so it may get wider publicity.

Sunday 22 May 1988

There could have been no better day than Whit Sunday (or Pentecost, as we are now supposed to call it) for the presence in the Cathedral of those attending the 25th Congress of the Federation Internationale des Confrères Bacchiques – in other words, the world's wine-growers. Evidently this is the first time the Congress has met in Britain and their host is Lord Montagu of Beaulieu, who is President of the British section.

They have come from all parts of the world, with very strong contingents from France, Germany and Spain, and this morning they wore the most exotic robes. Their procession to the Cathedral was quite a sight and, once inside, they – together with our own banners – created a feeling of great festivity. Some of the prayers and hymns were in French and the New Testament reading for Whitsunday, containing the accusation that the Spirit-filled disciples were 'filled with new wine', seemed entirely appropriate. I attempted, with no great success, to extend a welcome to our visitors in French, but the Bishop of Winchester preached an excellent sermon – in English.

After the service we repaired to the Guildhall for a lengthy lunch, a special feature of this being, naturally, the selection of wines. In order to demonstrate the world-wide character of the Congress, these were drawn from unexpected places. Thus, for the first, and possibly the last, time in my life I drank Indian whisky. An Australian Chardonnay was memorable. At the end of the lunch our local MP, John Browne, was – for reasons not altogether clear – admitted as an Associate of the Congress in a quite elaborate ceremony.

There was just one disappointment. I had anticipated that so large and so wealthy a congregation would yield a collection of equally ample proportion. But no; when I enquired of Harry Haysom, the Head Sidesman, this afternoon he told me somewhat dolefully that it was barely more than for a normal Whit Sunday morning. This is puzzling, and the only explanation I can find at the moment is that the majority of those present came from countries in Europe where there is no tradition of generous giving on church collection plates. I am relieved to know that Lord Montagu will pay for the printed Order of Service.

Monday 6 June 1988

At last signs of movement on the fund-raising front – small but highly significant. A meeting of the Trust Council was held this evening. Although the Council consists mainly of the great and the good of Hampshire – people who care a lot for the Cathedral – it has never been really active on the fund-raising side. The intention today was that Ronnie Taylor should outline the Trust's plans for the future and seek to enlist the aid of the Council members.

He spoke of the Trust's achievements so far and of a new effort to raise £600,000 for the restoration of the Tower. Some of this would come from the Trust's reserves and, hopefully, from a special appeal to Old Wykehamists, but more would be needed. Beyond this enterprise the intention was to raise £500,000 a year for further restoration work. Council members were therefore asked to (a) list all possible prospective givers known to them; (b) recruit willing helpers ready to give up time to send letters and make follow-up visits; and (c) offer to approach charitable trusts and business houses. All rather haphazard.

A number of questions and comments came from the floor but displayed little sign of enthusiasm. Whereupon General Sir David Fraser rose to his feet and, in the forthright manner of a military leader addressing his army, declared himself to be entirely lacking in confidence in the proposed strategy. There was, he believed, no possibility of its succeeding. The only way to raise large sums of money was to have a clearly defined target figure and employ professional fund-raisers to direct a major, well-organized Appeal.

This was music to my ears and to the ears of some others, for the speech was punctuated by 'Hear, hears', and after it ended the remainder of the contributors to the discussion favoured the General's line. All of which undermined the policy presented to the meeting and brought disarray to its organizers. Clearly the Trustees will have to think again and it should be possible for me to begin to have some influence on future policy.

Tuesday 28 June 1988

A difficult Chapter meeting. The Revd Maureen Palmer, who used to worship in Westminster Abbey before her ordination as a Deacon, came to see me yesterday. Her first curacy in Hereford has ended and there is no other job available for her in that largely rural diocese. John Baker, the Bishop of Salisbury, who also knew her at the Abbey, has suggested a curacy in a large parish in Poole, but she is none too keen on this and wondered if there might be a possibility of a Cathedral appointment here. The Bishop of Hereford has recommended her for this kind of work, for she is very bright – she has a PhD – and is also very good pastorally.

We could certainly make use of her, and there is the added attraction that she already owns a property in Winchester, thus solving the housing problem. Maureen emphasized the urgency of the situation – the Poole parish needs a decision from her – so I prepared a memo on the subject and distributed it to the Canons last evening in order that we might discuss the matter at today's Chapter. I apologized for the short notice.

My memo was not well received. Michael Manktelow led the opposition, suggesting first that I was holding a pistol at the heads of Chapter. This was absurd, for I was doing no more than requesting discussion of something that had come to hand unexpectedly and needed urgent consideration, though not necessarily a final decision. Michael added that it would in principal be good to have a woman deacon on the staff but he doubted whether this would be allowed by the present clerical quota system.

Roger Job thought there there was no job for Maureen to do; he would prefer someone who could assist him with the music. Paul Britton thought we should consider the principle, rather than the person, while Keith Walker was enthusiastically in favour and said it would be a pity if a great opportunity were not seized.

Sadly, the whole discussion was conducted on a rather sour note and I suspect this had something to do with the fact that Maureen is a woman. Had we been considering a man, we might not have felt it right or possible to employ him, but I am sure the debate would have been different.

It was decided to continue the discussion over lunch and possibly at a Chapter committee in a fortnight's time, but after the lunchtime exchanges it is clear that Maureen will have to go to Poole. Lucky them.

Wednesday 13 July 1988

With very considerable reluctance I have agreed to a weather-beaten statue of St Swithun, dating from the fifteenth century, being placed high on the South wall of the South Transept.

Earlier this year it became apparent that the new Triforium Gallery museum, due to be completed early next year, would be greatly improved by the addition of a large statue. This would not only crown the fine collection of sculpture fragments from the mediaeval Great Screen, it would also draw the attention of visitors down below to the existence of the museum.

The Treasurer and the Curator who are master-minding the whole operation then discovered in the Crypt a badly-worn stone figure of a bishop. This could only be St Swithun, our patron saint, and they deduced, correctly, that it had once stood high on the West gable of the roof. About nine feet tall, it would serve the Triforium Gallery purpose admirably, and an outline cardboard model indicated that its scale was near perfect. The Cathedral Architect agreed.

My own reluctance to use the statue in this way relates to the position it will have among the Cathedral's artistic and devotional treasures. If it were to be exhibited solely in the museum that would be fair enough – a very good place for it – but the idea of hoisting so battered, and scarcely recognizable, an object to a place of great prominence in the magnificent Norman Transept seems to me to be highly questionable. If anything at all is to go there it ought to be a piece of contemporary sculpture, and of course there is no money for this.

After a good deal of heated argument it was agreed that we would seek the advice of the Cathedrals' Advisory Commission and I agreed to abide by their decision. The Commission's delegation has now been to survey the statue and the site. It was led by its Vice-Chairman, Professor Peter Lasko, formerly Professor of the History of Art and Director of the Courtauld Institute, and included a professional sculptor and some other experts.

They were very enthusiastic about the proposal, declaring the statue to be a valuable, even if severely damaged, example of mediaeval work and opining that the South Transept is ideal for its display. I raised with them all my reservations, which are shared by Keith Walker, and while acknowledging that I had a point they were of one mind in recommending us to go ahead. So the statue must now go for conservation and the wall prepared to receive it.

This is a good example of a Dean's limited powers. The raising of a large statue to a prominent place in one of the most sensitive parts of the Cathedral is obviously a matter of the greatest importance. It may be there for centuries. The best available advice must be obtained, but what if this advice and the wishes of the majority of the Chapter run contrary to the views of the Dean?

Clearly I have a particular responsibility for what happens to and within the Cathedral, and I can if necessary use my power of veto to prevent the project going any further. But it isn't easy to do this in the face of specialist advice to the contrary, and what if I kill something that might come to be seen as one of the most imaginative things the Dean and Chapter has done this century? The only consolation I can find lies in the knowledge that if in the end the statue seems out of place it can be removed.

Tuesday 19 July 1988
morning

A nasty moment at the Chapter today when the Treasurer asked about the subject of my conversation last month with the architects Plincke, Leaman and Browning. This firm's office is on the edge of the Close and about once a month the entire staff gathers for lunch, sometimes with a guest or two.

The Treasurer was worried lest I had spent the lunchtime discussing with these architects the possibility of the Close houses being turned to better use – territory he regards as peculiarly his own. I was able to assure him and the rest of the Chapter that, while this subject had been mentioned in passing, most of the talk was devoted to cricket.

So all was well, but things have reached a pretty pass when the Dean is deemed to be answerable to the Chapter for the content of a lunchtime conversation.

Tuesday 19 July 1988
evening

The annual cricket match between the Choristers and a Dean and Chapter XI, held in idyllic surroundings, with the Cathedral and the ruins of the twelfth-century episcopal castle as the backdrop, was a great success. That is to say, the Choristers won by a single run and none of the Dean and Chapter players did themselves much physical harm. I missed tea, having been called from the field to write an obituary for a retired Archbishop of Wales.

So exciting was the finish that I felt moved to announce the result before reading the Second Lesson at Evensong – another innovation, amusing to the congregation but unlikely to become a permanent feature of the liturgy.

Tuesday 23 August 1988

We returned from holiday last evening and the Treasurer called on me this afternoon with the glad tidings that at the end of the current financial year (31 March 1989) we are likely to be faced with a deficit of £73,000; rough calculations suggest a deficit of £99,000 in the following year.

He apologized for breaking the news to me so soon after my return, but a quiet period earlier this month had enabled him to examine the accounts and these grim facts had come to light. Obviously I needed to be told as soon as possible. We talked for about an hour and I tried, successfully I think, to hide my extreme annoyance. I was told by Downing Street before I came that the financial position at Winchester was 'break even' and the Treasurer himself confirmed this when I arrived. In my Cathedral report at the Diocesan Synod I repeated these words, as indeed I have at a number of meetings up and down the diocese.

The truth appears to be that the Treasurer (on whom Downing Street obviously depended for information) was until the other day quite unaware of the deteriorating situation. So, apparently, was the Cathedral Administrator and the Accounts Department. The budget for the current year, which should have been prepared and approved in April at the latest, was not completed until the end of July and it was the sight of this in August that set the alarm bells ringing. The Treasurer blames the

Administrator, and he has a point, but of course it was up to the Treasurer to lean on him when he failed to produce the figures in good time.

The basic problem seems to be that there has been a steady decline in the number of visitors over the last three years, with the result that income from this important source has not risen to cover the effects of inflation. On an annual budget of nearly £500,000 inflation alone at a modest five per cent adds £25,000 to our costs. It is also the case that although Winchester Cathedral and Close look very prosperous, the Dean and Chapter have only small reserves, therefore no great investment income, and unlike many other ancient cathedrals we have next to no income from property. This place was truly fleeced by the nineteenth-century Acts of Parliament.

Everything is, in consequence, run on a shoe-string, so there is little scope for cost-cutting and, with five months of the year already gone, there is no way we can raise an addition £73,000 to wipe out the projected deficit. This is going to need some hard thinking and we must keep quiet about the figures until we know how we are going to deal with them.

What fun.

Thursday 8 September 1988

A visit to Jersey always produces a few surprises and this latest one was no exception. I preached this morning at the annual Legal Service in St Helier Parish Church. But first we went to the Royal Court where, in the presence of the Bailiff, the Jurats (honorary judges), Advocates (barristers) and other lawyers renewed their oaths of allegiance – all in Jersey French, the leading men in their robes, with French-style drum-shaped hats.

In my sermon I pleaded for a true sense of priorities in public life, pointing out that in the Christian scheme of things the proper order is God, Man, Things, Money, whereas in today's world this order has been inverted, with God as an optional extra. I don't know how well this went down with all the tax lawyers who were there. The Bailiff gave a lunch party at his home afterwards for about ten of us, and it turned out that he and I were the only ones present who did not own their own aeroplanes.

Last evening I accompanied the Dean to the institution of a new Rector. These ceremonies are always carried out by the Dean, rather than by the Bishop, because for over 200 years, between the end of the seventeenth and nineteenth centuries, the Bishops of Winchester never visited the Channel Islands. Having, of necessity, assumed a number of episcopal functions, the Deans have proved unwilling to let go of them. I wore my robes and was kindly welcomed by the Dean, who pointed out that the new form of institution service was largely the work of my son-in-law, Charles Taylor. Unfortunately, it contained a misprint: a prayer for 'the healing of our broken and divided society' appeared as 'for the healing of our broken and dividend society'. This would have made an amusing illustration in my sermon this morning, but I thought it best not to use it.

Thursday 15 September 1988

I have spent some time in the Accounts Department this week as the financial crisis has given me an excuse for poking my nose into every corner of our life. The Accountant is a good man, but it is a part-time retirement job for him and, although he is very good on VAT matters, he is not a high-powered finance manager and in any case devotes much of his time to simple book-keeping. The two women who assist him are efficient but also only part-time.

All the ledgers are hand-written, so the production of budgets and accounts is a laborious, time-consuming task. Hence all the delays. At Westminster I was very sceptical about the introduction of computer accounting, because this did not result in any reduction in the number of staff employed, but I am beginning to see that in a rapidly changing situation where quite large sums of money are involved it is necessary for a Dean and Chapter to know what is going on. I suppose that only computers can ensure this. Even so, I find it surprising that those working so close to the accounts were not aware that we were running into the red.

I was shown a paper that was highly revealing and at the same time depressing. Some years ago, when Alex Wedderspoon was the Treasurer, figures were produced which showed with crystal clarity that unless steps were taken to increase income the accounts would move into deficit by 1987. I wonder why this warning was ignored. There was perhaps the hope that increasing numbers of visitors and a few convenient legacies would save the day.

Besides raising our regular income substantially we shall obviously have to deal with weaknesses in our administration.

Tuesday 20 September 1988

One important way of increasing our regular income is through the building of a Visitors Centre. Virtually all the major cathedrals now have one and they serve the two-fold purpose of helping visitors to feel more welcome and of raising money – often substantial amounts. People who visit cathedrals like to buy souvenirs and many of them also like to have a cup of something or a light meal. This is a bone of contention at Winchester.

The main reason we do not already have a Visitors Centre is because there is no building available for adaptation to this purpose. Many of the centres in other places have been created within cloisters, chapter houses and other existing buildings, but at Winchester the shortage of local stone led to the dismantling of the monastic buildings during the years following the Reformation.

There is another reason, however. Back in the 1970s an architect post-graduate student at Sheffield University prepared his MA thesis on the reception of visitors at Winchester and included a design for a possible Visitors Centre. This thesis and design, nicely bound, is to be found in the Cathedral library, and very interesting reading it makes. But it did not win acceptance and my predecessor apparently greeted it with the remark, 'I did not find a Visitors Centre at Santiago de Compostela'.

Soon after my arrival here, Paul Britton, the Treasurer, presented me with a carefully considered paper which contained what he believed to be six good reasons why a Visitors Centre was not needed at Winchester. These included 'Winchester is different', 'There are many shops and cafés nearby in the City', 'There is no suitable site', and 'The return would not justify the high capital outlay'.

This afternoon the Dean and Canons were due to meet to discuss this paper. And we did, but without the benefit of Paul's presence because, having gone to spend a holiday with relatives in Canada, he mistook the day of his flight back and will not now arrive until tomorrow morning.

Nonetheless we had a good discussion and it was agreed that we should, if possible, build a centre. The example of St Albans was quoted, for they were in much the same position as ourselves, without a building. But after overcoming serious planning problems, they created what they call a Chapter House. This is now making a great deal of money from its restaurant.

The question of a possible site here was left open, for this raises a tricky problem. The Sheffield student proposed what certainly looks the most obvious site – not far from the South West door of the Cathedral and shielded by the high monastery wall. This would be clearly visible and accessible to visitors leaving the building, while making no deleterious impact on the environment of the Close. It is, I suppose, the only site where we might hope to obtain planning consent.

But the use of this site would involve taking a slice of land from the Treasurer's very large and now very beautiful garden, upon which he and his wife Clem have bestowed much time and energy. I don't think the land itself would be the problem, for this is attached to the Sub-Organist's flat on the North side of No 11 The Close, but the imposition of a substantial building there would inevitably affect the view from the house.

Tuesday 27 September 1988

The Chapter meeting today – appropriately William of Wykeham's Obit – was devoted entirely to the financial crisis and was mainly a brainstorming session in which everyone contributed possible, and some impossible, ideas. The general attitude was positive and I am pleased with the way things went.

I started the meeting on an up-beat note by saying that I welcomed the challenge: 'The problem is not so large as to be unmanageable but large enough to demand bold action. Tinkering will solve nothing.' I also made the point that a considerable array of fund-raising possibilities is open to us. No one demurred.

It was decided not to impose admission charges to the Cathedral but rather to encourage visitors to give more voluntarily. Cut-backs were also rejected because these would only lead to a reduction in the Cathedral's ministry. The Choral Foundation needs its present numbers of Choristers and Lay Clerks if the outstandingly high standard of music is to be maintained. An offer by the Librarian to undertake a sponsored walk from Land's End to John O'Groats was applauded for its spirit but I felt obliged to express my unhappiness at the prospect of his absence from the Cathedral for a possible fifty-one days. Token cuts in salaries were ruled out.

There is of course the need not only to balance the books but also to make provision for the expansion of our ministry and to replace the recently spent capital. In other words we are looking for quite a lot of new money, of the regular sort, but given the large number of people involved in the life of this Cathedral and the tremendous affection there is for it in Hampshire, it should be possible to turn things round. Winchester is surely the last cathedral in England likely to go bankrupt.

The priority now is to pursue this morning's ideas further, turn the best of them into some sort of recovery programme, then go public in a big way. It could be that this crisis will release the brakes on our developing life. We are all Marxists these days.

Monday 17 October 1988

Our problems with the Trust are by no means over. After we had decided, under pressure from the Council, to employ a professional fund-raising consultant, two companies were interviewed and the choice fell on Everald Compton International – the Australians who worked wonders at Ely and, against the expectations of many of us, helped to raise £4 million. They have conducted a preliminary investigation here, are favourably impressed with the situation and, if we choose to move forward, will carry out a feasibility study next spring.

Ronnie Taylor, the chairman of the Trust's Development Committee, has, however, circulated a paper in which he raises various points about the Dean and Chapter which I thought we had settled. The real problem is that he has no confidence in the Treasurer and wants the Fabric Committee, which oversees all our building operations, to be chaired by John Thorn, the Trust Director. Indeed, he wants some sort of monitoring committee that will exercise strict control over restoration projects and, if necessary, withhold money from the Dean and Chapter.

I had long discussions and correspondence with him about this during the summer and had to point out that it was quite impossible for the Treasurer to be divested of his responsibility (laid down in our Statutes) for the care and restoration of the buildings. It is good that John Thorn should serve on the Fabric Committee, both to represent the Trust and to make his own contribution to the decision-making, but the Dean and Chapter simply cannot hand over control to an individual or group that does not carry ultimate responsibility. And Canons cannot be sacked.

Most worrying, however, is the evident lack of confidence at the heart of the relationship between the Trust and the Dean and Chapter, and I have told him in a letter today that I don't see how we can contemplate the launching of a major appeal while this remains unresolved. I am suggesting a private meeting of himself, Jim Scott, Paul Britton and me at which all the cards can be laid on the table and, hopefully, we can resolve the problems once and for all.

In view of Ronnie's past experiences in the Close, and his inevitable comparison of these with what he has known over a lifetime in business, I can understand his anxieties, but it is no good harping on about matters which have now been brought under control.

Tuesday 25 October 1988

A day of considerable conflict and turmoil. Keith Walker brought me astonishing news yesterday about the statue of St Swithun which we were planning to put on the interior wall of the South Transept. The ever-diligent Brenda Kipling, a Cathedral Guide and local historian, has been examining back numbers of the *Hampshire Chronicle*, as she is wont to do, and came across two significant items about the statue.

The first, dated 1860, reported the removal of a statue of St Swithun from the West gable of the Cathedral and its replacement by a copy made by a Winchester firm of monumental masons. The second, dated 1908, reported the removal of this replacement statue because the stone had proved to be too soft to withstand the buffeting of wind and rain.

This, incredibly, is the object, believed to come from the fifteenth century, which we have been preparing for prominent display. There is evidently no doubt about its true provenance, for when the matter was drawn to the attention of the conservator he confirmed that the chisel marks on the statue were made by tools of the nineteenth rather than the fifteenth century.

All of which was made known some time ago to the group responsible for the museum, but they chose to go ahead with this part of the project in spite of the re-dating of the statue.

I was amazed and angry and expressed my feelings on the matter at this morning's Chapter meeting. I said that the group's failure to inform me and the rest of the Chapter of what had been discovered was a form of deception, since it was known that I had only accepted their proposal because of the statue's alleged historical importance.

This did not go down well with the Treasurer, who sought to defend himself by asserting that the date of the statue was unimportant. Its visual quality was the same, whatever its provenance, and the Great Screen contained many Victorian copies of mediaeval statues. The Bishop of Basingstoke thought the visual aspect was the main issue but the Librarian said that since the statue was not a genuine work of art, it could not be erected to call attention to an exhibition of mediaeval art. We were all getting hot under the collar and I was about to announce that I proposed to use my power of veto to end the project when the Chapter Clerk helpfully said that, since I had originally given my approval on the basis of quite different facts from those now known to be true, he did not see how the project could go forward. The Bishop and the Librarian agreed with him and it was decided that the project should be dropped. The £4,000 already spent on the conservation of the statue will, if necessary, be met from Dean and Chapter funds, rather than from the museum budget.

But this was not quite the end of the matter. Early this afternoon the Treasurer, having spoken to the Curator, came to see me in a somewhat emotional state. He is understandably disappointed that a project for which he fought hard has come to naught, but his chief concern was my use of the word 'deception'. He assured me that he and the Curator were jealous of their integrity and believed themselves to have been acting in accordance with the wishes and best interests of the Dean and Chapter.

After some talk I said that I accepted there had been no intention to deceive, but it had, to say the least, been very unwise not to inform me and the rest of the Chapter of a change of some 450 years in the dating of the statue. There we left it and I have written to the Cathedrals' Advisory Commission telling them of our discovery and decision. I don't suppose they will like it either.

This has been a bad business and illustrates yet again how difficult it is for clergy who have held a position of some responsibility in a parish or wherever to subordinate their authority to the Dean, or even corporately to colleagues, in a Cathedral set-up. But I must confess that I am mightily relieved that the statue is to remain in the Crypt.

Saturday 29 October 1988

Thanks to Dr John Patton and a number of other Cathedral people, William Walker, the Diver, now has a decent gravestone in Beckenham Cemetery, and one that records his great achievement. Certainly he deserves this, for he saved Winchester Cathedral with his own hands and is part of its folk history.

His story must be unique. When in the early years of this century the Eastern end of the Cathedral was in a state of near collapse, it was discovered that during the Middle Ages this part of the building was erected on a raft of beech logs. This was required because of the high level of the water table, something we are well aware of when the Crypt floods in the winter.

It was the deterioration of the raft, inevitable in the circumstances, that brought the building to a point of great danger. Photographs taken at the time show enormous cracks in the walls, some of which were leaning hazardously. The only solution perceived by the architect and the consulting engineer was to remove the raft and replace it with concrete underpinning. This involved working in a considerable depth of water and mud.

Hence the employment of a diver who, from 1906-1912, descended beneath the floor of the Retro-Choir in full diving equipment, took out the decayed beech and replaced it with 25,800 bags of concrete, 114,900 concrete blocks and 900,000 bricks. For this astonishing effort Walker was summoned by King George V to Buckingham Palace and made a member of the Royal Victorian Order. The Dean and Chapter gave him a silver rose bowl. Sadly, he died in the 1918 'flu epidemic.

John Patton, who has a great interest in Walker, wondered where he was buried and eventually tracked down his grave in Beckenham Cemetery. The whole thing was in a deplorable condition and it was apparent that the weather-worn headstone included no reference to his feat, in marked contrast to that of W.G.Grace, whose cricketing fame is recorded on a gravestone just a few yards away. Within a matter of weeks Dr Patton raised enough to restore the headstone and its surround, add a small stone bearing the figure of a diver and a Winchester inscription, and have something to spare for the grave's regular maintenance.

A bus-load of us went to the cemetery this morning where we were joined by members of the excellent Beckenham Church choir, which sometimes sings in the Cathedral when our own choir is away, and some other local residents. After a brief service in the cemetery chapel, we moved to the grave and I dedicated the new work.

Tuesday 1 November 1988

Yesterday's news conference on the financial crisis was very satisfactory. There was a good turn-out of the national and local press and I was interviewed by the local radio and television stations. I had constantly to make the point that the crisis relates to our day-to-day running costs and not to the restoration of the building.

The Times has a large picture of the Choristers, the staff and me standing beneath the Great Screen at the High Altar, and all the broadsheets are carrying the story. Some of the tabloids have a sentence or two about it, and no doubt the *Hampshire Chronicle* and the *Winchester Extra* will give it headlines at the weekend.

Wherever I have been today, in the Close and in the City, people have wanted to talk about the crisis, which has come as a great shock to everyone. The very idea that the Cathedral of affluent Winchester is broke is well nigh incredible. This, I'm sure, is the starting point for building confidence that we can put things right.

Wednesday 30 November 1988

The two meetings of the congregation and other supporters convened to consider the financial crisis were wonderfully well attended. Over 300 came to the Monday afternoon gathering in the Quire and almost 100 to the one held in the Deanery last evening. On both occasions I commented that it was worth having a financial crisis in order to have such meetings.

After a brief analysis of the causes of the problem, I devoted my somewhat lengthy speech first to confidence-building, then to winning support for the Dean and Chapter's fourteen-point recovery programme. I said that to cut back on the Cathedral's life would be a betrayal of all that we stood for and that we needed to approach the problem boldly and enthusiastically. If we did this we would bring new life as well as new money into our community.

The fourteen-point programme includes the expansion of the existing fund-raising activities, and quite a number of new ones, including the Triforium Gallery museum, due to be opened next April, a Visitors Centre, Sponsorship, Close Tours and Special Choir Concerts and Recordings. The Close will be thoroughly surveyed to see how the houses can be adapted and developed to yield more income and reduce their cost.

The Treasurer circulated a good leaflet outlining next year's accounts with their £99,000 projected deficit and spoke movingly of the need for individuals to increase their levels of personal giving and to make better use of Deeds of Covenant. Paul can be highly effective when he lets go of some of his inhibitions. This was followed by a good discussion and many suggestions, all of which we promised to consider. We also undertook to hold similar meetings, to report on progress, this time next year.

The only anxiety came last evening when a financier in the audience began to ask awkward questions as to how the Dean and Chapter came to be taken by surprise over the deficit. I gave him somewhat foggy answers but took him aside afterwards and suggested a private meeting to talk about this issue.

The other problem, not remarked on but obvious to me, concerned the management resources that will be needed to initiate and handle the fourteen-point programme. The existing administration is being taxed far beyond its capacity and in any event lacks the necessary drive. There is much hard work ahead and this means additional leadership.

Friday 9 December 1988

An interesting letter today from Nick France, the local Roman Catholic priest. Last month he and a large number of his people celebrated Mass for the first time in the Lady Chapel of the Cathedral. The possibility of their doing so was for some years a matter of dispute in the Chapter.

Long before I came it was agreed that they could celebrate Mass in the Gardiner Chantry, this having been designated a place of prayer for unity. But the Chantry can accommodate only a priest and about two other people, so the great majority of the congregation had to stand outside in the North Presbytery Aisle unable to see the action of the Mass. This was obviously unsatisfactory, but my predecessor felt quite strongly that the Roman Catholics should not be given a larger place in the Cathedral until they had themselves shown greater hospitality to Anglicans in their own St Peter's Church.

Bargaining of this sort held no appeal for me, but the Canons continued to hold this line until I was invited in Lent to conduct the Stations of the Cross and preach in St Peter's. Hence the movement to the Lady Chapel.

As it was their first appearance in the Chapel and a significant development, I went to the Mass to welcome them and said I was sorry the Chapel had no statue of Our Lady; doubtless it had one until the Reformation, and I looked forward to the day when a new one was installed.

Nick France writes:

> One of my parishioners, a discerning lawyer, listened with profound attention to your kind words of introduction during our Mass in the Lady Chapel of your Cathedral recently. He believed you were hinting at the possibillity of our community playing some part in providing you with an appropriate statue of Our Lady for your Lady Chapel. To back up his hunch, Peter George has now sent me £150 as a first contribution. Without rushing you, is there any way in which you could see us making a contribution to the Cathedral in this way? I am sure I would have no difficulty whatsoever in swiftly raising the money required for a statue, however expensive.

As a matter of fact, it had crossed my mind that this might be something they would like to do, but I wasn't going to ask directly at this stage. Obviously, we now need to respond quickly and I hope the Canons will be as thrilled as I am. A statue of the Virgin would enrich the Cathedral's devotional ambience and of course the ecumenical significance of such a gift would be considerable.

Monday 19 December 1988

More trouble at t'mill. I am confined to bed with what the doctor rather grandly calls an upper respiratory tract infection – in earlier times a cold on the chest – and have been afflicted also with a series of letters from Ronnie Taylor and John Thorn about a serious crisis in the Trust, for which I am said to be responsible.

At the end of last month the *Financial Times* sent their Christian Tyler to follow up the story of the financial crisis that came to light in August. He spent two days here interviewing various people and had a long session with me. His piece appeared in the paper last Saturday under a heading 'The Dean wrestles with Mammon'. It was mainly analytical and pretty perceptive, though the Canons may not be altogether happy with some of the comments on the past.

What I did not anticipate when I read the quite lengthy article was the massive offence it would cause some members of the Trust, Ronnie Taylor in particular. The offending passage reads:

The Cathedral Trust, having failed to meet its earlier targets, will next year launch an appeal for between £5m and £8m. The services of an aggressive ('thuggish' was one description) Australian fund-raising company will be employed. Here, too, cathedral politics can be tricky. The long-established Friends' organization at first resented the Trust when, having failed to woo sufficient corporate donors, it turned its attention to wealthy private individuals, some of them already Friends. Hard feelings have been assuaged by means of mutual exchange of committee members.

Ronnie objects (a) to the suggestion of failure to meet targets, (b) to the reference to a failure to woo sufficient corporate donors (It was, he says, never envisaged that much would come from corporate sources) and (c) to the implication that the Trust had acted in an underhand manner *vis-à-vis* the Friends. He says he has been trying to contain his anger and dismay, but the upshot of it all is that he has resigned from the chairmanship of the Development Committee and also as a Trustee. He feels there has been 'a ruthless public assault on my competence, but more important on my integrity'.

John Thorn is in a difficult position. He and Ronnie are good friends and he is aware of Ronnie's weaknesses as well as his undoubted strengths – and his generosity. He believes the resignation has been on the cards for some time and that the *FT* article was simply the last straw. He also feels some sense of responsibility towards me – a new Dean who finds himself struggling on several fronts. Thus he writes:

I think the whole thing is Hell for you, and you personally are much in my thoughts. I have nothing but the very greatest respect and admiration for you and for your efforts to bring order and purpose to the Cathedral's affairs. I have a strong feeling that out of the present trough we shall climb, given time, knowing much more clearly where we want to go and (to continue the metaphor) what form of transport we should use.

I am grateful for that. I cannot now recall the exact detail of my conversation with Christian Tyler, so it is impossible to tell to what extent he was quoting me, rather than anyone else he talked to. On the whole, his article was very fair, and another member of the Development Committee, Sir Charles Tidbury, has written to say how marvellous he thinks it is, but of course the nuances of interpretation are always tricky, especially when personal sensitivities are involved.

One thing is absolutely certain: given this debacle and the Dean and Chapter's financial problems, there is no possibility of our launching a major appeal next year. I am not sure there is any future for the Trust. Meanwhile, the most urgent need is for me to get fit for Christmas. Fortunately, it is the turn of the Bishop to preach on Christmas morning.

Tuesday 20 December 1988

The Chapter Meeting today was inevitably dominated by the problems of the Trust. I have a lot of support from my colleagues. My own view, initially, was that the Trust had outlived its usefulness and would best be disbanded. This was resisted by the Vice-Dean and others – probably rightly – on the grounds that it was not open to us to close down the Trust unilaterally and that a reconstructed Trust could well be important when the professional fund-raisers go into action.

We then discussed the timing of the Appeal. In the present circumstances there is no possibility of launching anything before 1990 and I went so far as to suggest that 1993 would be most appropriate. This will be the 900th anniversary of the Cathedral's completion, we should have its running costs properly financed by then, and we ought to have recovered from the strains and stresses of putting things in order.

Again – and again rightly, I dare say – my suggestion was resisted by the others and the discussion centred on whether 1990 or 1991 would be right. In the end I agreed that the Appeal should if possible be started in 1990, but only if the problems of internal finance are solved, and that 1991 should be seen as the latest time for launching. The desire to get on the move while the economic climate is favourable is perfectly understandable, but the Dean of Ely, to whom I spoke the other day, tells me that he had to take a whole year off from cathedral work while their Appeal was on and I am a long way from ready for anything like that. Obviously there is no point in Everald Compton conducting their feasibility study next Spring, so they will need to be stood down. I am to speak to Jim Scott about all this.

Well, I never! Everald Compton International, our prospective fund-raising consultants, are also miffed by the *Financial Times* article. Hugh Samson, their Managing Director in Britain, telephoned, and now has written, to protest strongly against the description of them (by one unnamed person) as 'thuggish'.

He believes this will gravely handicap any work they might be called upon to do for us – Who will wish to be interviewed by thugs? He even wonders if someone has deliberately used the term in order to undermine confidence in them from the outset. In any event, he wishes to defend the good name of his company, etc., etc.

Really, this is a great deal of nonsense. The concept of a tough-minded approach to fund-raising, in comparison with that of the gentleman amateur, is a compliment, not an insult. And no one knows this better than Australians, which is why they are so successful at it.

Nonetheless, this is the season of goodwill, I keep reminding myself, and we don't want another row breaking out, so I have spoken to the Editor of the Weekend Section of the *FT* and he has agreed to print a letter from me exonerating Everald Compton from anything approaching 'thuggishness' and expressing our utmost confidence in their methods.

What next?

Although Christmas has been extremely busy, it has been a wonderfully happy festival and a mighty relief from all the financial pressures and conflicts of recent weeks. It is astonishing just how many people come to this Cathedral over the course of four days – it must be in excess of 10,000.

Every seat was taken, with some hundreds left standing in the aisles, for our two Carol Services on Thursday and Friday; the same was true of the Midnight Eucharist on Christmas Eve and there was another huge congregation on Christmas morning. The Nave was full for the Children's Gift Service during the afternoon of Christmas Eve and a lot came later for Evensong and the Blessing of the Crib.

The music is undoubtedly a great draw, for the Choir has performed superbly, but it is also the case, I am sure, that historic cathedrals such as this provide a shrine for the so-called folk religion which is still around in some strength, even though there are signs of increasing secularization in English society.

This folk religion is not something to be despised. Indeed, it needs to be kept alive and nurtured and cathedrals have the opportunity to do this. Our doors must be kept wide open.

Thursday 29 December 1988

Although it is still the festive season, it was necessary to have a meeting of the Trustees this morning. It was quite straighforward. Sir Eric Drake, a former chairman of BP, distinguished City man and friend of Ronnie Taylor, has also resigned – because of ill-health he says. It is sad that he should go in these circumstances, but at seventy-eight it is really time for him to retire.

It was agreed to postpone the Appeal until the way forward is clearer. In the meantime, Jim Butler, the Senior Partner of accountants KPMG Peat Marwick McLintock, is to be invited to become a Trustee; the Development Committee is to be enlarged under a new chairman; a renewal of its activities was authorized, on the understanding that these will not prejudice a major Appeal later; the Trustees are to have a meeting with the Dean and Chapter.

When the meeting was concluded we were joined by two thick-set men in good suits who had come down from London: one was the manager of the Odeon Cinema, Leicester Square, the other the head of a film company. They brought the glad tidings that the Duchess of York proposes to attend a charity premiere of a new film and wishes the proceeds to go to the Winchester Cathedral Trust.

The film *Slipstream* is of the space-age sort and the star, Mark Hamill, apparently became famous through his appearance in *Star Wars*. He is said to be a favourite of the Duchess. The premiere is on 10 February, and the men in the suits told us of the possibility of £100,000 being raised for the Trust. This is dependent upon two factors: we must sell 1,600 tickets at prices ranging from £10 to £100 and we must produce a programme for the event that will carry about £30,000 of advertising. They do not regard any of this as a problem.

I do. The Trust is in disarray. The possibility of selling in Hampshire in six weeks 1,600 highly priced tickets for a film in London that no one may wish to see seems remote. And where might £30,000 of advertising be found? My lack of enthusiasm was shared by the other Trustees, but Jim Scott said 'A Royal offer cannot be declined, otherwise we will never get another.' He then, valiantly, undertook to get together a group of people in the county to form a committee and to sell the tickets. Bryan Hoadley, the ex-marketing man who is about to succeed John Thorn as

Director of the Trust, undertook to find the advertising for the programme.

The year is ending on a strange note and I hope that 1989 may be less fraught with problems.

1989

This has been a harrowing day and I am glad it is almost ended. This afternoon we had a memorial service for the thirty-four people who were killed in an appalling rail crash at Clapham on the 12th of last month. The two trains involved – one from Bournemouth, the other from Basingstoke – were crowded with Hampshire commuters and the Cathedral was the natural place for a service that had a national as well as a regional significance. It was transmitted live on television.

A lunch at Wolvesey for the VIPs and chief participants in the service was inevitably a sombre affair. I sat next to Bob Reid, the chairman of British Rail, who was obviously feeling the great burden of responsibility for an organization which he believes to be grossly underfunded and in which disasters of this kind can happen.

However, the sombreness of the lunch was as nothing compared with the atmosphere in the Cathedral, which was packed to the doors with the relatives of those who were killed – their emotions still raw – some who had been injured, and a host of people who had in a variety of ways been involved in the rescue operation. The Duchess of York came, having arrived home only this morning from a holiday in Switzerland, and the Prime Minister and Paul Channon, the Transport Minister, were also there.

For the Order of Service we were greatly helped by the one devised for use in Canterbury Cathedral after the *Herald of Free Enterprise* ferry disaster last year. The lighting of thirty-four candles was particularly moving and introduced an important personal element for the families. The candles were lit immediately after the opening hymn by three chaplains of St George's Hospital, Tooting, who were on hand when the casualties arrived at the hospital. My only anxiety about this ceremony was its length, for the television people wanted the candles lit in a particular sequence and this required a period of silence that was just about too long to sustain. I think, hope, it was all right.

The compilation of the Bidding was a difficult task. How does one express in three or four sentences the feelings of those gathered on an occasion such as this? I said:

> We meet today to remember those who lost their lives in the tragic accident at Clapham Junction, and to commend their souls to the safe keeping of the God and Father of us all. We offer to God our sorrow, our grief and our perplexity, our wounded hearts and bodies, and renew our faith and hope. We give thanks for the devoted work of all who took part in the rescue operation, and became channels of God's love and compassion to those who were in distress. We pray for all who travel by land, sea or air and those who are responsible for their safety and well-being.
>   'The Lord is loving unto every man and his mercy is over all his works' (Psalm 145.9).

The Bishop was faced with a similar problem, on a larger scale, in his sermon. Words, though necessary, are not a lot of use when such deep emotions are involved and one can only hope that the experience of coming together with others, likewise afflicted, in the context of an act of worship offered in a great building, will assist the accepting, healing process.

The choir of Emanuel School sang the Twenty-Third Psalm and this was fitting because the school is located just above the cutting where the crash occurred and both pupils and staff were quickly on the scene. Our own choir sang '*Requiem aeternam*' from Fauré's *Requiem* and Edgar Bainton's anthem 'And I saw a new heaven and a new earth' – both tearjerkers, but none the worse for that – and we ended with the Easter hymn 'Jesus lives! thy terrors now can, O death, no more appal us'.

After the service the bereaved families were given a cup of tea in a marquee erected in the Outer Close and the Duchess and the Prime Minister went around talking to them. It was interesting to notice the difference. Poor Fergie was quite out of her depth, as indeed almost anyone of her age would have been. But the fact that she was there was important. In contrast, the older and highly experienced Margaret Thatcher was a sensitive mother-figure, listening patiently and offering, now and again, a carefully chosen, sympathetic word in response. She stayed for over an hour. Very impressive and I am sure helpful – and how different from the shrill, combative figure in the House of Commons.

A good meeting this evening with Tim and Anthea Fortescue who, to my great relief, have undertaken to become our honorary Development Managers – responsible for some of the most significant items in our fourteen-point recovery programme: sponsorship, promotion, Visitors Centre and the Close.

Tim and Anthea were commended to me by Philip and Jo Holland, good friends in the House of Commons and at St Margaret's. Tim was also an MP and served in the Whips Office during the 1960s and 1970s, but much of his career was spent in senior positions in the food and drink industries, finally as Secretary General of the Food and Drink Industrial Council. Anthea, a lady of elegance and charm, is somewhat younger and ran her own highly successful conference-organizing business. They retired to Winchester last year and live in a lovely house just outside the Close.

I took the opportunity of our first meeting earlier this month to ask them if they would become our Development Managers and, after sleeping on this proposition for a night, they agreed. Now they are brimming with ideas and have both the ability and the time to carry them through. Naturally, they have a particular interest in developing a catering facility, which must have high priority, but I have warned them that the ethos of the cathedral world is very different from that of the commercial sphere. Patience and perseverance are essential to success and I must try to see that they don't become disillusioned by the obstinacy and inefficiency they will encounter before long.

Wednesday 1 February 1989

Dick Sawyer, a retired surveyor and long-standing supporter of the Cathedral, has very generously offered to bring together a group of former professional colleagues to carry out a comprehensive survey of the Close and make proposals for the better use of the properties and their surrounding land.

This is precisely what needs to be done. Most of the houses were built during the seventeenth and eighteenth centuries; they are very large, and although some have been sub-divided they are far from convenient; they are expensive to maintain and a continuous drain on our funds, and some have very large gardens – the Deanery three and half acres, and two others almost two acres each. The stonemasons' workshop is a former stable and contravenes current health and safety regulations. The former

Deanery bakehouse is a listed building and seriously dilapidated. A site is needed for a Visitors Centre.

The need for a survey is among the fourteen 'recovery' points for getting our finances straight, but this has been regarded as a long-term project because of its likely cost. Now we have the possibility of getting it done for nothing, though doubtless practising professionals will have to be brought in if and when a final scheme is prepared. The main thing now is to see what might, and might not, be possible.

Dick Sawyer is an interesting man. He was for many years Surveyor to the Diocese, so he already knows the Close well, and although he must now be in his late seventies he is always full of bright ideas and is not constrained by tradition. His approach will be open-minded and his proposals are likely to be fairly radical. And therein is the main challenge, since the Close – a place of great beauty and the wonderful setting of the Cathedral itself – is a desperately sensitive site and one of national importance.

Any suggestion of changing this environment significantly is bound to raise an outcry, for although it has developed over the centuries it is now a vitally important part of our heritage. I suspect that our room for manoeuvre will turn out to be quite limited and I, for one, do not wish to go down in history as the Dean who destroyed, or even attempted to destroy, the Close at Winchester.

Yet our financial problems are serious, and unless they can be solved it may not be possible in the longer term to maintain the Close in its present form. We must therefore be ready to look at any reasonable proposals.

Tuesday 7 February 1989

When I was installed as Dean, two years ago today, it was apparent to me that this great Cathedral was not open to rapid change for the simple reason that institutions with so much history behind them cannot be altered overnight. At this point I was not in any case aware of what, if any, changes might be needed.

I thought therefore that if over a period of nine years – this assuming that I am here until retirement at seventy – I were to make one substantial addition or improvement to the life of the Cathedral every year, this might add up to something significant. Not overly ambitious, maybe, but realistic and hopefully creative.

This is not, of course, how things have turned out. The financial storm that blew up last summer, apparently out of a clear blue sky, has driven this great ship off course. What is more, there has been a mutiny among a section of the crew. The future looks uncertain.

One thing is certain, however: the course must be changed. Money alone is insisting that we cannot carry on as before, and the fourteen-point recovery programme will require much new activity, and indeed a new outlook on the Cathedral's whole life and mission.

This, I am persuaded, is no bad thing. As the first half of the year progressed I became increasingly conscious of the extent to which our corporate life is in thrall to complacency and inertia. The worship and the music were, and remain, marvellously good. And to have as many as 500 volunteer workers is, I suspect, unique in the cathedral world. Yet within the inner circle of the Chapter, Keith Walker excepted, there has not been the slightest desire to branch out in any new direction. In fact, the lengthening of the Chapter agenda and the need for additional meetings to deal with necessary business has been causing resentment.

I realize it is difficult for those who have become settled in their pattern of life and the scale of their actitivity to change simply because a new Dean has arrived on the scene. I think it is also very difficult in these demanding days for anyone to remain enthusiastic and creative for much more than a decade.

But changes there must now be. What was impossible six months ago is now compulsory, yet – returning to the analogy of a ship in a storm – we must sail ahead with more or less the same crew. This may be difficult, but I think the financial crisis and the explosion in the Trust will mark important turning points in my ministry here.

Wednesday 8 February 1989

The main front-page headline of yesterday's *Southern Daily Echo* screamed 'Marquee Plan Causes a Row' and the sub-heading explained 'Tent by cathedral "a monstrous carbuncle" claim'. Alongside was a photograph of a model of what, from the angle taken, certainly looked a curious structure.

This is our project for supplying refreshments to visitors next summer. Rather than await the building of a Visitors Centre, dependent upon a successful appeal and many other factors, I suggested that we might erect a tent on the Outer Close and serve tea, coffee, sandwiches and buns there, spreading out on to the lawn in good weather.

Keith Walker has picked this up and discussed it with a firm that specializes in catering at cathedrals, art galleries and other institutions where there are large numbers of visitors. They are keen, and when they consulted the City Council about planning consent and so forth they were told that consent will almost certainly be forthcoming provided the proposed tent is no ordinary marquee of the sort often seen at village fêtes and sporting events but rather something interesting.

Enter Plincke, Leaman and Browning, the imaginative architects whose office is on the edge of the Close, who undertook to design an interesting tent and generously offered their services free as a donation to Cathedral funds. Last week they produced a model of their design, based on the concept of a mediaeval castle, and the appearance is very striking indeed. So also is the cost at £25,000, but the proposal is that the catering firm will meet all the costs and pay us an agreed percentage of the turnover.

This seems a very good move and the shrill complaints of local businessmen suggest to me that it is likely to be successful. Leading the opposition are the proprietors of Brann's Restaurant in Great Minster Street, overlooking the Close. This is an up-market establishment which has been given very complimentary reviews in London's weekend papers and charges £60-£70 for dinner for two. It is hard to believe that tea and buns in our marquee will rob them of many customers. But they also make the point that our 'monstrous carbuncle', as they call it, will spoil the view of the Cathedral normally enjoyed by their customers when they are tucking into the viands. What is more, they say, our project will heighten health fears and create a food-poisoning threat.

It is very interesting that in these days of the free-market economy the proposed opening of almost any retail enterprise in Winchester provokes cries of 'unfair competition'. But, as I told the *Daily Echo*, 'It would be ironic if wealthy Winchester proved to be the only cathedral city unable to cope with the creation of a small refreshment tent for visitors.' What many of the business people do not seem to realize is that without the Cathedral Winchester would not be much more than a large market town, of no particular interest to visitors and therefore much reduced in its commercial potential. It is in everyone's interests that the Cathedral should flourish and draw more and more visitors to the City. In these days the possibility of enjoying a cup of tea or whatever after visiting a cathedral is regarded as part of the total encounter with the building and its community.

Saturday 11 February 1989

Last evening's film première at the Odeon, Leicester Square, was the most extraordinary event I have ever attended. First things first: the cinema was almost full. Jim Scott, who can never be refused because he has himself helped so many, persuaded Judy Colman, wife of the chairman of Reckitts, to chair a committee of Hampshire people, charged with selling the tickets. Which they did with great success. And Bryan Hoadley also did exceedingly well with the advertising for the programme. So although the proceeds, after expenses have been paid, will be nothing like the £100,000 first mentioned they should, I am told, be well in excess of £50,000.

As instructed by the organizers, I was on parade in dinner jacket in the cinema foyer soon after 7.00 pm. After twenty minutes or so of greeting the assembling audience, my attention was drawn to a line of men, also in black tie, and women, attired in what I took to be the latest fashions, some distinctly revealing. These turned out to be the film stars and others involved in the management of the enterprise.

I was then supplied with a paper listing their names and informed that it would be my duty to present each of them to the Duke and Duchess of York. Since I was unacquainted with any of the company, and was fast approaching a state of panic when I caught sight of a clock, I requested that the line be ordered in exactly the same sequence as indicated on my list.

This accomplished, we awaited the arrival of the Royal patrons, who stepped out of their car to the cheers of onlookers on the pavement and, doubtless to the astonishment of the same onlookers, were greeted by a cathedral Dean. A small child presented a bouquet and I presented the film stars. The Duchess seemed to know some of them already and stopped to chat. This was helpful inasmuch as it enabled me to consult my crib from time to time, but the irregularity of movement caused me some confusion and I shall never know if I attached the right names to the right stars.

So, appropriately, to the Royal Circle – the audience standing and clapping a welcome, and the Cathedral Master of the Music playing the long-ago hit song 'Winchester Cathedral' on the cinema organ. Appreciative laughter all round and, it might have been said, a good start.

The film *Slipstream* is, the programme helpfully informed us, a space-age adventure story set in a world where nature has gone mad and flying, fuelled by the wind, is the principal means of travel. Much of the filming evidently took place in central Turkey where the spectacular barren landscape and the capacious caves helped to create the illusion of another planet. Microlight aircraft darted from place to place with remarkable facility and whenever they crashed, which was quite often, the Duchess, seated on my left, leaped in the air some inches – evidently more nervous than I had realized.

But what the story was about I could not even begin to fathom, for it was without rhyme or reason. There seemed no thread of continuity; only a sequence of unrelated, albeit dramatic, events. In desperation, I ventured to ask my right-hand neighbour, a small man, if he made anything of it. He assured me he did, which was perhaps not surprising for I learned later that he was Mark Hamill, the film's leading actor. Since I had not been to the cinema for about a quarter of a century I came to the conclusion that film, as an art form, had advanced well beyond my comprehension, in the same way that most contemporary expressionist painting has.

Eventually we saw the final air crash and I thankfully returned the Duke and Duchess to their waiting car. The Duke said he had enjoyed the film, the Duchess was non-committal, and it was a relief that neither enquired about my own reaction. But with them safely out of the way it was possible to canvass the views of the audience, now streaming into Leicester Square. These ranged from the bewildered to the angry, though someone reported that two Wykehamists had claimed to understand the film.

Sally James, the Bishop's wife, kindly offered me a lift back to Winchester in her car and we grumbled for much of the way. And today there have been telephone calls from people who were there and felt badly let down. They had bought expensive tickets, encouraged others to do the same, in support of the Cathedral, and their only reward had been a frustrating, wasted evening. I sympathized with them, and I wonder at what ultimate price the financial success of the occasion has been purchased.

Friday 10 March 1989

Although the *Slipstream* film première was, from the entertainment angle, a fiasco and did our relations with our County supporters no good at all, the event had some benefits. The profit amounted to £60,000, which is not to be sneezed at, and the Lord Lieutenant, having recruited Jim Butler and Bill Heller to help with the selling of tickets, has now persuaded them to join the Trust Development Committee and lend a hand with the reconstruction of the Trust's work.

Jim Butler has in fact agreed to be its chairman and seems ideal for the job. As the senior partner of the British section of KPMG Peat Marwick McLintock, the largest accountancy firm in the world, he knows everyone in the City of London and many other financiers and industrialists far beyond. He also has a quiet, attractive personality – probably better with figures than with words – and, I gather, a tremendous capacity for hard work. Once he has determined that something needs to be done, it gets done, they say.

Bill Heller has a quite different, extrovert, personality. He is a local businessman who came to Winchester twenty or more years ago to start a small factory for making cables. This proved to be very successful and is now a sizeable firm. Yet Bill remains very much the boss who exercises personal control and has, I guess, considerable leadership skills. He is full of ideas and enthusiasm for raising money for the Cathedral.

The great advantage of these men over those who have gone before them is that they are still active and influential in the business world. They know people with money, or who have access to corporate money, and in some cases are in a position to claim the support of others whom they have assisted with their appeals. Retired people have ample time to give to fund-raising but they no longer have the clout to bring in big money. We are going to need more like Jim Butler and Bill Heller and, again, this points to the need for a short, sharp effort because people of this sort have only limited time to give.

Monday 20 March 1989

A difficult assignment today. Corinne Bennett, the Cathedral Architect, has served the Dean and Chapter for the last fifteen years. She is a distinguished, albeit highly conservative, conservation architect and the only woman architect to be responsible for the care of an English cathedral. She is a devout Roman Catholic, yet shares fully in our life and we all like her very much.

But now that we are moving towards a major restoration programme, extending over a decade or more, we feel it is time for a change. New eyes may see the building differently and a younger architect should bring new energy. In most departments of a cathedral's life today there is a lot to be said for ten-year, rather than open-ended, appointments.

So I was asked to have a discussion with Corinne about her future here and tell her of the way our corporate mind is working. I don't suppose anyone in management enjoys this kind of assignment – I certainly don't – and it was made all the more difficult by the fact that only recently we congratulated her on the award of an MBE (for her work on the Brighton Pavilion) and we are such good friends.

I thought it best to send her a preliminary letter, warning her of the nature of our discussion, so she came prepared. Not surprisingly, she is upset, for she has a great affection for the Cathedral and has been proud to be the architect for such a building.

During our conversation, however, it emerged that she has just been appointed architect for the restoration of the Albert Memorial in London. This is a £6-7 million project and it is a sign of her standing in the conservation world that she has been given this job. It is hard to believe, however, that she could cope with this as well as Winchester Cathedral and a number of other buildings.

The way was therefore opened for us to agree that she will retire from the service of the Dean and Chapter later this year. I am sure this is right for us, and perhaps also for her, but it was a painful decision and I hope our friendship will survive it.

Tuesday 11 April 1989

A letter of complaint from a colonel at Newbury about the Nave banners on display in celebration of Easter. I have had a number of these during the last twelve months.

The large banners, sixteen of them, are the work of Thetis Blacker who, I am told, is the world's leading batik artist. They were created in 1979 as part of the 900th anniversary of the starting of the building of the present Cathedral and they have divided the camp ever since. They evoke either enthusiasm or hatred.

The eight banners on the North side represent the Genesis creation myth, from the creation of light to the Fall, while the eight on the South side represent the new creation, from the Incarnation to the New Jerusalem. They are very striking, for Thetis Blacker has Latin American blood in her veins and it shows in her work. She is also very much caught up into mythology and archetypal images and is herself something of a visionary. Thus, set against vivid yellow backgrounds, we have extraordinary and powerful representations of trees and birds, animals and people, mythological beasts, the sun and the moon, all invested with a swirling, exuberant vitality which is an expression of Thetis's own personality.

Michael Stancliffe, my predecessor, commissioned them and, being himself a symbols man, was closely involved in their creation. He persuaded the Friends of the Cathedral to find the £25,000 they cost and, wisely perhaps, got the money before revealing the designs. They are brought out for the major festivals, Christmas, Easter, Whitsun, and other big occasions. So far, their appearance has thrilled me and they certainly heighten the sense of festival. On the other hand, I am equally pleased when they are taken down and the austere beauty of the Nave is once again revealed.

The colonel is furious – outraged, in fact. He has never seen anything so appalling in any church, least of all in a cathedral. He believes the banners to be yet another example of the influence of trendy clerics; the Nave now reminds him of nothing more than a street in Hong Kong.

In my reply I explained the origin and purpose of the banners and said that good contemporary works of art tend to speak more helpfully to some than to others. As for trendy clerics, I pointed out that the banners are actually hung from brackets first used for twelve Flemish tapestries displayed at the wedding of Mary Tudor and Philip II of Spain on 25 July 1554. And I could not resist, though perhaps I should have done, the temptation to suggest how nice it will be for him to be reminded of Winchester Cathedral when next he walks down a street in Hong Kong.

Saturday 15 April 1989

Our Theology Days, now into their second year, are obviously meeting a need. Today's was the fourth and the attendance has never been fewer than 100.

We have borrowed the idea from Birmingham University's Extra-Mural Department where, for several years, they have had days in which two theologians working in the same field engage in public dialogue and after a time encourage their audience to participate. It is important not to have two scholars with diametrically opposed views or two who are in complete harmony; there needs to be enough difference to make it interesting and at the same time constructive.

Today was ideal. The subject was 'Evil and the God of Love' and the speakers were Professor Ulrich Simon, who taught me at King's, and Dr Michael Wilson, who was with me on the staff of St Martin-in-the-Fields in the 1960s and subsequently taught at Birmingham. I was delighted to see them both.

Ulrich, the fiery prophet, whose father was murdered at Auschwitz and whose brother perished later in the Soviet Union, spoke with his customary passion about the human tragedy and the unfathomable depths of human depravity. Michael, the gentle priest-doctor, emphasized the healing power of God's love at work in every situation, no matter how evil, and the need to cultivate every sign of love, however small. There was a fascinating exchange between them and plenty of thoughtful audience participation.

Keith Walker runs these days extremely well and the weekly seminars held in the spring and autumn are also attracting good numbers. This is, I am sure, just the kind of thing cathedrals ought to be doing, for well-educated laypeople often get spartan theological fare in their parishes.

Thursday 27 April 1989

The Duchess of York came today for the official opening of the Triforium Gallery Museum. She was her usual bouncy self and was very chatty with all the people who have been involved in the creation of this major addition to the Cathedral's life.

The project was under way by the time I arrived on the scene, so it has taken a long time to bring to completion – partly because of the delays in the manufacture of the tall display cases in Germany and partly because of poor planning here. It has also cost a great deal of money – about £400,000 – this being provided by the Trust, the Friends, the EEC and a marvellous gift of £100,000 from an American, Al Gordon, who is also a benefactor of Winchester College.

The result is superb and has transformed what used to be an untidy dump into a place of elegant beauty. The sculptured heads of kings and bishops, torn down from the Great Screen at the time of the Reformation and recovered from various places during the early years of the present century, are displayed at heights commensurate with their former positions on the screen. They belong to the late fifteenth century but could easily be portraits of men alive today.

Also striking to me is the evidence of the degree of violence used by the iconoclasts. Not only did they pull the statues down, they chopped off their heads and limbs, gouged out their eyes, and used the pieces for the building of walls. Thus the exquisite Winchester Madonna holds a headless child. Religious fanaticism and violence often go together.

A bonus for visitors will be the museum's setting, high above the South Transept, with dramatic views of the Cathedral's interior. It is the brainchild of Paul Britton, the Treasurer, and John Hardacre, the Curator, and they deserve all the congratulations they are now receiving, especially from the arts and museum world, and though it has been an expensive venture it should yield £15-20,000 a year of additional income.

Friday 28 April 1989

Our third Royal occasion in two days; it's getting like Westminster Abbey. The Duchess of Gloucester came yesterday morning for the Hampshire County Council Centenary Service; she was followed by the Duchess of York opening the Triforium Gallery museum during the afternoon; and today we have had Princess Margaret for the opening of the new Stancliffe Building at The Pilgrims' School.

This building, comprising a fine hall and several groups of classrooms, is a notable addition to the school and has been very sensitively designed for its Close site. It seemed a good idea to invite Princess Margaret to perform the opening ceremony, for she came on a private visit to the Cathedral one Sunday last year and stayed on to hear the Choir sing Evensong.

But as the day drew nearer there seemed some uncertainty as to what she was, and was not, prepared to do. Varying signals came from Kensington

Palace, the latest this morning indicating that, as the weather forecast was for bright sunshine, Her Royal Highness would not wish to step out of doors on to the terrace – the site of the ceremony – but would perform the opening through a nearby open window.

This seemed distinctly odd and it would have been a great disappointment to the assembled crowd of boys and their parents. I am aware that Princess Margaret can be difficult, though I have myself never found her anything other than pleasant and co-operative. When she arrived, in blazing sunshine, this morning's conversation with her secretary, Lord Napier and Ettrick, had apparently been forgotten. 'Might Your Royal Highness be prepared to carry out the ceremony on the terrace?' I asked tentatively. 'Yes, of course, it's a lovely afternoon, isn't it,' came the reply. And throughout the afternoon she could not have been more friendly and charming. Very mysterious.

Monday 1 May 1989

David Hill has now completed his first year as our Organist and Master of Music and proved to be a remarkable acquisition. This is a key job and it is hard to believe we could have done better, for he is a brilliant organist and equally good as a choir trainer. And, most unusually for someone of his quality, he is a joy to work with, entirely devoid of the prima donna temperament. Very rare, this.

There was a strong field for our post when Martin Neary moved to Westminster Abbey at the end of 1987, but the Lay Clerks were united in their hope that we would appoint David and our specialist advisers, James Lancelot and Lionel Dakers, agreed with them.

Although we were near-neighbours at Westminster, I never actually met David there, nor did I ever see or hear him in action. Simon Preston so dominated the music scene at the Abbey that none of us was aware of what was going on at the Roman Catholic Cathedral down the road.

In fact, a good deal was going on and in the music world David was winning widespread acclaim for the special quality of the choir's sound. This was confirmed by a coveted *Gramophone* award in 1985 and, in the nicest possible way, Canon Oliver Kelly expressed his dismay at our taking him away from a place where he was making an outstanding contribution.

When he came for interview it seemed that a boy had entered the room by mistake. He was actually thirty-one, but his appearance was, and remains, exceedingly youthful. A patch of fair hair on the crown of his head gives the impression of a tonsure.

Robert Cross has produced an excellent report on the future development of the Cathedral bookshop. The shop is located in the South West corner of the Nave, near the door where visitors leave the building, and it makes an annual profit of about £30,000. It has reached a point, however, where further increase in turnover and profit is impossible without fairly radical change. For one thing, the selling area lacks room for additional goods; for another, the management and assistants, under the admirable Captain James Pertwee, RN, are entirely amateur and many are elderly. They do amazingly well and they can't do more.

Robert Cross I have known for almost twenty-five years. When I was editing *New Christian* he was a director of *Studio Vista*, one of Tim Beaumont's few financially successful enterprises, and we occupied adjacent offices at the foot of Highgate Hill. We met again about ten years ago through our membership of the General Synod's Publishing Committee, by which time he was in charge of the bookshops at the Natural History Museum – a sophisticated enterprise with an annual turnover of £1 million. By chance, he lives in Winchester, already does some work for us in the Cathedral, and readily agreed to my request that he should examine the workings of our own bookshop with a view to increasing its profits.

This morning he presented his report to myself and the Canons. It contains five recommendations: 1. There should be a management board consisting of three senior Cathedral people, a businessman and an accountant. 2. A new professionally-trained manager should be appointed. 3. The shop should be enlarged. 4. A new programme of musical recordings should be started. 5. There should be stated financial objectives and proper budgeting – this covering the next three years, after which the shop should be moved to a carefully chosen site outside the Cathedral.

We had a good discussion. Obviously expansion will involve investment of money, but Robert believes that our 400,000 visitors provide considerable scope for increased turnover and profitability. He also made the point that if, as hoped, the shop is moved into the new Visitors Centre three years from now, professional management will already be in place. We accepted his proposals.

Throughout the meeting there was, however, what I took to be an ominous silence from the Treasurer, who has already made it known that he is opposed to any radical change in the running of the shop. He was, I suspect, unwilling to confront a professional head on. Now the report, with our endorsement, must go to Winchester Cathedral Enterprises –

the company we formed to oversee all our commercial enterprises and to keep us on the right side of the law.

Tuesday 30 May 1989

A very unsatisfactory meeting this afternoon with the directors of Winchester Cathedral Enterprises about Robert Cross's report on the bookshop. Although the Board oversees our commercial operation, the company was established to meet the requirements of charity law and to protect us from taxation on profits. Its members are drawn from the Dean and Chapter, the Friends and the Trust and are amateurs in commercial matters. The one professional present at the meeting was Bryan Hoadley, the Director of the Trust, and his experience lies mainly in the selling of butter.

The report was very severely criticized on the grounds that it does not take account of the Cathedral environment, that it is unrealistic in its costing of the proposed professional manager, that financial planning and budgeting are unnecessary, and that the present management committee is quite capable of running the show. No fundamental change was their message and I found myself fighting a losing battle, with the Treasurer among the opponents. The most desperate moment was when the chairman suggested that James Pertwee's replacement as bookshop manager could well be a retired colonel.

Faced by such complacent, conservative opposition, it is plain that we cannot make much progress in this area of our life, and I'm not sure what I am going to say to Robert Cross, who went to a lot of trouble over the compiling of his report and may well wonder why the Dean and Chapter cannot simply force it through. The reason is of course that, at this particular moment, the price would be too high. The only hope is that some minor improvements will be made to the running of the shop and that we shall have a Visitors Centre under professional management sooner rather than later. Even so, I find it all very frustrating.

Sunday 25 June 1989

Last Sunday evening, when I was on holiday, the Hampshire Freemasons had a service in the Cathedral and apparently it went very well. The local Press tried to turn it into a controversial event and managed to find one or two protesters, but there was no disturbance. The tricky aspect of such services is that the General Synod only recently decreed membership of the Freemasons to be incompatible with membership of the church.

This is a matter on which my mind has changed. Until about ten years ago I felt Freemasonry to be undesirable, partly because of its esoteric rites and ceremonies but chiefly because of its social and economic influence. Both, I am now persuaded, are much less serious than I then imagined. Many Freemasons seem to be Churchwardens and Church Councillors in their local parishes and regard their Lodge as a kind of social club.

The rites and ceremonies, with their bloodthirsty allusions and other curious elements, are, it seems, not taken literally but are demythologized in much the same way that most Christians treat the Old Testament – a bloodthirsty volume if ever there was one. And on the economic front the demands of the free market leaves little scope for private favourable deals, since these could be too costly.

In general, I believe that cathedrals ought to be open to all who choose to use them, unless there are strong reasons to the contrary. In this particular instance I thought it right to ask the Freemasons to restore to their draft Order of Service the references to Jesus Christ that had been excised and they made no bones about doing this. The service was basically Evensong and the collection generous.

Tuesday 11 July 1989

We have not yet received the report of Dick Sawyer's group on the future development of the Close, but there is an urgency about finding a site for the hoped-for Visitors Centre. Today the Dean and Chapter received a proposal from the group and from Tim and Anthea Fortescue, our Development Managers, that the Centre should go on the much talked about site on the edge of the garden of No 11.

As anticipated, the Treasurer opposed this idea. He said the Centre should be attached to the Cathedral and much more visible than it would be if it were to be erected on the garden site. He also reminded us that he and his wife, Clem, had undertaken the restoration of the garden of No 11 on the basis that a previous proposal for a Centre there was dead and buried. He would, he said, be deeply unhappy if this assurance were broken.

I said that the proposed site was clearly the most suitable and the one most likely to gain planning approval. The main part of the garden of No 11 would be untouched. A Centre attached to the North side of the Cathedral would raise formidable architectural problems and insuperable planning difficulties.

Apart from the Treasurer, there seems to be broad agreement that the garden site is the right one, and it is obvious that the needs of the Cathedral must have priority over the personal interests of members of the Chapter. But there was no readiness to make a final decision today so we asked for a more detailed plan of the site and the way it might be used.

Thursday 7 September 1989

We have appointed a new Cathedral Architect – Peter Bird, who is a partner in a firm that has been looking after churches and cathedrals for over 100 years. The fact that he is young, but has a highly-regarded partnership behind him is just what we need and we had no difficulty in choosing him from a fairly large field. The only embarrassment was that one of his senior colleagues wanted the job.

There is a problem – of at least there can be – with the best of the cathedral architects inasmuch as they tend to take on too much work. Peter Bird is already the architect for Exeter Cathedral and for three smaller Welsh cathedrals, and he is responsible for several National Trust properties, including Stourhead, in Wiltshire. So he will have his hands full when, as we hope, our £5 million restoration begins. Naturally, we discussed this with him and were reassured by his telling us that Exeter and the Welsh cathedrals have little money available for making heavy claims on his time.

The philosophy of conservation has changed considerably during the fourteen years in which I have had some responsibility for two major buildings. At Westminster Abbey, where the Victorian restorations carried out by Scott and Pearson survived barely 100 years because of a wrong choice of stone, Peter Foster is carrying out a programme of stone replacement that will, when completed, produce externally a new building.

Here at Winchester, however, our new man, like his predecessor, will replace stone only when it is absolutely clear that it has but a limited life ahead of it. This led to some interesting discussions with the candidates at the interviews because Keith Walker and I would like to see some of the old, decayed gargoyles and grotesques replaced by contemporary creations. Lydia Kirk, our Head Mason who is also a very good sculptor, is keen to do some, but quite apart from the conservation issue there is the difficulty of finding appropriate late-twentieth-century symbols to live on a mediaeval building.

Tuesday 26 September 1989

Dick Sawyer and his team of retired surveyors and town planners have today presented to the Dean and Chapter their report on the future of the

Close. A highly competent and interesting document it is, too. I am glad we have not had to pay for it.

As anticipated, the proposals are quite radical. The whole of what we call Dome Alley, consisting of four very large and much divided houses, two small cottages, several garages and some open space, should, they say, be leased to a property developer for a substantial sum of money. He would turn the existing houses into properties attractive to the wealthy and build four additional houses, also attractive to the wealthy.

The money thus realized would enable the Canons and others displaced to be rehoused in new properties erected in other parts of the Close. These would be much easier to manage and responsibility for the late-seventeenth-century houses in Dome Alley would fall to the developer. New workshops should be built in a distant corner of the Deanery garden and the old bakehouse turned into the Cathedral Office. A Visitors Centre should be built on a long strip of the garden of No 11, largely concealed by the high, former monastery wall, yet clearly visible to visitors leaving the Cathedral. For the purposes of Planning 'benefit' a new footpath, open to the public, should be created along the banks of the stream between the Deanery and Wolvesey, the home of the Bishop.

All of which hangs together and makes a good deal of sense. Besides the Visitors Centre issue, the sensitive points are those involving the building of new houses away from Dome Alley and the erection of workshops on a site that is at the moment particularly tranquil and where it would be necessary to make a new road and break through an ancient wall in order to gain access. There is also the point that handing over Dome Alley to a developer would increase the population of the Close by the introduction of a new element that may, or may not, wish to be associated with the Cathedral. The character of our community life would inevitably change.

Whether or not all or any of these proposals would win the approval of the Planning Authority, English Heritage and other interested parties is far from certain. A natural tendency would be to require us to leave the Close as it is. We did not discuss the report today, but confined ourselves to asking questions for the purpose of clarification. We shall consider it fully in due course. Meanwhile, it is absolutely imperative that the contents of the report be regarded as strictly confidential. Any leakage will cause the balloon to go up, not only in Winchester and Hampshire but far beyond, then rational consideration of the proposals will become impossible.

The thirty-six-hour colloquium on 'The Church and the Visual Arts today: partnership or estrangement', organized by Keith Walker, has been very successful. It is many years since an encounter of this sort was held and about fifty artists and theologians came.

The lectures and discussions were of uniformly high quality, though I think many were disappointed by the final lecture, given in the Cathedral by Roger de Grey, the President of the Royal Academy. The three main topics, addressed in varied ways, were: Is all true art religious? Is there such a thing as sacred art? How far are the churches sensitive to the needs of artists and why do they not make more use of contemporary artists in the adornment of their buildings?

Quite the most interesting, and surprising, contribution came from Peter Fuller, editor of *Modern Painters*. He was brought into the programme in order to introduce a sceptical, agnostic note. But he did nothing of the kind. I don't know his work, so I cannot tell if his mind is changing, but the artists were astonished when he said 'it is absolutely essential that some element of the transcendent is brought back into art. Modernism has refused to confront the transcendent; it has only used religious symbols in a degraded, sentimental or ironic way. Ever since the Pre-Raphaelites, Christian symbolism has ceased to make a significant contribution to British art. The secular institutions are morally and ethically and spiritually and aesthetically bankrupt, so the church now has a tremendous opportunity to give aesthetic leadership.'

Among the assembled company there was, however, no lively expectation that such leadership will be forthcoming. Several of the artists told of their unhappy experiences at the hands of church authorities who seemed to have not the faintest idea as to the nature and purpose of art, or of the true needs of their buildings.

A number of the theologians present said that, with the best will in the world, very few churches today have sufficient money to enable them to commission high quality works of contemporary art. To which the artists responded: money need not be a problem; where there is genuine understanding of what an artist is trying to do there is nearly always a willingness on his or her part to be generous to churches exercising patronage. Instances were quoted of artists who had virtually given their work away.

The whole colloquium was very stimulating and Keith Walker was asked to arrange another in two to three years' time.

The fund-raising consultants told a joint meeting of the Dean and Chapter and the Cathedral Trust this evening that they believe it is possible for £7 million to be raised by a major appeal (or campaign, as they prefer to call it) starting next year. In the course of their feasibility study conducted at the end of last month they interviewed about fifty carefully selected people and, although they met some tough nuts and had some disappointments, there was enough positive response to encourage the setting of a £7 million target.

I am frankly surprised. When we stated our needs – £5 million for restoration of the Cathedral, £1 million for the building of a Visitors Centre, and £1 million for the endowment of the Choir – I thought that after the feasibility study they would indicate a maximum target of £5 million, itself a substantial figure. But no, they say £7 million provided we start next Spring and recruit the necessary committees – a Major Gifts committee to obtain gifts of £100,000 and over; a Key Gifts committee for gifts between £25,000 and £100,000; a Community Gifts committee for everything below £25,000.

It is obvious that I shall have to play a leading role in the appeal, not so much by asking individuals to give, though there will be some of that, but more by my presence at every fund-raising meeting and event, by speaking to groups convened throughout the length and breadth of the Diocese, and by acting as the public spokesman of the whole enterprise. Experience shows that unless the Dean himself is seen to be 100% committed no one else will feel the need to be committed or to give. Which is fair enough, so I must start clearing my diary of non-essential engagements next year and, I suspect, 1991 as well. It will be a miracle if we can get the money in twelve months.

Thursday 2 November 1989

A pouring wet day for the official opening of the Trinity Centre's new venture on Romsey Road for the homeless and the drop-outs of our rich community. Two adjoining houses, neither very large and both sorely neglected, have been acquired – one will be used as a day centre, the other as temporary accommodation.

After lunch with the clients and staff, I made a short speech, then the Mayor and I stepped outside and, in some haste because of the atrocious weather, cut ribbons in the doorways of each house.

This is a significant development, since the Centre now has its own premises and is no longer beholden to anyone else. But this accommodation is totally inadequate for the need. It is heartbreaking to be with young couples and single mothers with their babies who are thankful to have as a bed-sit just one small room, poorly furnished and horribly cramped, with a communal bathroom and loo along the corridor.

Some have come from areas of high unemployment in search of work, but there is not the slightest possibility of their earning enough to rent or buy a house or flat at Winchester prices. The staff and helpers are doing heroic work, but there is something desperately wrong when young people are driven to this.

Tuesday 7 November 1989

At last the Care of Cathedrals Measure has won the approval (reluctant but given all the same) of the Cathedrals and of the General Synod and is ready for Parliamentary approval. It has been a long and tedious haul and it was a great relief to end all the discussion at yesterday's meeting of Deans and Provosts in Westminster.

The conservation lobby, spotting a loophole which hitherto exempted Deans and Chapters from Planning laws, has used its not inconsiderable influence to bring us under control. From now on we shall be required to submit all our plans for changes to the Cathedral to a local Fabric Advisory Committee and when the proposals are significant they will go to a central Fabric Commission in London.

There is nothing wrong with any of this. It may even be useful to us once we have learned to cope with the inevitable bureaucracy it will spawn. But there is no escaping the fact that it represents a major transfer of power. No longer will Deans and Chapters have sole responsibiliity for their cathedrals: they must petition for approval of even the smallest changes.

We were tackled skilfully with stick and carrot. The stick was a scarcely veiled threat that unless we agreed, more or less, with what was proposed, a much more draconian regime would be imposed upon us by Parliament. The carrot consisted of a hint that Government money might shortly become available for cathedral restoration purposes, but only if we accepted some degree of control.

So after much huffing and puffing the Deans and Provosts have agreed to a scheme that will shortly be invested with legal authority. This should be all right. In any case, few if any cathedrals have money enough to attempt anything outrageous.

It was reported to Chapter this morning that Tim and Anthea Fortescue have made considerable progress in the development of No 10a The Close as a place for serving refreshments to visitors from next Easter onwards. They are now looking for a large team of volunteers to help run it, under a professional manager.

The great marquee venture, which created so much excitement early this year, was abandoned, not because of the protests of local business interests, but because it proved to be neither practicable nor financially viable. The catering firm that was to be given the franchise found it to be too late in the year to get the marquee approved, manufactured, erected and into action this last summer, and they then told us that, from their point of view, it would be financially worthwhile only if the Dean and Chapter purchased the marquee. Costed at £25,000 this was obviously not on.

Further evidence of the lack of co-ordination and the poor communications in the Close came with the discovery that, while the plan for the marquee was in its early stages, Tim and Anthea Fortescue, our Development Managers, were working on a plan to turn No 10a into a coffee shop/tea room. When this plan emerged they were asked to put it on one side in favour of the marquee proposal, but after this was dropped they went back to their original scheme and have been working on it ever since. Three elegant first-floor rooms, probably of eighteenth-century creation, will provide seating for about sixty people, there is a good kitchen and, very important in these days of heavy regulation, adequate loos.

The Fortescues have had to fight many battles to get thus far. Every conceivable obstacle has been put in their way. Early on a retired professional caterer advised that the project was not financially viable, at which point I stepped in to insist that her figures be re-examined. With 400,000 visitors passing through the Cathedral every year, many commercial undertakings would surely give a great deal to be able to set up shop within easy reach of them. The next problem concerned the current use of the building. Designated some years ago as the Pastoral Centre, it is used occasionally for meetings and one room is rented by the Friends for use as a common-room by Cathedral voluntary helpers. It is, however, in a very shabby condition and only one volunteer is known to use the facility; still, there is a reluctance to give it up.

The Administrator is against the project, chiefly I suspect because he is not in charge of it, and the Treasurer is also opposing on the grounds (a) if it does not attract enough visitors it will lose money, and (b) if it attracts a large number of visitors it will become unmanageable and also disturb the tranquility of the Inner Close. The City Council is concerned with legal matters – change of use of the building, advertising signs, health and safety, and so on.

The whole thing must be something of a nightmare for Tim and Anthea and anyone less tenacious and committed than they are would have given up long ago, but now they are winning and are in touch with the head of the Diocesan Mothers' Union about the recruitment of volunteers to prepare and serve the food. They would like to be able to offer them travelling expenses, but needless to say, this is being opposed.

We also made the decision about the Visitors Centre. This is to comprise a restaurant, shop, meeting/changing rooms, storage, lavatories and an educational facility. And it is to be built on the edge of the garden of No 11 The Close.

Today the long-drawn-out, painful, dispute with the Treasurer had to be concluded because the fund-raising consultants have warned us that an artist's impresion of the proposed building will be needed for inclusion in the Campaign literature, and before anything is published it will be necessary to have an indication that the building is acceptable to the Planning Authority.

The Treasurer first dissented from the inclusion of an educational facility, then asked that his dissatisfaction at not being consulted in the early stages of the Visitors Centre proposal be minuted. The ensuing discussion inevitably covered all the old ground again but in the end the site was approved – the Treasurer abstaining and the Precentor dissenting, mainly I think in sympathetic solidarity with the Treasurer, whose views on most things he shares.

It is a great pity that such an important decision was not unanimous, but the needs of the Cathedral are too urgent for us to wait until we have reached a common mind. In any case, there is within the wider Cathedral community overwhelming support for the proposal and it would not have been easy to explain further delay.

Wednesday 29 November 1989

This year's meetings of the Cathedral congregation and other supporters, held yesterday and today, were just as well attended as those convened last year at the time of the financial crisis, so it looks as if something of this sort might become an annual event, though the agenda will need to be widened to encompass more than money.

It was good to be able to report that in the final four months of the

1988/89 financial year the projected deficit was reduced by £42,000 to a final, actual figure of £31,000 – still a substantial deficit, but things are now moving in the right direction. As a result of the steps taken after the crisis meetings, Visitors' donations increased by 4.5%, bookshop income by 43%, special services collections by £7,034, congregational giving by £16,000, with smaller amounts from calligraphy and the new votive candle stand. Other projects will begin to yield new income in the current year and I hope we may move into surplus.

Not surprisingly, all this was very well received and, best of all from my point of view, we have established a momentum for change which even the Chapter will not be able to resist. Thus I talked about the need for the planning of a new Visitors Centre, incorporating a restaurant, gift shop and educational facilities, to move forward as quickly as possible, so that as soon as the money from the Appeal becomes available building can start.

I spoke also of the need for the altar frontals, vestments, carpets and furnishings to be renewed, for the signs in and around the Cathedral to be replaced, for our educational work to be further developed, and for our relations with the parishes of the Diocese to be greatly strengthened. I ended:

Our task is to enable the Cathedral to do its great work, to fulfil its vocation, as an important centre of Christian worship and mission. There is enormous scope for this, tremendous opportunities for helping others to share the faith which inspired those who built the Cathedral and those who have served it across the centuries to our own day. This requires vision, energy and resources – all of which are to hand or within reach – and it must be a shared task, involving all who care for Winchester Cathedral and recognize its importance in the life of our region and nation. This is why I appreciate your presence here today.

I am grateful for the achievements of the past year.

I am full of hope for the future, and

I am an impatient Dean who believes it is still necessary to apply the accelerator, rather than the brake.

Friday 1 December 1989

So Winchester Cathedral is now floodlit – probably the last of the English cathedrals to be so illuminated. The possibility of this was on the agenda of my first Chapter meeting, a year last February, when the prospects were by no means promising because of the cost. But in the end the City Council, the Chamber of Commerce and the Wessex Hotel rallied round to provide what turned out to be more than £20,000, and this evening we gathered in the hotel, on the edge of the Close, for the switching-on ceremony.

I made a short speech, thanking the donors and pointing out – unnecessarily, but one has to say something on these occasions – that Winchester's night-time darkened central space would now be replaced by a truly magnificent sight, which would be good for the Cathedral and even better for the City. Then, to prove my point, the Mayor switched on the lights, but most unfortunately the building was shrouded in fog and the effect of the lights was distinctly eerie – the outline of the building faintly perceptible here and there, and the scene of no use whatever to the assembled Press photographers.

It should be better tomorrow, for although this low-lying area is vulnerable to fog, it is only rarely as dense as we have it this evening.

1990

We started the final decade of the twentieth century by the ringing of the Cathedral's bells and the usual annual ceremony in the Tower. The ringers and their families, a total of about forty, came to the Deanery for refreshments at 10.30 p.m.; they were joined at 11.00 p.m. by the Virgers and other Close residents, then by the Bishop and the Mayor. The ringers left soon afterwards to start the ringing out of the old year with muffled bells and at about 11.40 p.m. the rest of the company climbed the narrow, winding staircase to the ringing chamber – none too easy in an ankle-length cassock.

About three minutes before midnight I said a few words of thanks to the ringers for their efforts during the past twelve months, then led some prayers related to the year that was passing and to the year about to arrive, the Bishop blessed the City and the County, the bells, now minus their muffles, rang merrily, we wished one another a Happy New Year, there was handshaking and some kissing, and those of us who were not ringing descended to ground level and, in my case, thankfully to bed.

Although I spent fourteen years in the North of England where the advent of the New Year is taken very seriously, I have never been able to work up any enthusiasm for the occasion. For some reason, the ending of one year and the beginning of another doesn't move me in the slightest and I would much prefer to be in bed at midnight. My colleagues on the Chapter, apart from Keith Walker who is a ringer, evidently feel the same about it because they steadfastly refuse to attend the party or the Tower ceremony.

Tuesday 2 January 1990

The New Year finds us without a Deanery gardener, the last incumbent of this office having officially retired on health grounds on the last day of 1989. In fact he has done nothing to the garden for quite a long time and it would be more unkind than untrue to say that he retired some years ago.

He always arrived in good time in the morning but the lighting of his pipe was attended with great difficulty and the surveying of the three and a half acres occupied much time. Indeed before he could turn over more than a few spadefuls of soil the mid-morning break demanded attention. This accomplished and the spade once again prepared for action, the call of the betting shop necessitated a stroll into the City.

A gardener thus exercised required a hearty lunch, and afterwards another pipe of tobacco, carefully packed and patiently coaxed alight. There was barely time for the tea-break before the fading light of the winter afternoon made it impossible for the keenest of gardeners to distinguish between a prize plant and a weed. And there was the pressing matter of which horse had won the 3.30 at Newbury.

Inevitably, the weeds won the race for occupation of the Deanery garden and they gained a further advantage when the gardener was accused by a neighbour of having an affair with his wife and was so injured in the ensuing assault that he needed six weeks' sick leave – this coinciding exactly with the spring season of sowing and planting.

The recovery of the gardener, and also of the garden, was protracted and the injuries to the lower part of his body were succeeded by acute breathing problems, induced surely, by the pungent fumes generated by his pipe, rather than by excessive exertion. The hot summer came and went, autumn turned out to be a season of mellow fruitlessness and the garden, like the gardener, had lain fallow for year.

Never has a gardener entered into retirement better prepared.

Tuesday 16 January 1990

It is a great relief to me that a design for a Visitors Centre has now been formally accepted. The building of it depends of course on the success of the £7 million Appeal, and there will be many planning hazards to overcome, but at least we now have a firm project to work for and an important incentive for fund-raising. I hope also that the opposition to the proposal will gracefully accept defeat.

Plincke, Leaman and Browning, the architects who are so conveniently placed on the edge of the Close, have great flair and a considerable reputation for designing appropriate new buildings for historic sites. They offered us a choice of three designs – one of fairly modest-size that would not really have met our needs; another an ambitious scheme that would separate the shop from the restaurant by creating it beneath the flying buttresses on the South side of the Nave; and a third which makes ingenious use of the long strip of garden near the West door of the Cathedral, by converting the eighteenth-century coachhouse into a two-storey shop, linking it to a pavilion-like restaurant, and making a cloister alongside the high mediaeval wall to give independent access to the education centre.

They believe this third scheme can be built for just under £1 million and completed in just under twelve months. It looks very attractive and should meet our needs admirably, so now we must begin the long process of obtaining the necessary consents. There will be no avoiding an archaeological dig of some sort, so the sooner we can get things moving, the better.

Wednesday 17 January 1990

We have decided to reject the advice of the Cathedrals' Advisory Commission regarding our wish to place Peter Eugene Ball's sculpture *Christus* high on the North wall of the North Transept. This fine piece came to us by accident. The Visual Arts Colloquium last October was accompanied by an Arts and Crafts Exhibition in the Cathedral and almost at the last moment we were asked if the *Christus* might be included. It had been made in 1989 without any destination in mind, Dorchester Abbey had a look at it but thought not, so it came to our exhibition and was placed on the North Transept wall simply as the best display setting. Here it immediately seemed at home, so much so that when the exhibition ended Pat Broughall, a member of the congregation, offered to pay for it so that it might remain.

Part of the explanation, undoubtedly, is that Peter Eugene Ball, who lives in Nottinghamshire, has been deeply influenced by the Romanesque elements of Southwell Minster. Thus his long, slender robed figure of Christ, open-armed as if crucified, yet without a cross and symbolizing also embracing and accepting – this fits most happily into the magnificent Romanesque architecture of our transepts. The figure is actually made from two pieces of oak, recovered from an old house that was being demolished, and it has golden motifs, inspired by Van Gogh's clouds, which suggest resurrection.

We all like it very much, and so does Peter Bird our new architect, but the Cathedrals' Advisory Commission who have to be consulted in these matters are against our installing it in the North Transept. They say it is slightly too small for its setting, but more importantly they believe the North Transept to be so important architecturally that it should be left in its stark simplicity and have nothing whatsoever added to it. Herein lies the great problem with bodies of this sort: they want buildings or parts of

81

buildings to be frozen at a particular moment in their history, quite overlooking the fact that prior to the Reformation our North Transept was a blaze of colour and replete with ornamentation. What is more, they seem unable to accept the priority of worship and devotion, for the *Christus* will add something significant to the devotional ambience of the Cathedral and we also intend to bring it down to the Nave on Good Friday for the Veneration of the Cross.

Fortunately, the CAC still has only an advisory role and although it is not easy to reject its advice, the case for doing so in this instance seems overwhelming. The figure is therefore to be accurately sited and sensitively lit and it is good that we can do this before the successor body, the Cathedrals Fabric Commission for England, can bare its teeth.

Wednesday 7 February 1990

The last twelve months, comprising my third year as Dean, have been messy, but some progress has been made. The income for our day-to-day running costs has increased dramatically and we should have a surplus this year. The serious problems of the Trust are now behind us and, under new leadership, we shall be launching an appeal for £7 million in July. There is also a firm commitment to build a Visitors Centre as soon as the necessary money becomes available.

It is, I suppose, unrealistic to believe that developments of this sort can be achieved without a great deal of conflict and some upset. Although I have been in the full-time service of the church for nearly forty years, I still tend to think that it ought to be possible to make progress smoothly and efficiently along the lines of the best secular organizations. But of course the Church of England is not like Sainsbury's or Marks and Spencers.

The devolution of power, inherent in our organization, is designed to preclude concentration of authority, so there is bound to be pulling and pushing in different directions. It is interesting to compare a Chapter Meeting with a Bishop's Senior Staff Meeting. Both are made up of the same sort of clergy and in both there is a desire to reach a common mind before decisions are made. But because we are an episcopal church, the Bishop is acknowledged to have a leadership role and therefore a higher degree of responsibility and authority than everyone else at the meeting. This affects the dynamics of the process considerably, in marked contrast to those of the Chapter, where the Dean is no more than *primus inter pares* and where everyone claims equal authority, even though the Dean has to carry the can publicly.

This is how things are, and there is no point in becoming a Dean unless one is prepared to live and work with such a structure. And in spite of all the problems and disappointments we are actually moving forward. Certainly we are now getting a lot of attention from the media and there seems widespread approval of the direction we are taking.

Wednesday 21 February 1990

I have bought my first painting at a Sotheby's auction. When one of their representatives came to advise on the painting of William Laud, which turned out to be a copy of the famous Van Dyck portrait, not an original, I lamented the fact that the Deanery has no portraits of former Deans apart from a small one of Thomas Rennell who was here from 1805 to 1840. During the seventeenth, eigheenth and nineteenth centuries most of them must have been painted, but their families probably carried the portraits off when they died.

The representative undertook to let me know if any such portraits ever came on to the market and about three weeks ago he sent a catalogue containing details of a portrait of George Abbott, who was Dean from 1600-1609 and eventually became Archbishop of Canterbury. He was a Calvinist, much involved in theological controversy, and his career ended tragically when he accidentally shot and killed his gamekeeper while hunting in Hampshire. Canon Law decreed that no one with blood on his hands could be in Holy Orders, so Abbott was suspended from office and, although he was eventually granted a Royal pardon, he never recovered his reputation and influence.

John Hardacre, the Curator, went to see the portrait and thought it would be worth up to £1,500 but would require additional money for its cleaning. The Dean and Chapter agreed that I might spend this amount from the Deanery furnishing fund, now in healthy credit, so I went to the auction this afternoon. Very interesting and highly efficient it turned out to be, too. I was greeted by a glamorous young woman who entered my name and address in some sort of computer and handed me what appeared to be a table tennis bat, but she called it a paddle.

Soon I caught sight of my distant predecessor – a rather grim figure in episcopal robes and wearing a Canterbury cap. It is a large painting of about the same size as William Laud and, like him, very dark, even when allowance is made for the necessary cleaning. But well worth hanging in this Deanery. It took about an hour to reach Abbott, by which time the silky auctioneer had disposed of many other English portraits, including one of Charles II which went very cheaply and which I now wish I had bought, though of course the price might have increased somewhat had I started bidding.

I was, and still am, intrigued to know who else was interested in Abbott. The auctioneer started him off at £400. I raised my paddle, bearing the number 68, and immediately there was another bid at £500. I bettered this by a further £100, only to find myself challenged to make it £800. This I did and there was a pause during which the auctioneer's hammer was raised and I was half-congratulating myself on having secured the picture for well below my top limit. But bidding started again and at £1,000 the silky auctioneer very kindly advised me that I was bidding against myself. This was sorted out (a good thing I went in my clerical collar) and at £1,500 the hammer fell, number 68 was noted, and by the time I reached the accounts department the bill was ready. Now I must find some way of getting the purchase from Bond Street to Winchester.

Tuesday 27 February 1990

Antony Gormley, a leading British sculptor, has offered us as a gift a remarkable piece of his work and, after a certain amount of humming and hawing, the Chapter has agreed, somewhat ungraciously, to accept it on a year's trial.

Gormley was one of three sculptors we invited to submit maquettes for a statue of the Virgin Mary for the Lady Chapel, but his entry was disappointing, indeed somewhat puzzling. Modelled on a very small scale in clay, it portrayed Mary as pregnant. This was perfectly all right, yet it seemed so entirely lacking in grace – positively ugly, I thought – that it was impossible to see how in its final form it would ever enhance the spirit of devotion in the Lady Chapel. I wonder if he really wanted the commission?

During a visit to Winchester, however, Gormley was much taken by our twelfth-century Crypt which, as is usual in the winter, was flooded. This connected with a figure he created in 1986 with the intention that it should stand in or near water. It was exhibited in Bath for a time but did not find a permanent home there.

Called 'Sound II', it is a life-size figure of a man made of lead. Apparently the artist first got someone to cover him with plaster. When this set he was cut out of it and the plaster figure remaining was reinforced with fibreglass and resin before being clad in lead. The result is striking indeed. The figure is partly filled with water and holds a stoup of water on which it appears to be meditating.

Just why it is called 'Sound II' is far from clear but it has something to do with the fact that water is one of life's basic elements and has a divine source. Standing in the water and framed by a Romanesque arch, the figure has both power and serenity, and even without permanent lighting, which it certainly needs, the reflection in the water adds a great deal to its impact.

This is a wonderfully generous gift, valued at £80-90,000, and not unreasonably Antony Gormley's offer is subject to certain conditions, e.g. it must be adequately lit, accessible to the public, not removed to another site, fully insured against theft or damage. Keith Walker, who has secured the gift, is naturally very enthusiastic about it, and so am I, but the rest of the Chapter see all manner of problems. Who will pay for the lighting and for the wrought iron railings on the viewing platform? What about the loss of income if the public is allowed to view the figure, and therefore part of the Crypt, without charge? Who does Antony Gormley suppose he is, wishing to impose a piece of his unplaced work in one of England's greatest cathedrals? And who is going to pay for the additional insurance cover?

All very depressing and displaying that lack of vision and enthusiasm which is such an impediment to the development of this Cathedral's life. After a year here, and subject to the approval of the new Cathedrals Fabric Commission, it will surely stay and come to be widely admired, but getting the Chapter's agreement to anything unusual is a wearisome business and greatly saps one's energy.

Tuesday 6 March 1990

At mid-day I performed the official opening ceremony of Cathedral Refreshments – our first excursion into the realm of providing physical as well as spiritual sustenance for our 400,000 visitors, and making some much-needed money as well. It was a modest enough occasion but one of some significance, I think, because it will prepare the way for the opening of a Visitors Centre in two to three years' time and provide valuable experience of providing for visitors' needs.

I must say that Anthea Fortescue, who combines energy and enterprise with impeccable taste, has made a wonderful job of converting the shabby old Pastoral Centre into a most attractive place for anyone to eat and drink. The rooms themselves, being part of an elegant eighteenth-century house, gave her a good start and now, with just the right colours on the walls, ample use of Liberty's fabrics, and stylish furniture, we have something rather special. It has cost just over £5,000 to set up.

Recruiting Elizabeth Hewlett, the butler at the Judges' Lodging, to manage the enterprise was also an astute move, and the response from the parishes of the Diocese to our request for volunteers to serve the refreshments has been astonishing. Already, 90 parishes have produced 600 volunteers and offers are coming in every day. This is, I am sure, a clear sign of the perceived need for the Cathedral to have a facility of this kind, and I should like to think that the involvement of so many people in the development will strengthen the link between the Cathedral and the parishes – something most urgently needed.

Tuesday 20 March 1990

I have just had my first encounter with the military might of Russia. A telephone message this morning announced that General Sir David Ramsbotham, Commander of the UK Army, is entertaining the Deputy Chief of the General Staff of the Soviet Army and wished to bring him to the Cathedral this afternoon at 4.00 pm. Might the Dean be available to greet them?

They arrived at the West door dead on time and presented what for me was an astonishing sight. I had last seen David Ramsbotham more than thirty years ago when his father was Bishop of Jarrow and he a Cambridge undergraduate. Now he stands well over six feet and looks every inch a distinguished soldier. In marked, almost absurd, contrast his Russian guest was a diminutive figure, his height increased slightly by what seemed an over-large cap, of the sort worn by soldiers appearing in opera. His style suggested the Royal Army Pay Corps (no insult intended) rather than the leadership of an army whose strength has determined Western foreign policy for the last four decades.

Guiding him around the Cathedral with the aid of an interpreter was not altogether easy. At first I wondered if he might not be remotely interested in a building of religious significance, but it turned out that he was greatly interested both in its history and current use. His questions were perceptive.

The visit lasted the prescribed twenty minutes, and as the two Generals moved away to their next port of call I felt immensely reassured.

Saturday 16 June 1990

The parishes and people associated with the Renewal Movement in the Diocese came to the Cathedral this evening for a service of celebration – Praise for Pentecost. Whit Week was an appropriate time for them to come, for they have a particular concern for the work of the Holy Spirit in the church and in the lives of individuals. Sometimes they are known as the Charismatic Movement because they express their response to the Holy Spirit's presence in their lives by ecstatic utterances, speaking in tongues, informal prayer and acts of healing. About ten years ago I formed the impression that the movement had peaked and might well go into decline, but in fact it soon took on a new lease of life and it is becoming increasingly influential in the Church of England and in most other churches.

The Cathedral was packed mainly, but by no means exclusively, with young people. There was a good deal of electronic equipment for the making and amplifying of sound and before the service started there was a healthy sense of expectancy. I gave them my usual warm welcome, taking care to emphasize the importance of attention to the Holy Spirit, for so long neglected by the church. Unfortunately, I was not heard because the organizers had chosen to use their own equipment in preference to the Cathedral's sound reinforcement system and this was not effective with the spoken voice.

My own theological outlook and spirituality is miles removed from theirs, but I hoped for an act of worship that would be refreshing and renewing. Perhaps it was for them, but for me it proved to be extraordinarily boring. The service consisted of a sequence of some sixteen or seventeen hymns and choruses, the latter very repetitive, interspersed with prayers of varying length, and with a good sermon from the Bishop of Southampton in the middle. The content of everything was expressive of personal, evangelical religion, there was much hand-waving and, at times, a very great deal of noise. Occupying more than one and a half hours, the service had a lack of variety that became monotonous and, for me anyway, tedious.

Question: If, as I believe, the Holy Spirit is God in action, always seeking to enliven, invigorate and illuminate, why does he choose to bore me stiff? The answer must be that he doesn't, and that those who came to the Cathedral this evening are concentrating on only a small part of the Holy Spirit's activity at this time.

This movement seems to me to be markedly similar to eighteenth- and nineteenth-century revivalism – a phenomenon that has emerged at different times in the history of the church and always been sectarian rather than truly Catholic. It may well be helpful, for a time, to those who are caught up in it, but its focus is altogether too narrow to represent a comprehensive expression of the Holy Spirit's activity in the exciting, yet in many ways frightening, world in which we live.

This afternoon and evening the Diocesan Synod, meeting at Chandlers Ford, debated a report *A Church for the World,* produced by a small working party set up by the Bishop to consider the implications for the Diocese of a projected fall in the number of full-time clergy – about eight per cent by the year 2000. There are good things in the report, but it is badly flawed at one key point and poor Michael Manktelow, who presented it to the Synod, took a fair hammering.

The general thrust of its recommendations is that the policy of solving the clergy shortage by amalgamating parishes should cease; in fact, be reversed. Every parish should have its own minister – ordained or lay. If a full-time parson is not available, or cannot be financed or justified on other grounds, a retired priest might be appointed, or a non-stipendiary priest who has a job in the secular world, or a lay reader, or a local man or woman who is well-regarded and ordained to exercise a local ministry.

This is, I am sure, the right approach. The amalgamation of parishes has not worked well and the concept of a peripatetic clergy is alien to the Anglican tradition in England. So also, for that matter, is the ordaining of a local man or woman, and the training of a large number of these will almost certainly need more resources than are likely to be available. But it could be started on an experimental basis in one or two areas of the Diocese.

The great weakness of the report, however, is that although it has the comprehensive title *A Church for the World,* it concentrates entirely on the parochial system and takes no account of the fact that in these days most people spend a great deal of time outside the places where they reside and that the church already has other forms of ministry which engage with people in extra-parochial situations – chaplaincies in industry, education, hospitals, social services, youth work. Nor does it display any awareness of the existence of the Cathedral, which has considerable resources and is potentially, if not actually, the most powerful agency of mission in the Diocese.

Twenty-five years ago there were the beginnings of an understanding that if the church is to exercise a mission to the whole of society, in other words to be *A Church for the World,* it must cease to confine its ministry to residential chaplaincies and branch out into a more diverse pattern of ministry that embraces every part of life. The training of men for the non-stipendiary ministry was then seen as a way of offering a certain kind of priestly witness in the workplace, but now it is regarded as a way of providing cheap substitutes for full-time parochial clergy.

It was some of the clergy involved in non-parochial ministries who exposed the weakness of the report at the Synod and drove members of the working party on to the defensive, but as the parishes are now providing most of the money I fear that they will continue to be given priority in the allocation of resources.

Sunday 1 July 1990

The dedication this afternoon of the *Pietà* created for the Lady Chapel by Peter Eugene Ball was a very special occasion. The Cathedral was absolutely crowded. Besides our own congregation, a large number of Roman Catholics came, together with members of various societies that encourage devotion to the Virgin Mary. The placing of such a statue in the Lady Chapel after an interval of over 400 years has rung bells in all kinds of places and of course the ecumenical significance of the event has not been overlooked. It is curious how a chance remark (though it was, I must confess, slightly calculated) in a sermon can spark off a response and a sequence of events that leads to something really significant.

The Choir sang some of the finest music in praise of the Virgin, we had a lot of incense, Crispian Hollis, the Roman Catholic Bishop of Portsmouth, preached an excellent sermon and the Dedication was carried out by our own Bishop. Another curious little element in the occasion was provided by the fact that it was the previous Roman Catholic Bishop – Anthony Emery – by no means a dedicated ecumenist, who suggested in a sermon in the Cathedral shortly before he died that devotion to the Virgin Mary in the Lady Chapel might become a focus of unity for all Christians. This could hardly have appealed to the Methodists, Baptists and other Free Church people who were present, but it has borne fruit for Anglicans and Roman Catholics in a way that the old Bishop could hardly have anticipated.

Crispian Hollis is a very different kettle of fish. Tall, elegant, quintessentially Oxford (Balliol), Somerset Light Infantry, former BBC Religious Broadcasting Department – everything that Anglican bishops are made of. He is very much at home on the ecumenical scene, although if it came to a crunch I am not sure that he would be much more accommodating than old Bishop Emery ever was. However, he certainly rose to the occasion today.

The *Pietà* is a characteristic piece of Peter Eugene Ball's work and very successful in its setting. Mary is portrayed as the middle-aged peasant woman she was, mourning over her crucified son, and some people at the service found this surprising and difficult. The traditional image of Mary as youthful and beautiful is so all-pervasive that most of us have forgotten that by the time of the Crucifixion she was probably in her mid-fifties. This *Pietà* makes no attempt to idealize her, and it is clearly right that she is portrayed in relation to Jesus, on whom her place in Christian history depends.

Monday 9 July 1990

Very gratifying news today: in the National Heritage Museum of the Year Awards for 1990 our Triforium Gallery has been given the award for the best museum of fine and applied art. The citation reads: 'An exemplary gallery which has been beautifully carried out to a well considered plan.' The prize is £1,500, which is useful and so is the publicity. I'm glad, too, for Paul Britton and John Hardacre, and it is good for those who paid for it to know that their money helped to create something which has won national praise.

Tuesday 10 July 1990

The Treasurer reported to the Chapter this morning that the accounts for the year ended 31 March showed a surplus of £148,000. This represents of course a massive turnaround from the projected deficit of £99,000 forecast just two years ago and indeed from the 'small surplus' the Treasurer talked about at the meetings of the congregation last November. The explanation is that a number of the Recovery Programme projects are now bringing in additional income, Cathedral Refreshments made a clear profit of £25,000 in six months, and there have been some useful legacies.

The news of the surplus was, naturally enough, greeted with pleasure and congratulations all round, but I rather spoiled the festive spirit by blowing up with frustration. I pointed out that, while the surplus was most welcome news, it was not until the accounts were produced that we had the faintest idea whether we were in surplus or deficit. The Treasurer might well have appeared this morning with grim news of another deficit. This was, I said, totally unacceptable and we simply could not continue to run our costly operation in such ignorance.

Somewhat to my surprise, the point was taken and after some discussion it was agreed that we would take steps to bring in management consultants to make recommendations for the proper organization of our accounts department and also the overhaul of our whole administration. As the scale of the Cathedral's activities increases, the pressure on the administration inevitably becomes more intense and its inefficiencies are exposed. At the moment virtually everything requiring a decision has to cross my desk, there are no clear lines of reporting and accountability, little in the way of devolved responsibility, and the Administrator is simply not coping with the volume of work we are generating.

The decision to bring in expensive management consultants was eased by the availability of money from the surplus, though most of this will have to be used to replace last year's loss and to provide for forthcoming capital expenditure, and I am to approach Jim Butler, whose firm has a large management consultancy division. He will recognize the danger in raising £7 million for an organization with a highly inefficient administration.

Thursday 12 July 1990

Today marks the opening of our £7 million Appeal and we launched it with a news conference in the Deanery that attracted a good number of journalists and broadcasters. I think we have made a good start. Jim Scott, the Lord Lieutenant, spoke of the vital importance of the Cathedral's work and called on the Hampshire community to rally to its restoration and development, I spoke at somewhat greater length on why the money is needed and how it is to be spent, and Jim Butler, chairman of the executive committee, made a considerable impact when he announced that £912,000 is already in hand or promised.

A great deal of work has been going on behind the scenes since the beginning of April, recruiting people for the committees, preparing lists of likely major donors, setting up an office with full-time secretarial support, designing publicity material, and securing a number of substantial preliminary gifts to enable us to announce about £1 million at the launch.

The whole basis of the Appeal, which has 'Funding the Future' as its slogan, is direct, face-to-face giving. Enthusiastic supporters pledge a certain gift themselves then go to ask a few friends and colleagues to do the same. Matching like with like is crucially important: those who give, say, £100,000 go to others who are in a position to give on the same scale. There is to be no mass mailing, and although a certain number of events are being organized, these are chiefly for publicity purposes, rather than for fund-raising, though doubtless they will bring in useful money as well.

A meeting at Wolvesey, convened by the Bishop at the end of May for the recruiting of the Major Gifts Committee, was both instructive and fascinating. The aim of this committee is to raise gifts of £100,000 and more, and its members must therefore be in a position to donate this amount themselves. A committee of twelve giving at this level and each recruiting just one other person or institution to do the same will, without a great deal of work but with much generosity, raise £2.4 million. I wondered just how such a committee might be recruited, but I arrived at Wolvesey to find quite a crowded gathering in the Bishop's drawing room.

Here were many of the leading people in Hampshire society, most of them quite unknown to me but evidently concerned about the Cathedral and ready to lend a hand. The Bishop welcomed them, I spoke of the Cathedral's needs and Stefan Lipa, the Appeal Manager, talked about the fund-raising method to be employed. A short discussion followed, the Bishop's wife served tea, and out of the gathering ten members of the committee were recruited. At its first meeting in the Deanery it was apparent that the members knew a great many people with money who might be prepared to give to the Appeal – 'I will approach X because I supported him when he was running the Mary Rose Appeal'; 'I will ask Y because I let him have some shooting in Scotland'; 'I will go to Z because I fagged for him at Eton'. And so on. I am learning fast how big money is raised.

Stefan Lipa, our Appeal Manager, is an impressive man in whom I have great confidence. Although he has a Polish name (his father being a Pole) he is a New Zealander by nationality and before turning to fund-raising was trained as a lawyer. His style is that of a gentleman, but inside the velvet glove is a steel fist and his blend of courtesy and firmness is just what is needed. He and I are getting on exceedingly well and he is becoming involved in the general life of the Cathedral as well as in the managing of the Appeal.

We are fortunate also to have the active, not just the nominal, support of Jim Scott. He must be just about the best, certainly the most popular, Lord Lieutenant in the country and people seemed prepared to do anything for him. And Jim Butler, who is effectively the chairman of the Appeal, is hugely efficient, influential – and generous. So all in all we have very good leadership and the different committees have first-rate chairmen.

Whether or not we shall raise the £7 million in twelve months remains to be seen. It is certainly a tall order, and the economic climate is deteriorating quickly, but we must keep St Swithun's Day next year as our target date and display the utmost confidence that we can achieve it. The psychological element in fund-raising is, I think, much more important than is commonly realized. While we believe we can succeed, the possibility of success remains; once we lose confidence, failure is certain. At the moment there is no shortage of doomsters, including some on the Chapter, who are predicting failure to reach £7 million, so my main job, I can see, is keeping morale high. At the moment I am finding it all very stimulating and certainly I am tremendously encouraged by the number of people who have already offered to help and whose number is increasing daily.

Sandwich   Wednesday 1 August 1990

I enjoy coincidences, though I don't invest them with theological significance. Today I experienced one, the odds against which must be in the realms of millions to one. Walking along the main street of this ancient Cinque port to collect the newspapers I passed, as I do every day when I am here on holiday, a hut that houses a low-grade antiques shop. Hanging on the opened door of the hut was a water colour of a large church.

On closer inspection this turned out to be Winchester Cathedral, clad in wooden scaffolding and with some of its walls supported by huge beams. I asked the owner of the shop if he recognized the picture; he thought it was probably Canterbury Cathedral or some other large church in Kent.

Having put him right on this, I enquired about the artist – Ellen Eaton. He knew nothing about her, except that she spent the latter part of her life at Sturry, near Canterbury, and that a portfolio of her paintings had recently been found. He then consulted a small volume containing the names of painters and this revealed that Ellen Eaton worked during the early years of the present century and that her paintings were exhibited at the Royal Academy and many other reputable places.

My picture – I paid £75 for it – is of the Cathedral during the great Edwardian restoration when Diver William Walker underpinned the East end of the building with concrete and bricks, placed in position manually while wearing a diving suit to cope with the water and sludge present in the foundations. Quite apart from being an unusual and attractive picture, it is of particular significance as a record of what the Cathedral looked like at that time. So I suppose that when I leave the Deanery I ought to give it to the Dean and Chapter as it should remain in Winchester.

Question: What are the chances of a Dean of Winchester walking past a hut in a small town 150 miles from Winchester and noticing there such a painting of his cathedral which has probably not seen the light of day for eighty or more years?

Tuesday 11 September 1990

We have appointed the Revd Catherine Milford as one of our Honorary Chaplains, so she becomes the first woman to serve on the Cathedral's ordained staff. As a deacon, she will be of limited usefulness, but there are a number of ways in which she can assist and the symbolic value of her presence in the Cathedral is going to be important for us and for her. She is an excellent preacher.

Cathy's father, Sir John Cockcroft, was one of the nuclear scientists involved in the making of the two atomic bombs dropped on Japan in 1945, and this has had a profound effect on her, leading to a deep Christian commitment and the embracing of pacificism. She came to Winchester as the Diocesan Adult Education Adviser in 1988 and she is also the Moderator of the Movement for the Ordination of Women, now very active in campaigning for women to be admitted to the priesthood. This creates some difficulties for her as the Bishop of Winchester is firmly against it and the two of them obviously view each other with a good deal of suspicion whenever questions relating to women's ministry arise.

I don't think her ministry in the Cathedral as a deacon will cause any problems with the congregation, but if she becomes a priest during her time with us there are sure to be some objections to her presiding at the Eucharist – and from within the Chapter.

Tuesday 25 September 1990

The report of the archaeologists who have been working on the Visitors Centre site is now in and it is clear that the Centre will have to be re-designed. The site has turned out to be no more than a mediaeval burial ground and below nine feet there are a great many human remains. Quite a lot of bones have already been brought to the surface from the trial digs, and we have two options.

If we go ahead with the proposed two-storey building, requiring deep foundations, we shall be required to have a full archaeological excavation. This would seriously delay the building operation, it would be expensive, and there would always be the possibility of the archaeologists discovering deep down something really significant that would preclude our building on the site.

The alternative is to have a longer, single-storey building with shallow foundations that do not disturb the human remains and whatever else may be there. This would be more expensive to build but it seems the best way forward. Interestingly, it is the one favoured by the archaeologists, whose hands are already more than full with excavations in Winchester. Their chief concern is that we shall not destroy anything.

Wednesday 17 October 1990

Today's meeting of Deans and Provosts at St Paul's was concerned mainly with the appalling crisis at Lincoln. Last Wednesday the Bishop, Bob

Hardy, published the report of his official Visitation of the Cathedral which has been going on since February. This was initiated after the publication in the *Church Times* of details (supplied it seems by Brandon Jackson, the new Dean) of the circumstances in which the taking of Lincoln's copy of the Magna Carta to Australia led to the loss of a great deal of money – about £80,000 in fact.

The Visitation admonition is more concerned, however, with relations between the Dean and the Canons than it is about the Magna Carta, and it must constitute one of the most devastating attacks ever made by a Bishop on the Dean and Chapter of his Cathedral:

> The plain fact is that the Dean and Residentiary Canons have been at odds with each other, and the intemperate language and indiscretions on both sides have simply added to the sense of conflict. There does not seem the will to change. I consider the attitude of the Residentiary Canons to me to have been on occasion reprehensible and that they and the Dean have conducted themselves shamefully in the media. As far as I am concerned, the past eight months have been the saddest period of my ministry. The whole Chapter seems to have little perception as to how all this comes across to the general public. It all seems a very long way from Jesus of Nazareth.

This situation is analysed in detail in another 20,000 words and the Canons are invited to 'consider their position', in other words resign, so not surprisingly, the whole thing has been given massive attention by the media. Curiously there was no mention of it at the Deans and Provosts meeting until the chairman, Patrick Mitchell, raised the question of what subjects we ought to be considering at future meetings. Whereupon David Edwards and I joined forces to make the point that there is at the moment one subject above all others claiming attention, namely the Lincoln crisis and its implications for the rest of us.

Coming so soon after the Mappa Mundi controversy at Hereford, the revelation that the Head Verger at Exeter had stolen over £25,000 from collections and other offerings, and news of more administrative troubles at St Paul's, it is obvious that if the cathedrals do not put their houses in order others will press reforms upon us. The cathedrals have few friends in the General Synod, where they are seen as a non-conforming, uncontrollable element in the church's life, and some will see these public scandals as a golden opportunity to bring us to order.

I also made the point that in many other cathedrals a crisis of the Lincoln sort is just waiting to happen. A form of organization that might have been suitable when Deans and Chapters did little more than collect and share the revenues from their considerable estates now positively encourages non-collaboration and bloody-mindedness. But the difficulty of discussing this in a general meeting of Deans and Provosts becomes apparent whenever the Provosts speak, since their cathedrals, created during the last 100 years, have retained much of the organization they had when they were parish churches – the Provost has the authority of the Rector and the governing body is a Council on which there is strong lay representation.

In the end it was decided to set up a working party to make proposals for capitular reform and it looks as if this will be one of the most important items on the agendas of the cathedrals during the next few years.

Saturday 20 October 1990

The Diocesan Synod has given the Appeal a good boost by committing the parishes to contribute at least £650,000 to the £7 million target. Gordon Macpherson, a prominent member of the Synod, made a powerful speech proposing the motion and confessed that he had been converted to the Cathedral as an important agent of mission in the Diocese. Until comparatively recently, it seems, he regarded the Cathedral as a bit of a drag on the church's life and an extravagant waster of money. The Bishop spoke of the many different ways in which the Cathedral serves the Diocese and the wider community, there were a number of affirmative speeches from the floor, and I wound up the debate by saying how grateful I was for the many people in the Diocese who were already working for the Appeal and for the 1,000 volunteers from the parishes who were helping with Cathedral Refreshments.

This Diocesan commitment brings the Appeal total to £1,850,000 and it will assist further our approach to other bodies. Not surprisingly, when we go to companies and trusts for help we are asked what the Church itself is contributing to the funding of its Cathedral. Now we can explain that the Dean and Chapter has pledged £350,000, the Friends of the Cathedral £100,000 and the Diocese £650,000, making a total of £1.1 million – a not unimpressive figure. This should make it easier for others to support us.

Friday 26 October 1990

Lunch with Donald and Jean Coggan in their tiny flat was, as always, a great pleasure. Since they moved to Winchester in 1988 they have become very popular figures in the City, and Donald has a considerable following. Wherever he preaches or lectures he draws a crowd.

It is not simply that Winchester loves a retired Archbishop and a Lord, though that is true: he displays a most attractive combination of Christian piety, simplicity and friendliness. Pure Christianity, in fact. He and Jean showed us two tapestry cushions, the making of which they obviously enjoyed, and he is always ready to play the piano for services in St Swithun's Church, over the Kingsgate arch at the entrance to the Close.

What he offers, people seem to find helpful and reassuring. He has a good mind, steeped in the Bible, and unusual teaching gifts. While not indifferent to contemporary problems, he never seeks to analyse them deeply and always leaves his audiences with the possibility of hope – all articulated in a splendidly rich voice that demands attention, but does not hector or manipulate.

He is wonderfully encouraging to me in my work here, though we have not always seen eye to eye, especially when he was Archbishop of York in the 1960s and early 1970s. This coincided with my spell in journalism and broadcasting, and in those heady, turbulent times Donald's 'Call to the North' and other evangelistic enterprises tended to bring the worst out of me and I wrote and said things in ways that were unkind, even if true. I now try to make up for this by allowing him an allotment in the Deanery garden, which must surely make me the only person in the world to have an Archbishop as one of his gardeners.

Donald's six years as a caretaker Archbishop of Canterbury got off to a bad start with his 'Call to the Nation', and the time was too short for him to be really effective. The Archbishopric of Canterbury is too important a job for a short-term appointment. Yet having said this I am bound to admit that, when viewed in the light of the present situation in the church, the Coggan years were much better than some of us believed them to be at the time.

I shall remember him now for his attractive retirement years in Winchester, for his steadfast support of the movement for the ordination of women, and for his courageous, even if naive, call for intercommunion between Anglicans and Roman Catholics when he visited the Pope in 1977.

Friday 9 November 1990

Welcome signs of movement on the textiles front. When I came here I was very shocked at the poor state of the altar frontals and vestments. Apart from the fine gold and orange copes commissioned in 1979, some good

Ninian Comper vestments on loan from the Sisters of Bethany, and the splendid Creation frontal made by Belinda Scarlett last year, we have only off-the-peg vestments of the poorest design and a number of frontals that are badly worn. The Nave altar carpet is threadbare and has holes in its corners. It is hard to believe that any other cathedral in England is as badly off as we are in this visually important area of our life.

Money is the problem, of course, because these things are not cheap and the last three years have not been the time for moving in this direction. Nor does the present £7 million Appeal for other needs leave us with much room for manoeuvre. Keith Walker has, however, undertaken to do some preliminary work on our requirements and the ways in which these may be met when the money eventually becomes available.

He has had a meeting with Southern Arts, who recommended that he should consult Ann Sutton, who lives at Arundel and is probably the leading textiles designer in the country. And such is her experience and reputation that she knows just about everyone who is working in this field, mainly in secular design. Keith has had a meeting with her, she is keen to help, and the general idea now is that a small committee should be formed to determine precisely what we need, to identify artists who could be invited to submit proposals for frontals and hangings in the various chapels, and hopefully to find ways and means of financing the project. If, as is now being proposed, the textiles of the entire building are to be renewed and enriched in one great programme of activity a lot of money is going to be needed.

As to the vestments, Ann Sutton put to Keith the quite revolutionary idea that these should be entrusted to a Japanese man named Issey Miyake who is, apparently, the world's leading clothes designer. I had not previously heard of him, but I have now seen an article about him that appeared in *The Times* last September and he certainly sounds interesting.

> Issey Miyake's accordion-pleated robes regularly supply the spectacular flourish at the end of the fashion show he stages twice a year in Paris. Corrugated suits of armour with sharp-angled elbows and knees articulated by pleats, science-fiction space suits and dresses falling in asymmetric concertina folds that billow down the catwalk – these are his showstoppers, inspiring stunned gasps of amazement from the fashion world since his first experiments with the movement and shadow of pleating in the Eighties.

On the face of it this sounds some distance from the requirements of Winchester Cathedral, but it seems that many of his designs for women's clothes have close affinity with classical Eastern robes, so the concept of full, flowing eucharistic vestments would not be entirely foreign to him and he would obviously have to be briefed about our needs.

Evidently Issey Miyake is in such great demand worldwide that he would not easily be engaged for our project, but it might just appeal to him as something quite different from anything he has previously been famed for. The advantage from our point of view, so we are told, is that not only would we get vestments of outstanding, even if somewhat unusual, design, but the fact of Miyake's involvement would so excite the Japanese business interests in this country that they would immediately wish to be identified with the project to the extent of providing all the money needed, both for the vestments and for the frontals and hangings. This could be accomplished quite independently of the current Appeal.

A very big idea of this kind is not something I wish to discourage. When the need is great there is everything to be said for taking big, bold steps to meet it. I hope the Chapter will agree to the committee exploring the proposals further and, since Issey Miyake is seen as a key figure in the whole exercise, it would be sensible to sound him out to see if he is interested.

Meanwhile, two matters need to be made crystal clear. The first is that Roger Job must be deeply involved in the explorations and decision-making. He is both Precentor and Sacrist, which means that everything to do with furnishings and fabrics and ornaments is his direct responsibility. This is not simply a question of protocol: Roger's liturgical knowledge and concern will provide an important counter-balance to the enthusiasms of those whose approach is from the secular side.

The second point is that there can be no fund-raising of any kind, in any part of the world, for this project until the £7 million Appeal is successfully completed. The faintest hint that we are planning another appeal for money for something quite other than the three Appeal items would fatally undermine the massive effort now under way. Hopefully, the textiles money can in due course be gathered in without too much fuss, though it would be unreasonable to expect Issey Miyake and his financial backers to operate without some publicity. We must keep this pot boiling but take great care to see that it doesn't boil over.

Tuesday 13 November 1990

I went to the Wykeham Arms at lunchtime for the launching of an effort to raise £60,000 for the endowment of a Lay Clerkship – a substantial contribution to the £1 million we are seeking for the endowment of the Choral Foundation. This old pub, which stands just outside the Close, has become a remarkable centre of community life and action since Graeme Jameson became its landlord just a few years ago. Previously he had been a personnel manager in one of the big oil companies and he brought to his new job as a Licensee an entrepreneurial spirit and quality of service that has appealed greatly to the middle-classes of the area. Having the Cathedral and the College on the doorstep has obviously helped and the place is fizzing with life. Last year it won the prize for the Best Pub in England and it is highly praised in all the tourist guidebooks.

The point about the endowment of the Lay Clerkship is that our Lay Clerks are among Graeme's best customers, as singing in the Cathedral tends to make them thirsty and they gather in the Wykeham Arms after rehearsals and sometimes after big services. It has become a kind of common-room for them. True to form, Graeme has organized his appeal with imagination and flair, and there was a good Press turnout. Every table now has a brass-mounted opening for customers to insert their change, an attractive leaflet is on hand, photographs of the Cathedral and the Choir adorn the walls, and a leatherbound book will record the names of those who contribute £25 or more. Graeme has undertaken to match every gift with £1 of his own, so the effort will cost him £30,000 and he hopes to complete it in a year.

Monday 3 December 1990

At the suggestion of Cathy Milford, we have placed a large lighted candle in the North Transept beneath the Christus figure. This is to encourage prayer for peace in the Middle East and there are some suggested prayers for visitors and others to use. The invasion of Kuwait by Iraq has caused enormous tension in that region and there is a real possibility of a war involving the major powers. The United States simply cannot allow its oil supply to be threatened by a ruthless dictator like Saddam Hussain. Neither can the United Nations allow one sovereign state to be over-run by another, in defiance of UN resolutions, otherwise it will lose all credibility as an international force for peace. Having defied world opinion by occupying Kuwait, it is hard to see, however, how Saddam Hussain can now withdraw his forces and his claims without complete loss of face, both at home and throughout the Middle East. And he doesn't seem to be that sort of man.

Prayer on occasions such as this raises a number of problems for me, but that is no reason for refusing a candle which many people will find helpful.

This morning we discussed at the Chapter meeting the question of whether or not a volume of the Winchester Bible might go to America for display in connection with a fund-raising effort for the Appeal. The Librarian is keen to do this and has secured an offer from the Cleveland Museum of Art. But I expressed my considerable unease about the proposal. There is only one known occasion when the Winchester Bible has left the place where it was created in the twelfth century and that was for a major exhibition of Romanesque Art held in London about fifteen years ago. I am not opposed in principle to its being exhibited elsewhere, but in view of its unique character and priceless value there must always be an extraordinarily good reason for us to release it. Display in the Cleveland Museum of Art linked to a hypothetical and not-thought-out fund-raising effort seems to me to be a very long way from providing such a reason. It is in fact difficult to see how any significant amount of money could be raised in this way, since the only effective way of getting good donations is through face-to-face requests.

The Appeal has now passed the £2 million mark – £2,111,332 to be precise – which means that we shall not now reach the hoped-for £3 million by Christmas. This is disappointing, but when dealing in large figures of this kind the big gifts are not easy to time, since they usually depend on meetings of trustees and directors. It is very important, however, that we should reach the half-way mark, £3.5 million, by March when the Community Gifts element in the Appeal is due to be launched. £4 million would be even better for confidence-creating purposes. The main problem at the moment is in the Key Gifts area, as it was expected that the £25,000 – £100,000 range would be appropriate for Hampshire's commercial and industrial enterprises, but these are being hit very hard by the economic recession and at a time when they are laying off staff in large numbers they can hardly be expected to find money for a cathedral appeal.

The first report of the management consultants has arrived and is impressive. Although I was very much in favour of their employment, I wondered just how easily they would pick up the important differences between an ancient cathedral and the kind of secular institutions they are normally dealing with. But after one week here, spent interviewing members of the Chapter and the staff, they showed encouraging signs of understanding us, and their report exposes our weaknesses and needs with great clarity. On the management structure – if it can be so described – they identify:

poorly defined responsibilities

staff receiving conflicting instructions

poor communications

conflicts between personnel

staff feel poorly informed

Chapter meeting agenda not always completed

little business contact between Dean and Chapter outside bi-monthly meetings

Chapter members perceive Dean has little confidence in them

Visitors Centre project not formally managed, planned, communicated

dissatisfaction with Administrator

Administrator by-passed on many administrative and financial matters

informal reporting lines have evolved

lack of formal business planning.

In the light of all this it is amazing that we manage to run the place at all, and in their attempts to sort things out the consultants have quickly come up against a crucial difference between a cathedral and most other institutions inasmuch as the Dean and Chapter are quite different from a board of directors. Deans and Canons are not appointed for their management skills, they are not accountable to anyone, they may or may not accept the corporate discipline involved in team work, they cannot be dismissed.

The report is going to need very full discussion and the analysis will have to be accepted, either in its present or a modified form, before the consultants can make proposals for a new administrative and financial set-up. It is going to be very interesting to see how the Canons respond. I hope they will welcome more clearly defined responsiblities.

1991

There is concern among the Virgers and the voluntary helpers that a vagrant is spending a lot of time in the Cathedral. He is doing no harm but, for obvious reasons, neither his body nor his clothes have regular contact with soap and water and the position he takes up close to a hot radiator does nothing to improve the fragrance of the surrounding air. It was just such a problem that led the early church to use incense in worship.

Please can the man be removed – is the request from those who share his company in the Cathedral. Certainly not – is the response of the Dean and Chapter, but we will discuss the matter with the Trinity Centre staff to see if he can be helped in any way, especially with bathing. Would that all our decisions could so easily be made.

Thursday 24 January 1991

There was an important meeting this evening of the new Twyford Down Association and I have agreed to become one of its Vice-Presidents and to sign a letter to *The Times* about the M3 motorway. At the moment this ends just north of Winchester and the route south continues on the Winchester by-pass, created to deal with the traffic problems of an earlier age and now a highly dangerous stretch of highway on which there have been many casualties.

It is generally agreed that the M3 needs to be extended and continued to Southampton, but there is sharp disagreement over its best route. The widening of the existing by-pass would destroy the environment of Winchester's beautiful water-meadows and threaten the tranquillity of Winchester College and, to some extent, that of the Cathedral. It ought therefore to go further to the east, which brings it to Twyford Down – an area of outstanding natural beauty and listed by seven national bodies as being of special scientific and historic importance.

After a number of public enquiries, the Department of Transport has decided that the motorway shall cross the Down in a huge cutting that will divide it and destroy both its beauty and much of its special interest. The alternative, favoured by the Twyford Down Association and many others, is to take the road through the Down by means of a tunnel.

Although this would be several miles long, it is apparently quite feasible from the engineering point of view and seems the common–sense solution. But it would add £92 million to the motorway's cost and this is the sticking point for the Government.

We are pointing out, however, that in the context of the total cost of the M3 and its projected life-span £92 million is not a particularly large amount of money. Many defence projects cost more and the protection of a precious natural inheritance such as Twyford Down is an important test of priorities and therefore of the Government's philosophy. There is no doubt what the Italian and Swiss governments would do in these circumstances.

A long battle lies ahead and I suspect the chances of winning it are fairly remote. What is interesting, and surely significant, is that opposition to the cutting and support for the tunnel is not confined to the bearded and sandaled environment lobby but includes a large number of central Hampshire middle-class Tories. Anthony Trollope would not, however, be surprised to learn that the Dean and the Bishop are on different sides in the conflict.

Sunday 27 January 1991

It was my turn to preach in the Cathedral this morning so I thought it appropriate to talk about what has come to be known as the Gulf War, and in particular about relations between Christians and Muslims.

Ever since he invaded Kuwait, Saddam Hussain has made extensive use of religious language. He describes the war as a 'holy war', President Bush is 'the Great Satan', John Major is 'the Mother of all devils', the Western armies are 'the infidel at the gates', the holy places of Islam must be protected, and so on.

It is very doubtful that Saddam believes any of this, since he is not known to be a religious man and, unlike Iran, Iraq is a secular state in which religious leaders have no direct power. He is trying to exploit religion for his own ends and hopes to win the support of the Arab masses in other countries, especially where resurgent fundamentalism is looking for an international leader and a cause.

I talked about this and about the need to be aware of the vital place of religion in Arab culture and identity, even when unacknowledged. This may be compared with the situation in Northern Ireland, South Africa, Jugoslavia, and Britain at the time of the Reformation.

I went on to say that God never backs one side in a war. 'Whenever religion is used to justify violence of any kind, it is always wrong . . . The present war in the Gulf is a great evil and, while we may consider it to be a necessary action in order to prevent an even greater evil, we can look to God not for support but only for forgiveness.'

I then described the five 'pillars' of Islamic faith and, having pointed out that Islam is just about as fragmented as is Christianity, I said it was important for us to try to relate to it at its best and not in its most fanatical, distorted forms. Relations between Christians and Muslims, and indeed between Christians and the other great religious faiths, should always be characterized by friendship and never by enmity. We are all children of the one God. We are therefore all brothers and sisters in faith. We have much to share with each other, and we have things to learn from each other. If there is to be peace in the world, and if many other problems are to be solved, the high walls that separate the adherents of the great religous faiths will have to be taken down. And if we Christians are as confident in the truth content of our faith as we claim to be, we should have no difficulty in giving a lead in the process of demolition.

Saturday 2 February 1991

Farewell this evening to Michael Manktelow, who is leaving his Residentiary Canonry in order to concentrate exclusively on his work as Bishop of Basingstoke. He is only the second occupant of this suffragan bishopric, the first being Colin James, the present diocesan bishop.

When the possibility of having an additional suffragan bishop in this diocese was first mooted back in 1972 various difficulties were raised. Would there be enough work? How would he be paid and housed? In the end these problems were solved by combining the bishopric with a Residentiary Canonry of the Cathedral, the main benefit of this being that it provided the Bishop with an appropriate house and a base.

It was a common arrangement at that time but, as the cathedrals became busier and the demands on bishops became relentless, the tasks were seen to be incompatible, so that just two years ago only in two places were they still linked – Huntingdon in Ely diocese and Basingstoke here in Winchester. By last year it had been reduced to one, the Bishop of Huntingdon having suffered a heart attack.

There is no doubt that Michael Manktelow has found the dual role increasingly stressful and it was at his own request that he resigned from the Canonry. It seems that it worked pretty well until I arrived on the scene and the life of the Cathedral became more active. There is a monkish element in Michael which has made him an assiduous attender at the daily services, but every additional activity approved by the Chapter has been one more burden for him. Not that he was made responsible for implementing any of them, but there have been additional papers and meetings for him to cope with and a general burgeoning of ideas that required some attention. I think it is also the case that he has become tired and somewhat depressed. Fourteen years in a job of this kind is too long and Michael is disappointed that he has not been made a diocesan bishop. There is a fairly new problem here inasmuch as it used to be comparatively rare for a suffragan bishop to be elevated to the charge of a diocese. When professors, headmasters and other luminaries were becoming diocesan bishops, the suffragans who had often been first-class parish priests were seen as their pastoral assistants and were not encouraged to aspire to anything more than this. Indeed, most of them derived considerable satisfaction from a wide pastoral ministry that was not hampered by overmuch administration. But now they are the main breeding ground for diocesan bishoprics, and those who don't get one tend to believe they have been overlooked, under-valued and generally neglected. Hence the disappointment and depression.

Michael and his lively wife, Ros, and their three daughters have been a great asset to our community life and will be sorely missed. Now the time has arrived for them to go they, too, are dreading the arrival of the removal van. I think Michael really hoped he might have been allowed to leave the Canonry and yet stay in the lovely eighteenth-century house – the best we have – but Colin James wasn't prepared to wear this and it would of course have made it impossible for us to get a replacement Canon.

Thursday 7 February 1991

I have now been here for four years and by the summer I shall have completed half of my term as Dean, assuming of course that health or whatever permits me to stay until I am seventy. It is fortunate that I have a strong constitution because the work is getting heavier all the time – and not simply in volume.

My task would be ten times easier if the Chapter were capable of working as a team. We still get on very well at the personal level but always there is a strong undercurrent of conflict – partly through differences over the way the Cathedral is being run, but chiefly through lack of awareness of what is involved in teamwork. So often frustration, chaos and anger are caused because individuals fail to communicate with one another or do not think through the implications of their actions.

I sometimes wonder if my leadership is strong enough for this particular group. I don't like conflict and I try, but usually fail, to keep everyone happy. It might be better if I were to tackle head-on some of the problems created by members of the Chapter who are either not pulling their weight or are pulling in different directions. But this is not the right time for a showdown, even if I felt up to one.

At the moment I am greatly preoccupied by our £7 million Appeal and I can always raise a laugh at meetings by telling how as a young man I gave up my job in a bank and got ordained because I was more interested in people than in money; yet the greater part of my ministry has been spent dealing with money. 'Instead of becoming a manager in the Westminster Bank I became the Treasurer of Westminster Abbey.'

I don't regret this. The present Appeal is raising money for important work and doing this very successfully, though I cannot see how we shall reach £7 million by mid-July. And it is creating a lot of interest in the Cathedral as well as drawing more people into its service. Certainly it is enabling me to get to know people all over Hampshire and I am valuing this. Seeing the money rolling in also has its excitement.

I am worried, however, about the administration and the consequences of the management consultants' report. John Lamplugh, the Administrator, will have to go in order to make way for a more high-powered, finance-orientated successor, and so will the admirable Carola Stuart, who has served us very well as Cathedral Secretary and much else during the last two years but for whom there is no place in the new management plan. At this stage of a major fund-raising effort we cannot cope with the upheaval and pain of these staff changes but they must not be delayed beyond the summer.

Saturday 16 February 1991

I had an interesting talk today with Francis Lodge, a member of the Friends, who must I suppose be in his eighties but nonetheless wishes to sculpt a bust of me. Apparently he can do this from photographs and measurements of my head, so no long sittings will be required. He intends to enter the finished work in the arts and crafts exhibition which is being held in the Summer to mark the Diamond Jubilee of the Friends.

More importantly than this, however, was the conversation we had about the Silkstede Chapel. This was created in the South Transept by Prior Silkstede in the early part of the sixteenth century, but went out of liturgical use after the Reformation. Izaac Walton, the writer and angler who spent his final years in the Close, was buried in the chapel in 1683.

Standing unused, it was turned into a vestry for the Lay Clerks in 1816 and this has been its function ever since. There are some dreary cupboards, a desk and several cardboard boxes, and it is really a bit of a dump. An attempt to recover the chapel seems to have been made in 1902 when British and American fishermen paid for a large stained-glass window to honour Izaac Walton, but whenever anglers come to pay homage to the master of their art they are shocked by our apparent lack of reverence for him.

During the Friends' arts and crafts exhibition Francis Lodge, who is a former President of the Test and Itchen Fly Fishing Association, will display various items of angling equipment in the chapel and we discussed the possibility of using any money he raises to start a fund that will one day pay for its refurbishment and return to liturgical use. I would dearly love to do this and it shouldn't cost all that much to clean it up, and install an altar and appropriate seating. An appeal to the angling fraternity might raise the money quite easily. The chief problem is where to put the displaced Lay Clerks, but it may be possible to solve this when we have built the Visitors Centre and released the Bookshop store for another use.

Thursday 21 February 1991

John Crook, our Consultant Archaeologist, and John Hardacre, the Curator, have inspected the contents of one of the mortuary chests on the Presbytery screens. These contain the bones of Saxon kings and bishops which were gathered by Bishop Fox in the early part of the sixteenth century and placed in chests created for the purpose.

The chest that was opened proved to be filled to capacity with an assortment of bones – all packed in plastic bags, which must have been done comparatively recently. Apparently quite a lot of the bones show clear signs of arthritis, so this crippling affliction has a long history.

Other, less distinguished, mortal remains occupy fifty or more large cardboard boxes in a chamber above the Guardian Angels Chapel. These were exhumed when Martin Biddle was carrying out a major archaeological excavation on the West side of the Cathedral in the 1960s. Much of the area was evidently a mediaeval burying ground and all these bones had to be removed before the diggers could reach the Saxon and Roman periods.

I am sure they should be decently reinterred – human remains ought not to be kept indefinitely in cardboard boxes – but this will be a sizeable undertaking and Martin Biddle is against it as he believes the bones should be kept available for possible medical research. We have given him twelve months to arrange whatever research may be appropriate, then the bones must be returned to the ground.

Sunday 24 March 1991

The Cathedral was packed this afternoon for a service launching the Community Gifts programme of the Appeal. There must have been over 1,400 people present. Before and after the service it was possible to visit an exhibition 'The Living Cathedral', displaying almost every aspect of the Cathedral's life and work. This occupied virtually the whole of the Eastern part of the building and would be worth repeating from time to time when fund-raising days are over.

The whole event, organized by Carola Stuart, the Cathedral Secretary, and Virginia Allix, the Appeal Secretary, had a good feel to it and should generate a lot of new enthusiasm. We are now looking for about 200 people who will form 18 local committees and, by means of personal gifts and events in the under £25,000 category, raise £2.2 million. Mary Fagan is in charge of this operation and does not know the meaning of failure.

I preached a short Palm Sunday sermon on the meaning and significance of sacrifice, Jim Scott, the Lord Lieutenant, urged everyone forward into this new phase of the Appeal, and Jim Butler announced that we have now reached the £3 million mark – not quite half-way but an impressive sum all the same.

Wednesday 17 April 1991

The good news is that the Appeal has now passed the £3 million mark – £3.2 million to be precise – and the bad news is that Masons, the long-established local firm to whom we awarded the £1.3 million contract for the restoration of the Tower, have gone into receivership. The work has ceased.

In the present economic climate it seems that few, if any, building contractors are financially secure and they themselves are vulnerable to clients who are unable to meet their bills. Aware of all this, a good deal of enquiry preceded the placing of this contract, but it proved impossible to get close enough to the relevant facts. Banks, accountants and the like are bound by confidentiality rules and annual accounts become quickly out of date in the current unstable conditions.

The timing of the failure is quite convenient inasmuch as the erection of the complex scaffolding has just been completed and the actual restoration work has not been started. This should make the employment of another contractor a little easier. But there is alarming evidence that the scaffolding which we have purchased from Masons for £35,000 did not belong to them but was on hire from a firm of scaffolding contractors. In short, they sold us something to which they did not have a legal title. Since this constitutes gross dishonesty, the police have had to be called in. No doubt this is a reflection of the dire financial straits in which the firm found itself.

We are faced with several problems. We purchased the scaffolding for use not only on the Tower but also on the rest of the building as the restoration programme moves on, so it seems we have lost our £35,000 investment. What is more, the rightful owners of the scaffolding may well require it to be taken down and returned to their own premises for hiring out again. If, as seems most sensible, we place a new contract with one of the other firms that originally tendered we shall be obliged to pay their higher price. Inevitably there will be delay while things are sorted out and a new contractor is brought on board.

All of which is very disturbing. The restoration of the Tower is an important piece of publicity for the Appeal. It is highly visible and a dramatic advertisement (a) of the building's needs, and (b) of our determination to get the work done. The postponement of the work, if only temporarily, will not be encouraging to potential donors and the news that £35,000 has been lost in a dishonest transaction will do us no good at all, even though we are in no way responsible for what has happened. Fortunately, it will be some time before the case reaches the courts.

Saturday 4 May 1991

Alec Knight was installed as a Residentiary Canon this evening. He became Archdeacon of Basingstoke last year in succession to Trevor Nash, who has become a healing ministry specialist, and now he has succeeded Michael Manktelow on the Cathedral Chapter. He is, I think, a considerable acquisition to us.

With a background mainly in education and obviously very bright, Alec came to the Diocese in 1983 to unite four rural parishes in the Itchen valley – places not inhabited by country bumpkins but by some of the wealthiest people in England. Unfortunately, the parson whose removal from two of the parishes was necessary to the union failed to retire, so Alec was landed with a piece of work well below his capacity. He compensated for this by playing a leading role in adult education work in the Diocese.

Now he has a combination of jobs for which he is eminently well suited, though he has some anxiety about the claims the Cathedral may wish to make on him. I have suggested that he gives us about one-quarter of his time, leaving three-quarters for the archdeaconry, and this should work out satisfactorily. Archdeacons are now very much busier than they used to be and are almost mini-bishops. At one time they were concerned mainly with the care of the fabric of church buildings and a few legal matters, but the development of synodical government has drawn them into a multitude of committees, and the growing insecurity of the parish clergy has driven them to an itinerant ministry of hand-holding and cheering-up. I cannot think of any job in the church I would like less.

Sunday 5 May 1991

This morning I preached the University Sermon at Oxford – always a tricky assignment but one that vanity forbids someone like me to refuse. Although it is undoubtedly an honour to be a Select Preacher and suggests an opportunity to 'preach before the University of Oxford', it is in fact a very small-scale, down-beat affair these days. The congregation in the University Church at 10.00 am is very small, consisting mainly of the teaching staff of the Faculty of Theology in their doctoral gowns and hoods, and obviously there is no market for a thirty-minute sermon, preceded by a hymn and a long Bidding Prayer and succeeded by an anthem.

The previous occasion on which I did it turned out to be Remembrance Sunday and I found this particularly difficult. The sermon is supposed to have an academic flavour, so the kind of address normally given to the British Legion won't quite do, yet the occasion was essentially pastoral inasmuch as it was focussed on those who lost their lives in war and those who mourn them.

Either way, the University Sermon involves a fair amount of work as well as a journey to Oxford. I decided therefore on a subject – Cathedral Reform – which I have been thinking about a good deal lately and which, while of not particular interest to the Oxford congregation, might possibly find a wider audience through the media. In this way it may contribute something to the debate about cathedrals which is now gathering steam and has led to the appointment of an Archbishops' Commission. The pressure for reform cannot be too strong and my ploy seems to be working. *The Daily Telegraph* and the *Church Times* have already asked for a copy of the sermon, and I will see that members of the Commission also get one.

The second half of the sermon contained a fair amount of quotable material as I suggested four areas of cathedral life in urgent need of reform. First, the appointment of skilled laypeople to cathedral chapters. They would bring the managerial and financial skills now required for the effective running of the business side of a cathedral and at the same time release the clergy to undertake scholarly research or whatever else they have been trained to do.

Next, deans must be given the opportunity to exercise effective leadership. The role of *primus inter pares* is not appropriate in a dynamic organization. Which doesn't mean that deans should be given dictatorial powers: effective leadership and management requires close consultation and the winning of arguments; but equally it needs freedom from the millstone formed by the maverick and the indolent.

The method of appointment of canons also requires attention. Most of these are in the hands of the bishops who may, or may not, be ready to give priority to a cathedral's needs. The temptation to a bishop to use a canonry in order to solve a diocesan problem is very great – often they are treated as a reward for services already rendered or as a perch for someone with diocesan responsibilities. Consultation between the bishop and the dean and chapter should become mandatory and the latter should be invested with the power of veto.

This leads to the vexed question of tenure and freehold. A priest appointed in his mid-forties has the prospect of twenty-five years' service in the same office and, while this may not have much mattered when cathedrals were enjoying a siesta, it matters a great deal now that they have become dynamic and need to be vigorous and flexible. A ten-year leasehold office, which might in special circumstances be extended to fifteen years, is what is now required.

The reaction to the sermon by the Dean and Canons of Christ Church who were present was not altogether surprising. Although I had specific-ally exempted Christ Church from what I was saying, on the grounds that its dual role as a cathedral and a college chapel made it unique, they were obviously uneasy at my suggestion that other ancient capitular institutions are now due for reform. Their academic life is of course miles removed from my own and we are bound to see things differently.

Saturday 11 May 1991

The band concert for the Appeal held in the Great Hall last evening was a great success financially and also enjoyable for those whose ears can cope with bands playing indoors. The Hampshire police band and an army band joined forces for the occasion and generously gave their services as a contribution to the Appeal.

The Duchess of York graced the evening, thus enabling tickets to be sold at a higher price than normal, and she made a short speech in support of the Appeal. Unfortunately, the lofty thirteenth-century architecture of the hall misled her somewhat and she began her speech by saying how nice it was to be in the Cathedral again, thus greatly mystifying the assembled company. It may perhaps have been a slip caused by nervousness – easily done.

I sat with her throughout the concert and, besides my duties as her host, had the task of enlisting her aid over our approach to two prospective donors. Andrew Lloyd Webber, the composer, and David Frost, the television interviewer, live in Hampshire and both are known to be very wealthy. The former made use of the Cathedral choir for the first performances of his *Requiem* and the latter is the son of a Methodist minister, so we think they may not be averse to giving to the Appeal. But so far we have found no way of making a direct, personal appeal to either of them. Perhaps the Duchess might know them and be willing to ask them?

This was the question I was to put to her. But the bands played so loudly and the intervals between items were so short, that there was no opportunity to talk about anything. Seizing a brief opportunity before the final item, I asked her if she knew the two gentlemen. Indeed she did. Whereupon the army band immediately struck up and made further conversation impossible. And as soon as the piece ended the Duchess leaped to her feet, moved forward to shake hands with the conductors and then made swiftly for the door. Thus the vital second half of my question went unheard and the opportunity was lost. Ah well.

Saturday 11 May 1991

This afternoon I preached at the re-dedication of the Winchester United Church. Eighteen years ago the Methodist Church and the United Reformed Church joined forces in the Methodist building – a very large, lofty edifice in the Victorian style, which soon proved to be unsuited to their needs.

So a few years ago they set to and raised £1.1 million to enable the building to be modified, to give them a reasonable-sized worship area, lots of meeting rooms, a coffee bar and facilities for social work, which is one of their specialities. The result is very good indeed and a model of what can be done with a large building when there is money available.

It was, as I pointed out at the beginning of my sermon, interesting that they should have invited an Anglican dean to preach at such a significant Free Church occasion. I decided therefore to return the compliment by devoting the sermon to an exposition of what I believe to be the distinctive Free Church witness at the present time, and I took as a text what must, I suppose, be the classic statement of the Free Church position – II Corinthians 3.17: 'Where the Spirit of the Lord is, there is liberty.'

It is, I said, the vocation of the Free Churches to remind the rest of us that Christianity is a liberating and not a constraining religion – faith comes before order, the gospel comes before the church, life is above organization. 'You remind us of the necessity of faith and decision, for the church is a fellowship of believers, a gathered community, of those who are on the pilgrimage from darkness to light. Such a church, living in the liberty which is the gift of the Lord in the Spirit, will never allow itself to become enslaved to fixed and final forms of liturgical worship, to binding credal formularies, to particular systems of church order, to a subservient relationship with a state.'

I went on to say that the Free Churches also testify to the truth that the church is the whole people of God – laity and clergy working together in partnership – and, since the majority of the laity exercise their Christian ministry in the secular world, the church is bound to affirm its concern for the whole of life and for the application of Christian principles to the organization of society. The contribution of the Free Churches to the social and political life of Britain has, historically, been quite out of proportion to their size. Free Church laymen in the House of Commons have been much more influential than Anglican bishops in the House of Lords.

At the tea party after the service I gathered that my sermon had rung a few bells and the local Baptist minister said I had delineated the Free Church position exactly. I hope therefore that I offered the Free Church people some encouragement as they embark on this new phase of their church's life. Their witness in this area is of the greatest importance and they can do all manner of things that are quite impossible in and from a cathedral.

Friday 7 June 1991

The annual Shipping Festival service at which I preached last evening is remarkable, not so much for its content but for the fact that it continues to take place. It was started in 1931 when both the Royal Navy at Portsmouth and the Merchant Navy at Southampton were of considerable strength. And with the exception of two or three years during the darkest period of World War II it has gone on without a break. What is more, the number of people attending the service seems hardly to have declined. Given the reduction in the size of the two navies, I would have expected the occasion to have been given a decent burial some years ago, but there is no sign of this. The service and the party on the Deanery lawn afterwards are greatly valued.

The memorial books in the Cathedral containing the names of those in the Merchant Navy who lost their lives between 1939-45 are in many ways more moving than those of the Hampshire and Rifle Regiments. The number of names listed runs to many thousands and they were in no sense fighting men, but simply civilian mariners who set sail in the most hazardous of conditions and for a long time with the bare minimum of armed protection. The youth of many of them is also striking – sixteen- and seventeen-year-olds employed on ships in some capacity or other – and the manner of their deaths in the North Atlantic is described only too vividly by Nicholas Monsarrat in his great novel *The Cruel Sea*.

Friday 14 June 1991

I am now recovering from four days spent on the fund-raising trail in New York. It was actually a quite enjoyable experience, the main event being a fund-raising dinner on Tuesday, arranged by our American committee and held in Christie's auction rooms in Park Avenue. I think this will prove to have been successful, though Americans are, I gather, becoming somewhat weary of English cathedral appeals, which is not altogether surprising.

My arrival in New York was slightly undignified. Thinking it desirable to save Appeal expenses, I chose from a 'budget guide' to the city what seemed to me to be a reasonably priced hotel. But when I sent last-minute details of my plans to Jim Butler's accountancy colleagues, who were to be responsible for my arrangements, they threw up their hands in horror and said it was impossible for me to stay in one of New York's most dangerous areas and in a hotel that was used mainly by welfare benefits people. They booked me into another hotel at about three times the price.

On the day of the dinner Jim Butler and I had lunch with Al Gordon in his club which overlooks the Hudson River. Al, who is either ninety-two or ninety-three, is a remarkable man and a most generous benefactor of the Cathedral and Winchester College, where his sons were educated. He has a fascination for English cathedrals and is President of the American Anthony Trollope Society. Evidently he made a great deal of money as a

Wall Street merchant banker, but his financial expertise is concealed by what is for me a delightful home-spun philosophy of the American frontiersman type. He paid the entire cost of the Christie's dinner and, handing me an envelope containing a cheque for $50,000 after lunch, advised me to pay it into the bank immediately – 'something you must always do when receiving a cheque from a man of my age'.

There were about sixty people at the dinner, quite a number of whom were Old Wykehamists now working in New York, including Sir David Hannay, the British Representative at the United Nations. There was also a Princess, whose royal lineage I was unable to unravel, and John Andrew, the Rector of St Thomas's, Fifth Avenue, whom I knew quite well from his days as Michael Ramsey's chaplain at Lambeth. The aperitifs were served to the accompaniment of recordings by the Cathedral Choir and when the time came for me to speak at the end of the substantial meal I was bidden to ascend the auctioneer's rostrum. I remarked that this seemed very much like a pulpit, and so in fact it turned out to be, having been acquired at some time from a disused church. I spoke mainly about the long history of Winchester and ended by inviting those present to lend a hand with 'maintaining this beacon of light which is the precious possession of the whole of the civilized world'. Afterwards I was told by someone on my table that a more direct approach would have been better – 'I've come from England for your money and this is how you can give it me' – but I find that difficult to believe.

Wednesday and most of Thursday were spent mostly in an accountant's office, thirty or more floors above Park Avenue, following up the dinner contacts, and as I gazed down on New York I could not help wondering what all but my most recent predecessors at Winchester would make of this role for a Dean. An hour in the Frick Collection, where virtually every painting is a masterpiece, was as always pure delight. The flights in both directions were without incident, but shortly before landing I was once again astonished to hear the captain of the aircraft expressing the hope that I had had 'an enjoyable flight'. Imprisoned for five or six hours in so confined a space, in close proximity to some thousands of gallons of highly inflammable fuel feeding the white-hot engines of a piloted rocket, there is not the faintest possibility of enjoyment. Only necessary endurance.

Monday 24 June 1991

Work on the Tower has re-started following the financial failure of the original contractors. We are, I suppose, lucky to have lost only two months over this wretched business, but the new contractors are more expensive

An aerial view of Winchester Cathedral.

Dean and Chapter, Canon Theologian, Cathedral Choir and lay staff, 1990.

John Crook

John Crook

Trevor Beeson working on a project at one of the Cathedral's
annual schools days.

Southern Daily Echo

Trevor Beeson with Diana, Princess of Wales, after a service marking the amalgamation of the Royal Hampshire Regiment with the Queen's Royal Regiment, 23 July 1992. A model of the projected Visitors Centre is in the foreground.

Trevor Beeson with a
Buddhist monk before the
Creation Harvest Festival,
4 October 1987.

Hampshire Chronicle

Sound II –
a life-size lead statue
by Antony Gormley,
installed in the
flooded Crypt in 1990.

John Crook

DESECRATION

Sublime to the ridiculous: Is Winchester Cathedral really an appropriate setting for a rave-up?

What kind of society lets the young trample on its hallowed heritage?

by PAUL JOHNSON

THE LACK of a sense of history is one of the outstanding faults of our time, for not knowing about the past is one reason why we so often get the present wrong.

It is doubly curious then that one of our oldest institutions, the Church of England, is also the most forgetful of the past.

In the wake of the Archbishop of York's extraordinary remarks about the Government and its belief in 'competitive success' feeding the criminal culture, we are to be noisily reminded of the values for which the modern Church of England seems to stand.

On April 24, the powers-that-be at Winchester Cathedral have decided to hold a 'rave in the nave' there. Three rock bands called Cross Reference, Azimuth Brainstorm and Fresh Claim will pour out deafening music for four hours, preceded by a period of 'disco fun' led by the Reverend Roly Bain, described, perhaps aptly, as a 'clown priest'.

The Very Reverend Trevor Beeson, Dean of Winchester, has decreed: 'The main thing is that the young people have a good time.'

It does not seem to have occurred to the dean that 'having a good time' is not the purpose for which cathedrals exist. A cathedral is, and has been for two millenia, a church which is also a centre of spiritual education. It is built as a solemn setting for the cathedra, or chair, from which the bishop instructs the faithful in Christian teaching.

cathedral, the core of the present building.

Winchester is thus the collective work of our Saxon, Danish and Norman monarchs, enlarged and embellished by generations of Plantagenet kings, bishops and noble benefactors.

They saw Winchester as the house of God, associated by its antiquity with the whole dramatic panorama of English history and with the origins of its government. None of them regarded it as a place of entertainment.

them to conquer the limitless world of knowledge and realise their own potentialities in the process.

By contrast, some Anglican churchmen today think the young can be bribed by pandering to the debased taste imposed upon them by television and commercial showbusiness.

But most young today are not like that at all. They know very well when they are being conned — and they do not like it. They're just as capable as anyone of becoming absorbed by the

plainsong to Benjamin Britten's Requiem. To belch out grotesquely amplified pop music there is to insult the very stones themselves, let alone the kings and bishops who erected them.

The spirits of these benefactors are still there, to register disapproval of the coming saturnalia. For there is no place in England, not even Westminster Abbey itself, which can match Winchester for tombs.

BURIED in and around the cathedral, in their hundreds, thousands even, are the famous, dead. Tomb-chests hold the bones of the Saxon kings, magnificent chantries the coffins of

The 'Rave in the Nave' controversy sparked off by Paul Johnson in the *Daily Mail*.

Hampshire Chronicle

Trevor Beeson in conversation with the Queen on the 900th anniversary
of the dedication of the Cathedral; the Bishop of Winchester,
the Right Revd Colin James, is in the background.

Hampshire Chronicle

The Visitors Centre.

Hampshire Chronicle

Trevor Beeson leading VE Day 50th anniversary prayers outside
Winchester City Guildhall.

Trevor Beeson batting in the annual Dean and Chapter v. Choristers match.

Hampshire Chronicle

A grotesque of Trevor Beeson carved by Lydia Gould, installed
on the West Front shortly after his retirement in 1996.

Southern Daily Echo

than the first and it seems that we have lost about £35,000 over the scaffolding swindle. Solicitors and the police are still investigating this. The rightful owners have generously offered to waive the rent on the scaffolding erected on the Tower provided they can be sub-contractors for the main contract. This seems fair enough and we have agreed. The sight of the restoration work on the Tower going ahead will be an important visual aid for the remainder of the Appeal.

Thursday 27 June 1991

I have now lost count of the number of times I have ascended the Cathedral Tower with parties of potential donors to the Appeal. At the moment it is averaging three times a week.

The aim of the exercise is to show as many people as possible why we need to spend £5 million on the restoration of the building. The parties are recruited by members of our local committees and usually consist of ten to twelve people. They arrive at the Deanery at eleven o'clock, are welcomed by me and then shown a seven-minute video about the Cathedral and its needs.

Now we go to see for ourselves. At the East End of the building there is enough decayed stone near ground level to enable me to break pieces off to make a dramatic point. This is followed by a slow climb to the belfry – not hazardous but requiring a certain amount of energy and agility – where the twelve bells are hanging and the huge wooden frame and the tower louvres are seen to be in urgent need of repair.

A few more stairs bring us to the roof of the Tower from where on a clear day it is possible to see the Isle of Wight and the Fawley oil refinery on the Solent coast. Here attention is drawn to more decayed stone and I explain that the restoration of the Tower will cost about £1.3 million.

We then descend to the ringing chamber, inspect worm-eaten timbers in the South Transept roof and traverse the longest mediaeval Nave in Europe on a walkway above the vaulted roof. Rusted bolts securing the roof bosses are pointed out, and so is the precarious condition of the West gable window. A door takes us out to the Nave roof where rotting timber beneath the lead covering is revealed and more decayed stone – some of the result of a low-quality restoration earlier this century.

The party returns to the Deanery, where I talk aout the projected Visitors Centre and the Choral Foundation's needs. Stefan Lipa explains how individuals can help, questions are answered and a light lunch is served. The experience is a revelation to virtually everyone who comes and, quite apart from the financial aspect, it is a good public relations exercise for the Cathedral. But it is hard work for a Dean who recently qualified for what used to be called the old age pension.

Tuesday 2 July 1991

I am pleased to have been invited to become the President of the Trinity Centre. This solves a problem for its committee and for me. I joined the committee soon after arriving in Winchester. It was formed a few years earlier by the local churches to help the City's homeless and drop-outs and after a difficult period of working in Holy Trinity Church Hall the Centre now has premises of its own – inadequate but better than camping out elsewhere.

The reputation of Winchester as a place of great wealth has, over the years, attracted to the City unemployed people from other parts of the country. Quite often they have, until the present recession, found jobs but never sufficiently well paid to enable them to rent or buy a house in the area. Thus they end up on the streets, homeless. Besides these there are the young victims of broken homes, and others released from psychiatric care without adequate support, who have nowhere to go and have turned to begging, drugs and sometimes crime.

The admirable chairman of the Centre's committee is the Rector of St Matthew's, Sir John Alleyne, a baronet of most liberal outlook who has a deep concern for social justice. I attended the meetings regularly for my first two years in Winchester but once the Cathedral's life began to claim most of my time Keith Walker began to represent me and has I think been a very useful contributor. It is now clear that I shall never be in a position to return to the committee, so rather than having a seat retained for me I am to become the President. This will keep me in touch and enable me to use whatever influence I may have in the City to support the Centre's work.

Friday 5 July 1991

This morning saw the beginning of the Diamond Jubilee celebration of the Friends of the Cathedral and Donald Coggan made a pleasant speech at the official opening of the Festival of Talents – one of several events taking place this weekend. Among the exhibits is a bust of the Dean sculpted by Francis Lodge. Although he worked only from photographs and a few measurements of my head, the result is considered very successful and certainly I wouldn't mind looking like the figure on show. I cannot, however, believe that anyone will purchase it for £400.

The starting of Friends organizations in many of the English cathedrals during the 1930s has turned out to be much more significant than originally visualized. The raising of additional money to enable deans and chapters to conserve and enhance the beauty of their buildings was the primary purpose, but eventually, and particularly during the latter part of the century, those who have paid their modest subscriptions have wanted to become more involved in cathedral life.

Over the last sixty years the Winchester Friends have raised almost £1 million which, given the effects of inflation during this period, represents a very large amount of money, and they are now busy raising £100,000 for the Appeal. But more important than this is the fact that in their membership are 3,700 people who have degree of interest in the Cathedral's life, and about 600 of these are actually undertaking voluntary work for us. Quite a lot of this work saves us money, inasmuch as we would otherwise have to pay people to do it, but the existence of this large band of helpers who demonstrate their love of the Cathedral by serving as cleaners, guides, stewards, bookstall assistants and so on is a wonderful advertisement to visitors and others who encounter not only a magnificent building but also a community of people who care about it.

When visiting French cathedrals I often think what a difference it would make if they had something like our Friends organizations. Many of them seem very neglected and unloved, with chairs stacked in disused side-chapels, a few artificial flowers on the altars and dust everywhere. And usually no one around who seems to belong and care. This is, I suppose, partly a result of the state accepting responsibility for the maintenance of the fabric of the French cathedrals, but it may also have something to do with the fact that in the Roman Catholic Church the laity have still not been given a truly responsible part in the ordering of the church's life.

Not that relations between deans and chapters and Friends in England have always been cordial. I gather that there have been no problems at Winchester, but there are a lot of stories of deans and chapters treating their Friends insensitively and some of the Friends trying to exert financial pressure to gain undue influence. The Dean of Worcester told me the other day that he believed the health of his cathedral required the abolition of the Friends, but this is quite the reverse of our experience and it is difficult to see how we could manage without them.

Monday 15 July 1991

Another St Swithun's-tide has ended and, as always, it has been a very happy Patronal Festival. The combination of the Friends' Festival, the Southern Cathedrals' Festival (held this year in Salisbury), the Liturgy of the Foundation, and the St Swithun's Day Sung Eucharist and lunch for the General Chapter – all in a space of nine days – makes a heavy programme for those of us who have to be involved in all of it, but the general air of festivity, expressed in worship and parties of one sort and another, makes this the high point of the Cathedral's year.

Today is the day on which the Appeal should have ended, with £7 million safely gathered in, but of course it hasn't. I announced yesterday that we have now reached £4 million and intend to press on until we have got the rest. I don't know if anyone, including our fund-raising consultants, really believed that we would raise £7 million in twelve months, but obviously it is necessary to have a challenging target and also a time-scale that will encourage busy, influential people to lend a hand.

I suspect that twelve to fifteen months is also about the right time for the employing of the consultants. We said goodbye to Stefan Lipa, our man, at a small dinner party on Saturday and we are certainly sad to see him go because he has served us exceedingly well. But these men do not come cheaply and he has taught us all we need to know about the method, so we just need to keep on with it. Stefan will be available to us for advice and will come to Winchester occasionally to review the situation.

The raising of £4 million in one year, in a time of severe economic recession, is no mean achievement. I cannot think that getting the rest is going to be easy, since we have now tapped most of the best sources, but there are still a lot of people in Hampshire who have not given anything, a number of major Trusts still have us under consideration, English Heritage money is now on stream, John Thorn hopes to raise a substantial amount from Old Wykehamists, and various other possibilities are being pursued. The main thing now is to keep the figure moving steadily upwards, so that the 200 people actively working in the Appeal have sufficient encouragement to enable them to overcome fund-raising fatigue.

Thursday 18 July 1991

My three-day visit to the Channel Islands, partly in support of the Choir tour and partly in the cause of raising money for the Appeal, ended drearily with a five-hour wait at Guernsey airport. A warm front brought heavy rain and fog and, since the airport is without modern blind-landing aids, no aircraft were able to land until late afternoon. Very tedious indeed. The Choir is not returning until tomorrow, so they should not be delayed, but I suspect they will have had an unpleasant crossing to Sark this morning.

I spoke at a number of receptions, some held in conjunction with Choir events, some not. The most memorable for me was held in a very large house in Guernsey. I arrived a little early in the Classical-style portico, rang the door bell and was greeted by an untidily dressed man whom I took to be a gardener or handyman but who turned out to be the host. He left me for a time on a comfortable sofa in the hall while he went to change.

Around me the walls were almost completely covered, from floor to ceiling, by paintings, and there was barely an inch of flat space that did not support a piece of porcelain. When the host returned he led me though a number of other rooms, equally crowded with paintings and porcelain, and the whole house was a veritable Aladdin's cave packed with works of art apparently bought without much sense of discrimination.

I learned that we – other guests were now arriving – were in the recently acquired home of a builder and property developer from Leeds who had made a great deal of money and was now settling in Guernsey for tax reasons. Sadly, his wife does not much like her new home. Their bank manager, who is a member of our local Appeal committee, asked them if they would host the reception and this was a good ploy, as they are keen to find a place in Guernsey society – none too easy for a builder from Yorkshire, I imagine – and many local people were anxious to see what was being made of one of the island's finest houses. The champagne and canapés also proved to be of a high order, as the ex-builder has bought a hotel in St Peter Port and the chef was in charge of the catering.

After walking and talking for a time in the rose garden we assembled – about sixty in all – in the conservatory, which was crowded with exotic plants and an over-abundance of cane furniture. I gave my usual speech, but it was only with difficulty that I could make myself heard, owing to the sound of running water from an indoor fountain.

As the guests dispersed I thought it prudent to pay more attention to the host, who obviously has the capacity to help us more substantially if he feels so minded. I suggested that, as an ex-builder, he might like to visit the Cathedral to see the restoration work in progress and have a private tour of the building. He readily agreed. Apparently he has already helped Ripon Cathedral, and we have a point of personal contact in his daughter, who has twice sung at Winchester with a visiting choir from Cheshire.

While we talked about these things he took me to what I believed to be the extremity of his large garden. But I was deceived: the land fell away sharply and below us, standing in an attractive lake, were sixteen pink flamingoes. There had, I was told, originally been eighteen of them, but two died; the survivors are fed on an imported shellfish, without which they would lose their pinkness. As I was leaving I offered to meet our host when he arrived at Southampton airport for his Winchester visit, and he informed me that he would be coming in his own aircraft. I hope this will come off, but sometimes people who host receptions feel they have done their bit.

Friday 19 July 1991

Today's interview with John Lamplugh, the Administrator, in which I had to tell him of the redundancy decision, went better than anticipated – at least from my point of view. The Treasurer was also present and I explained that the Management Consultants' report recommended us to employ a different kind of Administrator, with considerable financial expertise, to usher in and manage a new regime with financial planning and control. The development of the Cathedral's overall life also requires someone with stronger administrative skills.

John was obviously shaken, but he took the grim news with dignity. The position is certainly serious for him. He was twice made redundant before coming to the Cathedral and at fifty-nine the prospect of his finding another job must be bleak. Our severance package cannot exceed more than about £25,000, because we do not have the money to increase it, and poor pensions arrangements with his previous employers are bound to leave him badly off.

The situation is made all the more sad because his father, who was Bishop of Southampton in the 1950s, resided in the Close, and as a young man John actually lived in the house which is now the Cathedral Office where he has been working. But the post of Administrator is of crucial importance in our management structure and it is vital that it should be occupied by someone of the highest calibre.

There is a great difficulty when clergy are in hiring and firing roles. The pastoral instinct in us makes the imposing of painful management discipline very hard, and I suspect that often enough we don't do it very well. Equally, I think those upon whom the discipline is imposed find it hard to accept from clergy, because their image and normal experience of us is of people who are in the pastoral business and not therefore creators of pain.

Thursday 26 September 1991

The textiles project is making progress but getting more and more into a tangle. The Precentor has effectively backed off, leaving Keith Walker in charge. He and Ann Sutton, the consultant, thereupon invited about a dozen textiles artists to submit designs for altar cloths and hangings for all the chapels.

We have now seen the designs and many of them are, I must say, very fine. Obviously, a highly-gifted team has been chosen. There are, however, a number of problems arising from the fact that the artists have quite deliberately been drawn from the secular field. This means that they have little, if any, knowledge of the church tradition and it is by no means clear that they were adequately briefed before they got to work on their designs. Thus the proposal for the Venerable Chapel does not reflect the fact that this is the chapel in which the Blessed Sacrament is reserved.

At the moment there is no possibility of our moving forward with any of this, since we lack the necessary money. Wherein lies another problem. The total cost, according to Keith Walker, is likely to be about £500,000 and there is of course no possibility of our seeking this while the present Appeal is running. Keith, who is playing no part in the Appeal, is annoyed because it has been extended for a further year and has written a paper complaining that other needs are being held up because of this. Apparently there have already been informal talks with a representative of the Mercers' Company, which is tricky because Jim Scott, the Chairman of our Trustees and up to his eyes in the Appeal, is a prominent member of this livery company.

I have had to say in no uncertain terms that nothing must be done that will in any way jeopardize the raising of the £3 million required for the completion of the Appeal. We simply cannot get the two things mixed, and it is vital that no uncertainty be created among those who are working flat out in the Appeal. All this seems obvious, and the Chapter has readily agreed that there cannot be additional fund-raising without reference to me, but Keith is not happy, as he has the textiles bit between his teeth.

Saturday 12 October 1991

Another big Appeal event last evening – a performance of *The Merry Widow* by Pavilion Opera in the Great Hall. This talented company is obviously used to playing in a more intimate setting than a huge thirteenth-century hall, but nonetheless they were impressive. Not everyone appreciated the fact that they sang the opera in German. Mary Fagan, who masterminded the event, thinks it will have made about £30,000, and there can be no doubt that this owes something to the presence of the Duchess of York, who is still quite a draw.

She appeared in a bright crimson dress that was exceedingly short and contrasted with the formal attire of most of the other ladies present. I suppose Winchester has not yet caught up with the latest London fashions, though age may have something to do with it. I was in the official welcoming party and as soon as the Duchess arrived she rushed across to me, shook me by the hand and said 'Hello, Trevor, how are you?'. Which was all very well but hardly how a Royal Duchess should greet an elderly Dean on a formal occasion and I felt somewhat embarrassed. Her behaviour during the supper that preceded the opera was also a trifle odd, as she found it necessary to make a telephone call, and again during the interval. I don't know what all that was about. Her lady-in-waiting was ill, so her stepmother came instead.

Monday 21 October 1991

Issey Miyake, the celebrated Japanese fashion designer, came today to see the Cathedral and to discuss the proposal that he should design our new vestments. He travelled from Paris, where some of his latest work is on show, and was accompanied by an entourage of six or seven other Japanese, including a photographer.

He is an impressive man, quietly spoken and displaying the traditional oriental courtesy. There was much bowing. Apparently he is a Buddhist and told us that he felt very much at home in the Cathedral's spiritual ambience. Certainly his questions displayed the utmost sensitivity and were far deeper than those asked by most of our Christian visitors. And he seems very keen to undertake what will be for him a totally new challenge because he has never before ventured into the realm of religious robes.

Apart from the money-raising problem, I have just one anxiety about our employing him. He obviously tries to see things whole and wants to design robes that will harmonize with their environment. I can therefore envisage him producing wonderfully shaped, honey-coloured vestments that will match the stone of the Cathedral's interior and create a beautifully harmonious picture. With this evidently in mind, he is looking for a degree of influence on the work of the other textiles artists who are designing altar cloths and hangings for the chapels.

But we are of course in the liturgical business and need to make strong statements in red, green, blue and gold to mark the different seasons of the church's year. Naturally, Issey Miyake knows nothing about such matters and he can be instructed about our needs, but I suspect that the colours we are looking for will clash with his overall concept of what ought to be done. We shall see, and there is no point in opening up the subject until we have sight of the money with which to undertake this great project. I wish I could share the committee's confidence that it will be forthcoming.

Thursday 24 October 1991

I went this morning to the Wessex Hotel, on the edge of the Close, to receive a donation of £7,000 to the Appeal. This was welcome, but modest enough in all conscience, for when the Trust House Forte Group built the hotel on Cathedral land in the early 1960s they were given a ninety-nine-year lease by the Dean and Chapter. This has break clauses at thirty-three and sixty-six years, with the future rents already agreed, and even in the final period of the lease the ground rent for this large and popular hotel will be no more than about £800 per annum. Who on earth advised the Dean and Chapter on this matter I am unable to discover, but the agreement is depriving the Cathedral of a huge sum of money.

As the media were present I took the opportunity to announce that the Appeal was having its most successful week so far. Besides the hotel's donation, we have received an anonymous gift of £250,000, another one of £80,000 and £165,000 as a first grant from English Heritage towards the cost of restoring the Tower. This totals over £0.5 million and brings the amount raised or promised to about £4.8 million. It will be good if we can reach £5 million by Christmas, but we are now at the point where even donations of £50,000 don't seem to raise the total very dramatically.

Friday 8 November 1991

Keith Walker has produced another report on the textiles project. This is concerned mainly to explain and defend those designs about which the Chapter has expressed reservations and, in one or two cases, absolute opposition. It concludes, surely unnecessarily, that the purpose of the project is 'the glorying of God and mission'.

Unfortunately, this 'glorying' is now likely to cost £1 million, double the amount mentioned in September. Apparently the robes and uniforms to be designed by Issey Miyake will require £500,000, while the altar cloths and hangings will cost £250,000, and another £250,000 has been assigned to a display gallery in the North Triforium. This last proposal will raise all manner of problems not yet considered, since there is at the moment no adequate public access to the North Triforium and the creation of a stairway is bound to be a major architectural undertaking and exceedingly costly, even if visually acceptable.

I fear that Keith and his artist friends are allowing their enthusiasms to obscure reality, and this project must be kept in the background until the Appeal is successfully completed.

Monday 25 November 1991

Good news today: the Skaggs Foundation in California is to give $50,000 to the Appeal for the restoration and conservation of the wall paintings in our Holy Sepulchre Chapel. This Chapel is one of the Cathedral's gems. It was created in the twelfth century in the form of an open-sided sepulchre and has superb wall-paintings dating from about 1180. These were discovered when conservation work was undertaken in 1963 and, as might be expected in such a Chapel, include scenes of Christ's entombment as well as of his resurrected glory. The style is very close to that of some of the illustrations in the Winchester Bible, which is of the same period, and this has led to conjecture that the same artist might have been involved in both projects. Unfortunately, the conservation work in the 1960s was not done very skilfully, so very special care must be taken over the next attempt. David Park, a leading wall-paintings specialist on the staff of the Courtauld Institute, will be in charge of this and he was responsible for us obtaining the grant from the Skaggs Foundation.

Friday 20 December 1991

The Choir is safely back from its pre-Christmas tour of Brazil. When the invitation for them to go came from the British Council we wondered if it was right to accept. The first of the Cathedral Carol Services is scheduled for tomorrow evening and the music at Christmas is so important to so many people that the case for playing safe by keeping the Choir in Winchester was obviously a strong one. But the opportunity for the boys and the men to spend seven days in Latin America might never come again, so we decided to take the risk. David Hill reports that the services and concerts in Rio de Janeiro and Sao Paulo were hugely successful and attracted enormous crowds. The programme also enabled the Choir to rehearse all our own Christmas music, including the singing of 'In the bleak mid-Winter' in a temperature of 95°F.

Other points of note were: the father of one of the Choristers was the captain of the aircraft in which they flew from London to Rio; two of the Lay Clerks were mugged on the streets of Rio and lost their wrist watches and wallets; one of the concerts was televised for broadcasting throughout Brazil on Christmas Day; £18,000 was raised for the homeless in Rio and Sao Paulo, children with AIDS and a cancer hospital.

It was my turn to preach at Mattins today and in calling attention to the new Christmas Crib in the Retro-Choir – another notable work by Peter Eugene Ball – I took the opportunity to point out that the beauty of Christmas Cribs should not lead us to romanticize the circumstances in which Jesus was born. These must have been squalid in the extreme and are a sign of that self-emptying by which God stooped down to the humblest human condition in order that he might be the saviour of all.

I went on to point out, however, that the circumstances in which Jesus was born do not mean that poverty is something to be encouraged or even tolerated. On the contrary, one of the prime purposes of the ministry of Jesus was to inaugurate a new world order in which poverty is eliminated. Yet almost 100,000 people are spending this Christmas in Britain living in hostels or lodging houses, sleeping on park benches or on the streets. Jesus was born in the poverty of a stable to help us see the evil of this situation and to stimulate us to do something about it.

The fact that in this context I had announced earlier the great news that the Appeal has reached £5,020,104.32 was a vivid illustration of the tension some of us feel over the raising of £7 million for the Cathedral and its work while so many people in Britain and other parts of the world are living in dire poverty. Quite often I am tackled about this, especially by people who are raising money for Christian Aid and Oxfam. The answer I give is: (a) the money being raised by our Appeal would not otherwise be available for Third World projects, (b) those who are supporting the Appeal are also likely to be among the most generous supporters of other charities, and (c) while Christians must be deeply concerned about the relief and eradication of poverty we are also in the business of declaring that 'man does not live by bread alone'. It is therefore necessary to maintain cathedrals and other churches as signs of the spiritual dimension of life and to encourage the development of the generous, sacrificial spirit which is essential to the tackling of poverty.

1992

Thursday 9 January 1992

We had an interesting discussion at today's Chapter Meeting about the destination of the collections taken at services on Good Friday. For many years the money has gone to the Church's Ministry among the Jews, but a Mr Wood has written to me complaining that this organization conducts aggressive mission activity among Jews which he does not regard as appropriate and which should not therefore be supported by the Cathedral.

He has a point. Until comparatively recently, Good Friday was considered to be a specially appropriate day on which to pray for the conversion of Jews and to support those engaged in mission to Jews, since they were held responsible for the crucifixion of Jesus. But in these days of inter-faith dialogue it is increasingly recognized that the Jews, as a race and a religious community, carry no particular responsibility for the death of Jesus. Furthermore, Jesus was himself a Jew and the Christian faith has a special relationship with Judaism, out of which it grew. Serious dialogue with Jews is highly desirable but no attempt should be made to convert them.

It was against the background of this new thinking that the Church's Mission to the Jews changed its name some years ago to the Church's Ministry among the Jews, but there is a good deal of evidence to suggest that the change of name has not been accompanied by a change of method. Prompted by Mr Wood's letter, we decided therefore to donate Good Friday collections to 'the victims of twentieth-century forms of crucifixion through agencies assisting the poor, the oppressed and the exploited'.

Friday 10 January 1992

The prospect of a grant from the EEC has given a useful impetus to the plan for developing part of the Deanery garden so that it can become a place of beauty open to the public. The idea was first mooted by John Thorn, then taken up by Tim and Anthea Fortescue, but no money could be found and it had to be dropped. But now Patrick Daniell, himself a notable gardener, and Gilly Drummond, of the Hampshire Gardens Trust, have got together and recruited a few more enthusiasts, all of whom I met this morning.

The plan involves what used to be known as the Deanery Rose Garden – a large rectangular space which is separated from the rest of the garden and has wonderful views of the whole of the South side of the Cathedral. It also has an independent entrance. The garden itself, which has been neglected for many years, is on the site of the former monks' dormitory. During the years following the sixteenth-century Reformation virtually all the monastic buildings, including the cloisters, were dismantled, not I think as an act of vandalism but mainly because there is very little stone in Hampshire and what was regarded as surplus material at the Cathedral – this having been imported from France and the Isle of Wight – was a valuable resource for new buildings in the area.

The dormitory was evidently a two-storied building, with an undercroft which accommodated washing facilities and loos. The above-ground material was eventually carried away and after the collapse of the undercroft roof the remains of the building were in-filled, then covered with a layer of soil to make a raised garden. A painting of the garden during the Edwardian era shows it to have been full of lovely roses, but these do not flourish in chalky soil unless carefully tended – the fifty bushes I planted have been disappointing – and if the experts can now take the area in hand it will not only provide something the public will appreciate but also relieve the Dean and Chapter of responsibility for some of the three and a half acres that now constitute the Deanery garden.

The Dean and Chapter have no money to contribute to the project and of course we do not want to be landed with a garden that requires a lot of expensive maintenance, but the enthusiasts do not seem deterred by our warnings. They believe they can get good grants from various bodies and also have much of the work done by volunteers. Inevitably, the archaeologists will have to investigate the site, at considerable expense, before anyone can do anything.

Sunday 26 January 1992

At the beginning of Evensong today I admitted ('dubbed') three new Choristers – boys aged between eight and ten who have completed their time as Probationers and are ready to take their places as full members of the Choir. I always find this little ceremony moving and I never fail to marvel at the way in which Choristers, who are after all no more than children, come to occupy an international stage, alongside Lay Clerks who are professional singers, some of considerable distinction.

Obviously, the combination of Choir responsibilities and the normal academic requirement of The Pilgrims' School makes a taxing demand on the boys, but they seem to flourish, and by the time they are thirteen and ready to move on they have had a remarkable education. Most win music scholarships to public schools, though not all parents can afford further independent education, and some return to the state sector.

Our Choral Foundation, like that of most of the ancient cathedrals, dates from the Reformation era, but there were boys singing here during the Middle Ages. The records show that Mass was often sung in the Lady Chapel, with boys joining the monks to provide a treble line. They probably came from the monastery school in the cloisters.

Certainly the English cathedral choral tradition, unique in the world, is something special and to be treasured. It costs a great deal to maintain, since we pay one-half (about £3,000) of the boys' fees at Pilgrims' and stipends of about £4,000 to the men, but it is worth every penny, and at Appeal gatherings, when discussing the £1 million we are raising for the Choir, I often say that if it cost twice as much we would have to find the money somehow.

Friday 7 February 1992

My fifth year as Dean, completed yesterday, has been dominated by money-raising and I am getting a lot of sympathy from people who believe I would be better employed and happier if I were involved in more 'spiritual' tasks. But, truth to tell, I am rather enjoying it all. For one thing, the Appeal has been hugely successful: the raising of more than £5 million in eighteen months during a period of severe economic recession is remarkable and confounds the cynics who thought, and said, that we would get nowhere near £7 million. The remaining £2 million is not going to be easy to raise and we could do with a little luck, but I am sure we shall reach the target eventually and it is my job to keep confidence high.

I am also enjoying working with a really first-class team. Within Hampshire there is an extraordinary amount of talent and in the central area of the county there is a very real affection for the Cathedral. The combination of these two factors has enabled us to recruit as strong an Appeal team as could be found anywhere. There has been virtually no conflict between or within the committees – only a great deal of dedicated effort and real generosity. After all the problems with the Chapter, I find this exhilarating.

Money-raising is not generally thought to be a job for the clergy, but there is no possibility of raising substantial amounts unless those who are perceived to be the leaders are in the thick of things. And, as I see it, raising money to keep a great building like Winchester Cathedral in good order is an important spiritual task, as indeed is ensuring the survival of the Choral Foundation and the making of provision for visitors. This is, I think, an entirely proper use of a Dean's time, though it ought not to go on for too long, because there are other things he needs to be doing.

Another benefit of the Appeal is that it is bringing me into contact with a large number of people whom I would not otherwise meet, at least not in so short a time as this great corporate effort is taking. This I am greatly valuing and I hope it will contribute something towards the cementing of the relationship between the Cathedral and the wider community.

The other major project of these last twelve months has been the Visitors Centre and I hope that the decision to build is now settled once and for all. It would be wonderful to have it completed and opened by next spring, when we shall be celebrating the Cathedral's 900th anniversary, but there are still some financial problems to be solved and it rather looks as if we shall not be able to start the building for a few more months. Assuming about a year's work, the summer of 1993 seems the earliest we can expect completion. We must try to get the Queen to come for the 900th anniversary and to open the Centre at the same time.

One of the lessons of this project is that forward moves cannot be allowed to await unanimity. It would have been very good if the whole of the Chapter had given it their backing and it could then have been something excitingly shared. But that is not how things turned out, so there has been a lot of pain in the decision-making, and some resentment. Yet I am absolutely convinced that we need the Centre for the making of better provision for our visitors, for increasing our educational facilities, and for substantially increasing our regular income. Fortunately, the overwhelming majority of the Cathedral community support this view.

Friday 14 February 1992

The issue of protection for the Judges' Lodging and overall security in the Close when the Judges are in residence has surfaced again and is causing some concern. The history of the Lodging is extraordinary. Until about 1890 it housed a Canon in some style, though by then it was in urgent need of repair. Unable or unwilling to tackle this, the Dean and Chapter granted a lease to the then Southampton County Council for the house to be used by the Judge attending the Winchester Assize once or twice a year.

The annual rent was set at £10 and the lease was, according to the official document, for 999 years. But the minutes of the Dean and Chapter record that the lease was for only 99 years and some correspondence at the time indicates that 99 years was the figure envisaged. How the change came about is not apparent, though there is a story circulating among the Judges that two of their nineteenth-century predecessors generously wined and dined the Dean and got him to agree to an addition of 900 years to the lease. Whatever the truth may be, the fact is that the Crown has the use of a house which is worth at least £1 million for no more than a peppercorn £10 a year and this will continue until almost the end of the next millenium. To all intents and purposes the house was given away.

The present generation of Judges, for whom Winchester is the favourite Lodging, are very conscious of the anomaly – if this is what it is – and Michael Nolan, the current Presiding Judge of the Western Circuit, has been very active on our behalf during the period of the £7 million Appeal. But he has made no progress. It seems that the Lord Chancellor's Department is paying the Government's Property Service Agency about £9,000 a year for the use of the house, and doubtless this is held in an account to cover any future repairs. The point has also been made that a lease is a lease and the Government is not in the business of giving away tax-payers' money when they are under no legal obligation to do so. I sometimes tell the Judges, who are here all the year round and whose hospitality I always greatly enjoy, that I shall never refuse their invitations to dinner, since this seems the only way of getting back some of the Dean and Chapter's money.

Against this background, the security issue is a rather tricky one, because it might appear that, having failed to secure additional rent, we are now trying to get the Judges removed from the Close. This is not the case, but the decision of the PSA to install protective wires on certain windows of the Lodging has once again reminded us that the Judges are men at risk. The Winchester Crown Court is a modern building with a high degree of security and, being not too far from London and with a prison close at hand, is sometimes used for IRA and other trials where security risks are considered high. Last year the need to afford the Judges protection during their short journey from the court to the Lodging rendered much of the Close unuseable.

The point we are making is that if the occupants of the Lodging require this degree of protection, what are the risks for others who live nearby? And what are the responsibilities of the Dean and Chapter for the safety of the boys and staff of the Pilgrims' School, which is less than 100 yards from the place where bombs might be secreted or bullets fired?

Using the Establishment network, we have got the Bishop to discuss the problem with the Lord Chancellor, which he did in the House of Lords last week. This hasn't really got us very far on the main issue as the Lord Chancellor does not believe the presence of the Judges in the Close constitutes a greater risk for the rest of us than that experienced by the population at large when terrorism is threatened; indeed, he argues that we may actually benefit from the special protection afforded to the Judges. I hope he is right, but it doesn't really feel safer. Anyway, we have gone to the top and done as much as we can.

Ash Wednesday, 4 March 1992

Although this is a day of repentance in sackcloth and ashes, a letter this morning from a Southampton solicitor has dispelled all gloom and turned it into a day of rejoicing. It informed me that in the Will of the late Alfred Edgar Victor Day there is a legacy to Winchester Cathedral that will amount to at least £500,000 and possibly to more than £600,000 when the Estate is finally settled. It specifies that the legacy is intended for 'the repair of Winchester Cathedral', so it can be included in the Appeal. The Will was in fact drawn only last year when the Appeal was being widely publicized. The experts say that a successful appeal needs one big stroke of luck and one gift that amounts to about 10% of the total required. So this may be our moment.

But who was Alfred Edgar Victor Day? The name is unknown to me, and does not appear in the membership of the Friends. The solicitor has told me that he lived in Southampton and was a ships broker and freight forwarder, which is I gather a kind of middle-man in the export business. His total estate amounted to about £2.4 million, after payment of tax, and his only relative seems to be a nephew with a Germanic name who lives in Zurich. The solicitor is going to let me have his address so that I can write to him and there are one or two other leads that may be worth following up in the hope of learning more about our benefactor.

The Treasurer has been on sabbatical for the last two months at his country retreat in Wiltshire and this morning I had to decide if he would be more annoyed if I failed to tell him of the legacy than he would be if I broke into the peace of his sabbatical. In the end I decided to telephone him with the good news, but he seemed neither pleased nor excited by it, which was I suppose predictable enough. Jim Butler, the chairman of the Appeal, whom I telephoned first, was quite bowled over by the news, even though he is used to dealing in huge sums of money, and we calculated that the Appeal total now stands at just under £6 million.

The long, curious and exasperating saga of the textiles project has now ended, though the need for our vestments and altar furnishings to be renewed remains as urgent as ever. This is, I think, a classic case of ambition exceeding capacity, thus frustrating achievement and creating only disappointment. In retrospect, I think I should have stamped on it much earlier, but I have been almost totally preoccupied with the Appeal, I am desperately keen to see to see the textiles renewed, I believe in giving colleagues their heads, and the committee always seemed absolutely certain that the necessary finance, however large, would come from Japan in the wake of Issey Miyake's involvement.

The writing was, however, clearly on the wall in January when Keith Walker reported that the total cost of the project had risen to £2 million – about four times that of the original estimate. The explanation of the increase was that a developing project inevitably involved additional cost, but such was the enthusiasm of the committee that no one had paused to consider if it was actually appropriate to spend such a large amount of money on textiles. I felt it necessary to express also my fear that by aiming so high we might finish up with nothing: 'Those who will ride only in a Rolls-Royce, generally walk.'

The dénouement came strangely. It was always a tricky business managing the project in the midst of a £7 million Appeal designed to raise money for other items, and the only justification for permitting any kind of development was that the money would ultimately come from Japan. In the meantime, however, it was essential to maintain strict confidentiality, since any leakage of information could easily lead to misunderstanding and jeopardize the successful conclusion of the Appeal.

As is so often the case, a leak occurred and came from an unexpected source. Issey Miyake, once again in Paris for a fashion show, spoke about his involvement in Winchester Cathedral's textiles to the editor of a French fashion magazine. The story published in this magazine was read by a British journalist, and so it was that in early March the *Today* newspaper ran a headling 'The Cathedral of the Rising Sun'. The report that followed was more or less accurate and included details of likely costs. The *Southern Daily Echo* picked up the story from *Today* and soon it was common knowledge that we were planning to spend a vast amount of money on vestments and altar cloths.

Those involved in the leadership of the Appeal had to be informed immediately that the project was only at the discussion stage, that nothing would be done about its implementation until the Appeal was ended, and that, in any case, the money was expected to come from Japan. But there were now other problems, as letters of protest to me and to the Bishop soon indicated. Some senior parish priests, mindful of the difficulty being experienced over the raising of the Diocesan contribution to the Appeal, said the parishes would find it impossible to raise any money for the Cathedral if they believed money to be available for spending on vestments.

From Lincoln and Durham, where there had been announcements of cuts in the number of clergy to be employed because of financial constraints, there came protests that the Church of England had a wrong sense of priorities. Evangelicals, within and without the Diocese, complained that a non-Christian was to be employed on the making of robes for use in Christian worship. A number of older people were outraged that a citizen of a nation that had treated British prisoners-of-war so cruelly could be invited to work for Winchester Cathedral.

After spending some time in the dousing of these fires, it was necessary to have a number of 'crisis' meetings, and decision-making became much easier when it was evident that the professional fund-raiser, whom the committee wanted us to employ, stood not the slightest chance of raising £2 million in Japan.

Yesterday therefore the Chapter scaled down the project, so that it now embraces only altar cloths for the Wykeham Chantry and the Holy Sepulchre Chapel – these to be paid for by donors. The consultant and the fund-raiser are to be stood down – unfortunately at some cost in fees – and I am to write a diplomatic letter to Issey Miyake explaining our problems and much regretting that the project has been indefinitely postponed.

It is a great relief to have all this out of the way, but it is frustrating that so much time and money has been spent to such little effect. I got the Chapter to agree that all future projects requiring money, contracts or other obligations should have the Receiver General present at key meetings in order that financial, administrative and legal matters are not overlooked. It will also be important to ensure that projects approved by the Chapter are not subsequently developed so that they run far beyond what was originally envisaged.

Wednesday 24 June 1992

This afternoon I dedicated the three new bells which will shortly be hoisted up the tower to join the existing ring of twelve, some of which date from 1734. Two of the new bells have been paid for by the ringers, the other by the Friends, and the ring of fifteen will, I think, be the largest in the country apart from one of similar size at St Martin-in-the-Bullring, Birmingham. The new bells arrived on a lorry from the Whitechapel Bell Foundry and I had to climb on to the lorry – thus demonstrating my advancing years – to carry out the dedication. Television cameras recorded the event and quite a number of photographers from national and local newspapers were there, so we should get some useful publicity.

Immediately after Evensong Peter Lippiett, the admirable Vicar of Twyford, came to me pushing a wheelchair in which was seated an apparently severely disabled man. This turned out to be none other than the famous Professor Stephen Hawking, who was struck with motor-neuron disease some years ago but is still Professor of Mathematics at Cambridge and one of the world's leading scientists. His book *A Brief History of Time* is a best-seller and, although I have not read it, I understand that its conclusions point in the direction of atheism. Interesting, therefore, that he should have been ready to attend Evensong.

It seems that in his case, and most unusually, the motor-neuron disease has not progressed beyond a certain stage and, even though it has left him a physical wreck, his brain is quite unimpaired. Able to hear but not to speak, he has on his wheelchair a highly sophisticated piece of apparatus that enables him to tap out on a computer words which are then transformed through a synthesizer into speech. This enables him to hold conversations, but for obvious reasons these can be neither fluent nor lively. I welcomed him to the Cathedral and after a long pause a disembodied voice, coming from the back of the chair, responded 'I am glad to be here'. Another remark from me, another long pause, and another brief reply. It was by no means easy, but one could only marvel that it was possible at all. Running out of subjects, I told him that I had this afternoon dedicated three bells – long pause, followed by 'I do not like bells'. End of conversation.

The professor is not alone in his dislike of bells. The Bishop, Paul Britton and some others in and around the Close dread the arrival of visiting bands of ringers who come four or five times a year to attempt three-hour peals. I rather enjoy them, but now there has been inserted in the tower a sort of funnel which will project the sound of the bells more widely over the City, while reducing their volume in the immediate locality of the Cathedral. It will be interesting to see if we get more or fewer complaints in consequence.

Wednesday 15 July 1992

Today, being St Swithun's Day, is the second anniversary of the launching of our £7 million Appeal. Originally it was to have been completed in twelve months, but this was never a realistic possibility, and it was inevitable that another year would be needed. As we have undertaken a second year of considerable activity, it is now important that we should halt what we are calling 'the intensive phase', and this we can do quite easily, since we now have gifts and promises totalling £6,508,564. There are other anticipated gifts which have yet to come in and a number of money-raising events are scheduled during the remainder of the summer. Besides this, the interest on the large amount we have in hand will add quite significantly to the total. So, all in all, we should reach the target without too much difficulty. One of the many pleasing aspects of the enterprise is the £82,584 contributed by the Old Wykehamists. This has come through the indefatigable efforts of John Thorn, the former Headmaster of the College, who has written personal letters to hundreds of his old pupils and many others and secured a fine response. It is a moot point whether or not this could ever be repeated, for until comparatively recently the College used to have Evensong in the Cathedral once a month during term and, although I dare say many of the boys hated it at the time, it seems to have created in retrospect a real affection for the Cathedral. Now that the College comes only twice a year – for William of Wykeham's Obit and a Carol Service at Christmas – I doubt whether such an affection is being kindled in the present generation.

Thursday 23 July 1992

At midday we had the final service for the Royal Hampshire Regiment. Under the reorganization of the army, this regiment is being amalgamated with the Queen's Royal Regiment and will in future be known as the Princess of Wales's Own Royal Regiment, with its headquarters at Canterbury.

The service was a very moving ocasion and at the end I noticed tears in the eyes of some of the older people present. I can understand this, for the regiment was formed over 200 years ago, it has very close links with Hampshire, from which most of its members have always been drawn, and its proud traditions have been forged on the anvil of war. Today there were plenty of DSOs, MCs and MMs on show and inevitably the event aroused memories of comradeship in perilous times. The link with the Cathedral is also strong, for there are many regimental memorials on the South side of the Nave, the regiment has always regarded Winchester as its cathedral, and I have come to regard many of its senior officers as friends.

Yet there is a cause for rejoicing inasmuch as the amalgamation of the two regiments has been brought about because we no longer live under the threat of imminent war. The armed forces can safely be reduced in size and our prayers for peace have been answered. Prayer now should be directed to the proper use of the resources released by this change.

The Princess of Wales, who has been Colonel-in-Chief of the Hampshires and is to have the same office in the new regiment, came to the service and looked exceedingly glamorous in an outfit of striking blue. When the service was over there was about half-an-hour to spare while the regimental people went off to the Castle to prepare to receive her for lunch, so I was asked to keep her occupied in and around the Cathedral. This was not difficult, because she is the easiest of the Royal Family to talk to, so I showed her the various parts of the restoration programme which are now under way, introduced her to various members of the cathedral staff, and, with the aid of a model, explained the plan for building a Visitors Centre. We also had some general talk in which she told me what a battle there had been over the name of the amalgamated regiment and how she had insisted on the Hampshire element being recognized by the use of her title and by her becoming Colonel-in-Chief. When she moved off her great popularity with the general public became quickly apparent and the way in which she combines dignity and friendliness cannot be faulted.

Tuesday 28 July 1992

This has been a busy day. Meetings this morning, first with the Chairman of the Friends, Brian Cocup, then with the Precentor. At 3.00 pm I clambered up the winding steps of the Tower to its roof and, in full robes, conducted a brief act of thanksgiving and dedication to mark the completion of the restoration of the Tower. First, however, I congratulated and thanked the Contractor and the Clerk of Works and all who have been involved in the work, for the restored Tower is a splendid sight and a very visible symbol of the success of the Appeal. Fortunately, it has been a gloriously sunny day for the ceremony and for the press photographers who were in attendance.

At 4.00 p.m. there was an important Chapter meeting to decide the best way forward with the Visitors Centre. The Steering Group, under the chairmanship of Bill Heller, has served us exceedingly well in the planning of the project and in the detailed work of obtaining and examining the tenders for its building. This afternoon they provided us with a carefully compiled report on the tenders, of which there were eleven – all very close and much higher than anticipated. This is disappointing in a way but it probably means that, in the face of such fierce competition, the final price will be as low as is economically possible.

Even so, £1.2 million plus £350,000 for fitting out costs and initial stock, plus fees, is quite a long way above the £1 million now being raised by the Appeal for the Centre. The Steering Group presented us with five options: (1) proceed with the full project and finance the shortfall from Dean and Chapter reserves; (2) proceed with the project but postpone the building of the Education wing, thus reducing the shortfall by about £150,000: (3) build the scheme in phases, using no more than the £1 million available from the Appeal; (4) start again and ask the architects to design a different building within the £1 million available; (5) postpone the project to see if our needs might be met in other ways, e.g. by the purchasing of existing premises not too far from the Cathedral and turning these into a shop and/or restaurant.

The committee recommended the second course and in the end this is the one we agreed to take. But not before a full and appropriately serious discussion. The Treasurer, full of doom and gloom, said the taking of £400,000 from reserves would place the Cathedral's finances under an unacceptable strain and the ultimate financial success of the enterprise was a long way from certain. The Librarian was naturally disappointed by the prospect of losing the Education wing at this stage and with no indication of how and when it might be financed. There is also the question of whether or not the Church Commissioners willl permit us to reduce our reserves by £400,000 for a project of this sort.

With this in mind I have been asked to discuss the problem with Jim Butler and John Ashburton, of the Trust, to see how they feel about it and to seek their help.

Wednesday 5 August 1992

Today's meeting at Baring Brothers in the City of London to discuss the funding of the extra £400,000 needed for the Visitors Centre was wholly successful and in a way very amusing. I had thought to meet John Ashburton and Jim Butler alone, but the Treasurer, who is unhappy about the whole project, insisted on attending and decided that the Receiver General, Keith Bamber, should accompany him. Informing me of this he wondered if we might travel on the same train, but as I had other business in London I went earlier.

Just before 3.45 p.m. I arrived at Barings' discreetly signed office in Bishopsgate and was quickly whisked up by lift to John's office, where he and Jim were waiting. A secretary produced cups of tea and we talked about this and that, anticipating the arrival any minute of the Treasurer and the Receiver General. When it reached 4.15 p.m. and there was no sign of them we decided to go ahead, and it was soon settled that the Trust would loan the Dean and Chapter the £400,000 at an agreed rate of interest, with annual repayments from the Centre's profits. This will avoid the liquidation of Dean and Chapter assets and possible problems with the Church Commissioners.

We were just about to depart when the absentees arrived. Their train had caught fire near Woking and been delayed by an hour. We told them what had been decided, they – thankful to be alive, perhaps – seemed perfectly happy with the arrangement and the three of us returned safely to Winchester. Building can start next month.

Friday 4 September 1992

A major piece of behind-the-scenes work on the Cathedral's archives has now been completed. These are said to have been the largest collection of uncatalogued mediaeval archives in the country, consisting of over 100 charters and a multitude of manorial rolls and other documents from the days of the Benedictine monastery.

They had been catalogued in an amateurish way, but it was difficult for scholars to track items down, they were inadequately stored and many of the charters were simply pasted into books – a treatment that would in the long run have threatened their survival. It is greatly to the credit of Keith Walker, the Librarian, and John Hardacre, his deputy, that this was taken in hand and, over the course of three years, knocked into shape by professionals.

At no cost to the Dean and Chapter, for the Hampshire Archives Trust allocated a member of its staff to the task for a year, and grants from the County Council and the Radcliffe Trust enabled us to employ Dr Nicholas Vincent, a Research Fellow of Peterhouse, Cambridge, to deal with the charters. No doubt he will get a book out of his work here because he made a number of important finds.

Wednesday 10 September 1992

There is a problem over the painting that has been revealed in the course of the conservation of the wooden vaulting beneath the interior of the Tower. For 100 years or more the vaulting of the Eastern roof, all of which was constructed in wood by Bishop Fox in the early part of the sixteenth century, has been painted white to match the colour of the stone vaulting in the Nave. Viewed from the West end of the building, this gives the impression of a continuous sweep of roof, and in fact Fox imitated the tracery of the Nave.

But now the conservationists, in thrall to the distant past, wish to get rid of the white paint beneath the tower and return to the dark brown ribs of the original vaulting. I am not at all sure that this is a good idea because it will break the continuity of the interior roof line which is the Cathedral's greatest glory. And now it seems that prior to the application of the white paint in the nineteenth century there was an indifferent seventeenth-century painting in the circular space at the centre of the vaulting. This purports to represent the Trinity, but neither the sunburst nor the words around the edge – all seriously decayed – seem to me to have anything to express about any understanding of the Godhead.

But apart from Keith Walker and me, everyone is wildly excited about this 'great find' and insisting that, after a modest amount of conservation, it should be returned to its central place beneath the Tower. My suggestion that it should be carried away to the museum and Keith Walker's idea that it should be replaced by a modern painting (at enormous cost, no doubt) have failed to find any support and a mere Dean is in no position to enforce his own wishes in a matter of this sort. My only consolation is the assurance of the experts that the painting, when viewed from floor level, will not look as unattractive as it does at close quarters. Some future generation will, I dare say, call for brushes and white paint or possibly commission something rather special for a space which is, I believe, known technically as an oculus.

Thursday 17 September 1992

Carlo Curley, the renowned American organist, gave a recital this evening in aid of the Appeal. A giant of a man – physically and with a personality ten times larger than life – he has a remarkable following. The Cathedral was packed to the doors, people having come from far and wide to see and hear one who is advertised as 'The Pavarotti of the Organ'.

He chose not to play our own organ but a huge electronic instrument imported for the occasion. This was augmented by a mechanical bird-in-cage that was sometimes induced to cheep and cause amusement. The comments of the organist between items were also highly entertaining and Carlo Curley's avowed aim is to bring organ music to the masses, extending it far beyond the somewhat rarefied breed that normally attends organ recitals.

On the evidence of this evening he is, I think, succeeding, and although he is unashamedly a showman (is his name really Carlo Curley?), he is also a very accomplished organist. Not as accomplished as our own David Hill, however, for when David contributed a piece to this evening's programme on the Cathedral organ there was a noticeable heightening of quality and he was loudly applauded.

The commercial element in the Carlo Curley show is also interesting – plenty of CDs and cassettes on sale and a fan club to join – and when he autographed programmes it seemed hardly surprising that his signature covered the whole of a page.

Tuesday 22 September 1992

Over the last forty years I have dedicated many persons and objects, but not until today had I dedicated a chair-lift. It was well worth doing because it will enable a lot of disabled people to see the Eastern half of the Cathedral. The Quire, the Retro-Quire where the shrine of St Swithun once stood, and the Lady Chapel stand considerably higher than the Nave and can be reached only by ascending a steep mediaeval stairway. A number of invalids in wheelchairs are lifted up the stairs but this is a back-breaking task for friends and Virgers and really should not be attempted.

We have therefore raised about £20,000 from trusts, personal donations and the Friends and installed on the North stairway a lift capable of raising wheelchairs and their occupants. There was quite a large gathering of people from the trusts and organisations concerned with the disabled at the dedication and soon there was a queue of wheelchairs waiting to use the lift. It was moving to witness the delight of some who have spent all their lives in Winchester but never before seen the Eastern end of the building. Money well spent.

Wednesday 7 October 1992

I spoke about the Appeal this evening at the Southampton Deanery Synod and this proved to be a very tricky assignment – more difficult than anything else I have tackled so far. It was always going to be a challenge because Southampton, aware of its size and independent history, thinks nothing of Hampshire and is scarcely aware of the existence of Winchester Cathedral. The Southampton churches share this sense of independence of the Diocese and over the last five and a half years I have only once been invited to preach in a Southampton church.

The situation was not helped by the need to deal with a very long business agenda before reaching the Cathedral's needs and it was positively hindered by the presence of a bishop from Uganda who made a powerful appeal for money for his poverty-stricken diocese and wondered why the Cathedral was looking for £7 million when there were far more urgent needs in Africa. I don't know if the decision to invite the two of us to the same meeting was the result of lack of imagination or a deliberate ploy to put the Cathedral on the spot.

The problem I ran into at Southampton is, however, only part of a more serious problem relating to the involvement of the whole Diocese in the Appeal. At the outset, the Diocesan Synod pledged the Diocese to raise £650,000. This is of course a large sum, but divided among the 300 parishes, spread over four years, and taking account of tax rebates on covenant gifts, it ought certainly to be manageable. But, as always, only about 50% of the members of the Synod were present at the meeting when the pledge was made, and by no means all the parishes are represented anyway, so the Diocese as a whole doesn't seem to feel any commitment to raise the money.

Inevitably, a number of parishes are struggling to raise money for the repair of their own churches, but the main problem is that the parishes on the whole do not 'own' their Cathedral and feel no sense of responsibility for either its maintenance or its life. An additional factor is that giving by church members in this Diocese is by no means generous. Although Hampshire is one of the richest counties in the country, Winchester Diocese stands thirty-fourth in the league table of forty-three dioceses for the level of giving. The average is just over £2 per church member per week, whereas in poorer dioceses, such as Southwark and Sheffield, the average is over £4 per week. A clear case of comfort breeding complacency.

Friday 9 October 1992

I am still in a state of shock after the events of last evening. We went for dinner to Michael and Mary Callé, who live on the outskirts of the city. It was a delightful dinner party, with a Judge and a General and other interesting people among the guests. I talked a great deal and Michael, generously hospitable as always, kept the wine glasses filled.

We left for home at about 11.30 pm, having declined brandy in the drawing room, and as we approached the city centre I became aware of flashing lights in my rear mirror. These were from a police car which also displayed a sign calling me to stop. At first I thought that perhaps my rear lights had failed but when two young policemen reached the car door their first question was, 'Have you been drinking, Sir?'. Indeed I had, but since the glasses were always replenished before they were empty I could not say how much. I was thereupon invited to step outside and blow into a breathalyser, it first being explained to me that the gauge would start at green, change to amber if I had consumed any alcohol, and to red if I were over the legal limit.

The change to amber was swift and, in what seemed like an eternity while we waited to see if it would turn to red, my mind visualized the newspaper headline 'Dean on drink-driving charge' and all the disgrace that would follow. But mercifully it stayed on amber and the policemen, having taken my name and address (this was the first indication they had that I was the Dean, for I was not wearing a clerical collar), bid me goodnight, with the kindly advice, 'I should have one less next time, Sir.'

I asked them why they had stopped me and they explained that I seemed to be driving rather slowly and applied the brakes frequently, which must have appeared unusual for the driver of a BMW, though in fact I do generally drive somewhat cautiously. Curiously, they followed me almost to the entrance to the Close; perhaps it was to check that I really was the Dean.

I suspect that I escaped by about a thimbleful and that had I accepted the final brandy I would now be in deep trouble. Certainly I would have had to offer my resignation from the Deanery. Whether or not this would have been accepted I cannot tell, but of course it would have been extremely embarrassing, and life without the car for the next twelve months would have been very difficult, not least for Jo, who now depends entirely upon it for any movement beyond the Close.

This must not happen again and, quite apart from the possible effects on me, it is undoubtedly the case that drink-driving costs lives. I don't think I need go 'on the wagon', but two glasses of wine must now be my dinner-party limit.

Friday 9 October 1992

The funeral today of Jeanne Home drew a large congregation for she had a special place in the Cathedral's life. A diminutive figure, she was nearly always dressed in blue and never without a head scarf. The Cathedral was her daytime home: she rarely missed any of the daily services and between them was generally somewhere in the building except at lunchtime when she repaired to the Close to consume her sandwiches. Sometimes she would take a group of visitors on a guided tour, which was a memorable experience for them as she saw the Cathedral through eyes different from those of the rest of us. In some ways she seemed like a mediaeval figure re-incarnated in the twentieth century. I imagine that during the Middle Ages there would be a number of women like Jeanne about the place – devout widows, nun-like – who found meaning and purpose in their lives through their association with the monastic community. She always treated me with what in the present age is regarded as excessive respect – standing to one side whenever I approached and bowing as I passed. Only on rare occasions would she permit herself to engage in conversation with me and evidently regarded it as a high honour simply to be greeted.

Her background was mysterious. It seems that she spent some years in Africa and once said that her husband had been killed in the Mau Mau uprising in Kenya, but I am not altogether sure this was the case, as her grip on reality could be tenuous. What is certain is that she had hardly any money and lived in great simplicity. We shall miss her, and during a period of hectic activity in the Cathedral's life, with much emphasis on money, her presence has been a salutary challenge to our priorities.

Saturday 7 November 1992

The Bishop held a Eucharist in the Cathedral this morning to enable the Diocese to pray for the General Synod which next Wednesday will once again vote on a proposal that women may be ordained to the priesthood. The service was well supported, though the Cathedral was not full to capacity, and it was, I think, a good occasion. The Bishop was, and remains, in a difficult position, as he is still opposed to women priests, yet – on the evidence of the voting in the Diocesan and Deanery Synods – a good majority in the Diocese are in favour.

The service was carefully organized so as to express a strict neutrality on the matter. There was no sermon, the prayers were for unity and the guidance of the Holy Spirit, the main participants were drawn from both sides of the debate and we were all on our most tolerant behaviour.

The main aim, I suppose, was to try to express and reinforce the unity of the Diocese and thus help to stave off possible division after the vote. The difficulty about praying for the guidance of the Holy Spirit in this context is that when the result is known none of those who are disappointed will believe that the Holy Spirit has had anything to do with it. In theory the Holy Spirit could guide the minds of the General Synod members, but only if they are open enough to receive such guidance, and most are not.

Wednesday 11 November 1992

Marvellous news this evening: the General Synod has voted in favour of the ordination of women to the priesthood. Jo gave me the news when I came in from Evensong and I wondered at first if she had heard the six o'clock television news correctly, but it soon became plain that an historic decision was made in Church House, Westminster this afternoon.

It was evidently a near thing, as it was always going to be, but the securing of two-thirds majorities in the Houses of Bishops, Clergy and Laity in the coalition of religious interests that constitutes the Church of England was a most decisive judgment on which there can be no going back. It is a great triumph for people like Monica Furlong, Cathy Milford and Margaret Webster of the Movement for the Ordination of Women who have laboured hard and long for this day and have often been denounced and insulted for their pains.

In some ways I am surprised by the vote; in some ways not. An insufficient vote in the House of Laity at York in July suggested that entrenched positions had been taken up and that today the proposal would once again be narrowly defeated. At that stage and for most of this autumn I thought there would be further delay, for another four to five years. But during the last few weeks there were some signs of a change of mood and a few signals that the proposal might just get through. So I am not completely surprised by a decision which is long overdue. It is twenty-five years since I wrote in a *New Christian* editorial that the time had come for women to be ordained to the priesthood. That was considered pretty *outré* even in the reforming 1960s, though a few brave souls like Betty Ridley were also pleading the cause.

The opposition, led by the Bishop of London, have been unscrupulous in their tactics but I think that, from their point of view, they made a fatal mistake in 1986 when they supported the ordination of women as deacons. By so doing they supposed they would buy off a significant number of those who wanted to see women in the ordained ministry and would settle for them to be no more than deacons. But in the event the experience of women ministering as deacons in the parishes over the last five years has helped many people to accept the ministry of women and to recognise their vocations to the priesthood.

On the Chapter the only serious problem will be with Roger Job, the Precentor, who has always been firmly opposed to the ordination of women and never believed it would be accepted by the General Synod. He is bound to be deeply shocked. Keith Walker and Alec Knight are as delighted as I am and, rather surprisingly, Paul Britton is not greatly perturbed because, apparently, he was never fully convinced by the arguments against women priests.

I don't know what the reaction of the Cathedral congregation is likely to be, as I have never tested opinion on the matter and have not been able to gain a general impression of where people stand. Some, I know, are strongly against women priests, but I suspect that the majority are in favour – reflecting the broad outlook of the people in the parishes of this diocese. I am preaching at Mattins on Sunday morning, so I must try to say something that will help the wounded, though this cannot have priority over recognition of the importance and the rightness of what has happened.

Sunday 15 November 1992

I preached this morning on the General Synod's historic decision to authorize the ordination of women to the priesthood and I was very conscious of the fact that among those present were some who are overjoyed by the decision and others who are greatly distressed by it. I was equally conscious of the fact that nothing I could say would alleviate their pain, for the opposition to women priests is not, I think, primarily an intellectual matter. It runs much deeper and touches sensitive emotions.

I first pointed out that the decision had not been taken lightly or recklessly, that no parish would have a woman priest imposed upon it, and that our differences with the Roman Catholic Church were related mainly to the place of authority in the church, rather than to the gender of the priesthood.

Then I moved on to outline what I believe to be the heart of the Christian religion, namely the trinitarian faith expressed in the Apostles' and Nicene Creeds. In neither of these is there any reference to matters of church order and organization, since these are of secondary importance and may vary from time to time and place to place. It is, I said, perilous to raise these things to a level at which they become articles of faith, for 'it obscures the nature of true faith and causes disagreement, division and pain over matters which are legitimately open to differences of interpretation and practice'.

'In the Church of England we have for most of our history been ready to concentrate on the essentials of the Christian faith and we have therefore never gone in for heresy-hunting, recognizing the essential mystery of God's nature and being. We have tolerated wide variety in the expression of faith, and during the last 100 years we have accommodated a wide variety of worship and sacramental practice. The conflict over the ordination of women has been out of character, and now the decision has been made, we need to learn how women priests can be assimilated into our corporate life, not as an unfortunate aberration but as an expression of the richness of a developing Christian tradition ... The divisions and conflicts of the world will never be healed by a divided and squabbling church. May the Lord have mercy on us all.'

It is already apparent that, nationally, the opponents of women priests are not going to take the General Synod's decision lying down, and will use every possible means, including the Parliamentary debate and vote next year, to get it overturned. There is not, I think, the faintest possibility of this happening, so we are now left with the problem of how to deal with the opponents. Inasmuch as the battle has been won and women are going to be ordained, we can afford to let the opposition have their heads and not challenge them further. On the other hand, their outbursts and threats will continue to be much publicized, causing much pain to the women and a good deal of damage to the church. We shall have to see how things go, but in the long run tolerance is likely to achieve most.

Wednesday 2 December 1992

The new workshops which I officially opened and dedicated this afternoon are a notable addition to our resources and should enable the Cathedral and the other buildings of the Close to be efficiently and economically repaired for many centuries to come. Erected at a cost of £350,000, they must be just about the best cathedral workshops in the country, with up-to-date facilities and machinery for stonemasons, carpenters, plumbers, painters and other trades. There is also a good room for the displaying of plans and designs, and an attractive mess-room for meals.

The contrast with what went before is complete. For many years the stonemasons worked in and from an old stable behind No 1 The Close, but this was condemned by the Health and Safety Executive in 1989. The painter kept his ladders, paints and brushes in part of another disused stable and the carpenters had to improvise in whatever space they could find, substantial work being impossible.

So although the new building has cost quite a lot of money, it will eventually pay for itself as our own staff undertake much more of the restoration work at a much lower cost than that of outside contractors. The Cathedral Architect, Peter Bird, who designed the workshops, has also demonstrated that it is possible to erect a new building in an ancient Close without in any way diminishing its overall beauty and dignity. Indeed, it seems to me that the utilization in this way of an unused piece of land has actually enhanced the environment, and I believe the new Visitors Centre will do the same.

But we have been warned by the City Council's planning people that further new buildings will not be permitted until we have submitted an overall plan for the future development of the whole of the Close. In other words, no more piecemeal development, which is fair enough, but of course much of the charm of the Close is that it was developed in a piecemeal fashion in the seventeenth and eighteenth centuries.

Thursday 3 December 1992

Another two good annual meetings of the Cathedral congregation – again attended by about 400 people – with lots of good things to report. The Appeal is within £150,000 of its £7 million target; the Tower has been completed and so have the new Workshops; work has started on the building of the Visitors Centre and will soon begin on the Retro-Quire tiles – said to be the largest and most important area of mediaeval tiles in England; early in the new year work will commence on the West Front; the first stage of the new management plan has been implemented with Keith Bamber as an able Receiver General and Geoff Barker, a newly recruited Chartered Accountant.

The Treasurer reported that, while a surplus of £31,000 was achieved on the day-to-day running costs during the 1991/92 year, the outlook for 1992/93 is much less rosy and it will be difficult to avoid a substantial deficit. It has of course been impossible to give much attention to the increasing of ordinary revenue while the Appeal has been claiming such great attention.

I spent much of the meeting, however, trying to look beyond the Appeal and the current building and administrative developments to the future of the Cathedral's mission. Next year, being the 900th anniversary of the completion and dedication of the building, will be a year full of activity, mainly from Maundy Thursday until the autumn, and now that the Archbishops' Commission on Cathedrals is going into action the spirit of reform is in the air.

The Dean and Chapter are to review our patterns of worship, ministry to visitors, education work among young people and adults, preaching, music and relations with the wider communitiy. This leads inevitably to a consideration of the place of change in the church, and I said:

'We are living in a period of considerable change in the church – more than at any time since the Reformation of the sixteenth and seventeenth centuries. Change in the religious sphere is not, however, usually welcomed. However, it is often necessary if the church is to be a living, dynamic agency of mission in the world. Cathedrals are caught up in reforming movements because they are in the forefront of the church's mission and are tremendous assets in its encounter with the wider world. There are two approaches to change in the church – the first sees it as a tiresome business stimulated by those imbued by the spirit of a secular age and therefore something to be resisted; the second sees it as an attempt to respond to the work of the Holy Spirit in the church and therefore something exciting as well as demanding. After nearly six years as your Dean, I hope you know me well enough to recognize that my own beliefs lead me to the second of these approaches.'

Monday 7 December 1992

At a pleasing little ceremony this afternoon the Bishop dedicated a new stained glass window in the Nave in memory of Frances Chamberlayn Macdonald – a daughter of our big house, Cranbury Park, who was only twenty when she died suddenly at the end of a day's hunting in 1985. The window is actually a re-creation, for it incorporates a number of fragments of mediaeval glass. In his will, drawn up shortly before his death in 1404, Bishop William of Wykeham provided for the glazing of the Cathedral's Nave aisles and clerestories and the work is believed to have been carried out by Thomas the Glazier of Oxford – one of the finest glaziers of his time.

Virtually all of his glass was destroyed at the time of the Reformation, but some fragments, including a representation of St Agnes, a winged seraph supported by a wheel, the head of an Old Testament prophet or king, and a bishop's head, were subsequently recovered. When I arrived in Winchester these were lying around awaiting re-use, but now a donation of £25,000 to the appeal by the young woman's godmother has enabled us to have them mounted in a modern setting by Alfred Fisher, a leading contemporary artist in glass. The predominant colour is blue, and as the window is directly opposite my stall in the Nave I shall greatly benefit from its arrival.

Christmas Eve 1992

At Evensong we dedicated not only the Christmas Crib but also two icons which have been placed in niches of the feretory wall facing the site of the former shrine of St Swithun. This area of the Cathedral, once a focal point of local devotion and a magnet for pilgrims from all over England, is now something of a problem as it offers only emptiness and no encouragement to either reflection or devotion.

A statue of St Swithun by a top-class sculptor is, I am sure, the answer, but I don't see this happening during my time as Dean. Meanwhile the placing of icons in the niches which housed small statues of saints until the destruction of the shrine in 1538 will introduce both colour and objects of devotion. Those dedicated this evening portray the Archangel Gabriel and the Archangel Michael, and they are the work of a young Russian, Sergei Federov, who is said to be the finest icon painter currently in the West.

Certainly, they look exceedingly well and at £2,500 each are not at all expensive, which encourages me to believe that we shall have no difficulty in finding donors for another seven to complete a full sequence. First, however, we must convince the fundamentalists on the Fabric Advisory Committee who assert that statues should be replaced only by statues and not by icons.

We invited a Russian Orthodox priest from Southampton to carry out the actual dedication ceremony, which he did impressively, and it would have been even more impressive had his small silver censer not gone out at the critical moment of its use. It is interesting that the congregation at Evensong on Christmas Eve has more than doubled in number over the last few years, so that the service has to be held in the Nave, rather than in the Quire.

1993

The delegation from the Archbishops' Commission on Cathedrals completed its visit today, having arrived at lunchtime on Friday. Elspeth Howe, the chairman of the Commission, came and was accompanied by Canon Kenneth Riley of Liverpool Cathedral, Robert Aagaard, who runs Cathedral Camps, and Nigel Waring of the Church Commissioners, who is Secretary of the Commission. Michael Turnbull, Bishop of Rochester, came for part of Saturday.

They got through an extraordinary amount of work in the time available, our having set up a sequence of interviews for them in accordance with their requirements. These enabled them to meet representatives of every part of the Cathedral's life, including the Bishop, Honorary Canons, and others who look at us from a more detached position. How they will manage to keep this up for another seven weekends at other cathedrals is an interesting question and of course all the information and impressions they gather will need to be correlated and compared with that of the other delegations.

By the time they interviewed me they had seen many other people and picked up that my experience over the last six years has not been one of unadulterated joy. The problems in the Chapter are widely known about. Speaking frankly, I told them that while I regarded it as a great honour to be the Dean of Winchester and would always be grateful to have had the opportunity to serve this great Cathedral, I would not wish to undertake the task again under the conditions that had prevailed during my time here.

They seemed entirely sympathetic to my position and were obviously taking rather seriously the things I said in my University Sermon on the subject. Elspeth Howe has a sharp mind and her questions were very much to the point, though I suspect that she has brought to the enquiry a secular model of management that may not be entirely appropriate to cathedrals. I hope she is flexible enough to modify this as her tour of the cathedrals continues and no doubt there will have to be lots of compromises if anything is ever going to flow from the Commission's work.

Saturday 23 January 1993

I do not find it easy to get angry – it might be more healthy for everyone if I did – but the nearest I come to rage is often at Evensong, which would doubtless seem surprising to the devout souls, often quite a large number, who form the congregation at this marvellous daily offering of worship.

The contribution of the Choir is never less than superb and it is a wonderful thing that day by day the Psalms and Canticles and an anthem are sung at such a high level. The combination of words, music and architecture is truly glorious, inspiring and consoling. But the Bible readings appointed for the Lessons are often appalling and a denial of what we are about.

This evening for the First Lesson the Canon in Residence read, as prescribed by the official Lectionary, Leviticus 3. This consisted solely of ritual instructions for the sacrifical offering of animals in ancient Israel:

> If he offers a lamb for his offering, then shall he offer it before the Lord, laying his hand upon the head of his offering and killing it before the tent of meeting; and Aaron's sons shall throw its blood against the altar round about. Then from the sacrifice of the peace offering as an offering by fire to the Lord he shall offer its fat tail entire, taking it away close by the backbone, and the fat that covers the entrails, and all the fat that is on the entrails, and the two kidneys with the fat that is on them at the loins, and the appendage of the liver which he shall take away with the kidneys. And the priest shall burn it on the altar as good offered by fire to the Lord.

We heard these instructions three times in relation to different animals and it is impossible to believe that anyone present was edified by this reading. There was, unusually, an alternative reading that might have been used. It was from the I Maccabees 1, and described the frightful assault on the Jews by the army of King Antiochus Epiphanes of Syria in 168 BC:

> They kept using violence against Israel, against those found month after month in the cities. And on the twenty-fifth day of the month they offered sacrifice on the altar which was upon the altar of burnt offering. According to the decree, they put to death the women who had their children circumcised, and their families and those who circumcised them; and they hung the infants from their mothers' necks.

Would this have been preferable to Leviticus? Possibly, inasmuch as the reading ended with the heroic resolution of some of the Jews to stand firm against the assault.

When the *Magnificat* had been sung, I found myself required by the Lectionary to read the final section of chapter 14 of the First Letter of St Paul to the Corinthians. This consisted of instructions to the church in first-century Corinth about the ordering of worship and began with the way in which those who felt called to 'speak in tongues' were to be handled. It then moved on to the place of women in worship:

> As in all the churches of the saints, the women should keep silence in the churches. For they are not permitted to speak, but should be subordinate, as even the law says. If there is anything they desire to know, let them ask their husbands at home. For it is shameful for a woman to speak in church. What! Did the word of God originate with you, or are you the only ones it has reached?

In fact, I did not read this and ended the Lesson at verse 33: 'For God is not a God of confusion but of peace.'

It is true that all these readings are part of the Bible and show how particular people at particular times responded to God's revelation of himself to them. Serious study of the Bible cannot ignore the ancient Jewish sacrificial system, the Maccabean wars and St Paul's dealings with the Corinthians. But Evensong is not an occasion for Bible study: it is an act of worship in which the hearts of the worshippers are lifted to God and inspired for their daily encounters and the tasks in the world to which they return when Evensong is ended.

Readings of this sort reduce, rather an enhance, the spirit of worship and they are thoroughly misleading to any from outside the Christian community who chance to be present at Evensong. It is a fact that the cathedrals now attract people who are on the edge of faith. They are quite a long way from Christian commitment but they have some religious intuitions, and in the kind of worship offered in cathedrals find something to which they can respond. But how could they possibly be drawn closer to a faith whose adherents read in public the kind of material prescribed for use at Evensong today? Might they not be repelled by what they heard, as that most sensitive soul, Philip Toynbee, was once repelled by the content of the First Lesson at Evensong in Peterborough Cathedral?

The basic problem is that the liturgists who devise lectionaries are essentially theorists. They 'know' what is 'correct' and they are upholders of the tradition that the whole of the Bible, no matter what its content may be, should be read sequentially over a period of two years. What the effect of this in practice may be is of no concern to them, but it must be of concern to those of us who are called upon to read the Bible in public in cathedrals attended by a wide range of people who are at different stages in their religious pilgrimage. There ought to be a special lectionary for cathedral use.

Pending the compilation of such a lectionary, I have tried to persuade the Canons to use their discretion over the Old Testament readings, so that if the prescribed reading is, as today, manifestly unsuitable they substitute something else. But so far to no avail. Some of them believe that what is officially prescribed should be followed, whatever the consequences may be; others, I suspect, only discover the content of the reading shortly before reaching the lectern, by which time it is too late to find something more suitable.

Friday 29 January 1993

Alarming news today: the builders undertaking the construction of the Visitors Centre have gone into receivership. We had the same experience with the firm responsible for the restoration of the Tower, and the building industry is apparently so unstable that it has become impossible to tell whether or not appointed builders will complete the job. It must be a nightmare working and managing in this sphere.

Fortunately the Receiver General has set to work immediately and is hopeful that the valuations of completed work can be made quickly and the way prepared for the letting of a new contract without excessive delay. But there is bound to be some delay in the completion of the building and it looks as if we must now think in terms of late, rather than early, autumn. This may not be too bad because the Queen doesn't return from Balmoral until the end of October and if she is to open the Centre for us we cannot expect a date before about mid-November. The change of contractor will inevitably mean increased costs, though some of the other original tenderers were close to the successful bid and may be anxious to get the work.

Wednesday 3 February 1993

Disaster was narrowly averted when a huge section of the West wall of the Deanery collapsed during the night, depositing many tons of stone and rubble on the adjacent path and road. A car parked, illicitly, overnight was completely crushed, and had the wall collapsed during the daytime there would almost certainly have been deaths. The Choristers pass by every day to and from the Cathedral.

The wall, originally mediaeval, was apparently rebuilt in the early 1660s when a north wing was added to the former Prior's Lodging. At its base it is over four feet thick but it seems that its construction was not solid stone. Two separate walls were united by a chalk in-fill centre and with the passage of the years the outer stone surface, some eighteen inches thick, separated from the centre and last night crumbled. Annual tests gave no hint of this possibility and although I sleep on the west side of the house I heard nothing.

Sunday 7 February 1993

Six years have passed since I was installed as Dean, and these have been the most surprising years of my ministry so far. Although there was much talk of money and Cathedral restoration when I came, I never dreamt that by 1993 we should have raised £7 million. Flowing from this has been our embarking upon the most extensive restoration programme since the Edwardian days of Diver William Walker and also the building of a Visitors Centre at a cost of £1.4 million. A spin-off benefit from all this is that in a relatively short space of time I have become well-known throughout the Diocese and County, which is no bad thing for a Dean to be.

I think it is also the case that the success of the appeal has enhanced my reputation. In many ways this is unfair because the success was due to the leadership of Jim Scott, Jim Butler, Mary Fagan and others who had access to money and were able to coax it from their contacts. I suppose that my enthusiasm and optimism helped, and also my role as the frontman who was always on hand when arms were being twisted and always available for Press photographs whenever a major event was being launched or a major gift acknowledged. Hence the illusion that I was in some way running the show.

It would be comforting to suppose that this great effort and its success had in some way bound the Chapter closer together, but I don't think this has been the case. Indeed, the decision to build the Visitors Centre in the garden of No 11 The Close has made things worse in some respects, and my preoccupation with money-raising has meant that a number of tricky personal matters have had to remain unresolved or untouched. The problems run too deep to be solved by external events, and maybe they cannot be solved other than by change of personnel.

I hope, however, that the 900th anniversary celebrations, coming so soon after the Appeal, will help to raise morale and induce a more forward-looking approach to the Cathedral's life. There is no telling, of course, what hazards lie hidden in the extensive anniversary programme itself.

At the personal level Jo's health is a source of increasing anxiety to me. What seemed a year ago to be no more than the kind of memory loss that often goes with advancing years has turned into something altogether more sinister. Last autumn she began to forget to prepare supper – at first just now and again, but then more frequently – and, when she did remember, it sometimes seemed that she had forgotten what to do. We had some strange concoctions for meals, and over Christmas there were dangers of food poisoning from dishes that had been put on one side and were long past their safe consumption dates.

At the same time she was becoming increasingly confused over shopping – forgetting what to bring and experiencing difficulty over paying at the check-out till. So I have now taken over responsibility for cooking and shopping, and curiously Jo doesn't appear to think this unusual. Which is very odd, because cooking and shopping have always been among the chief interests of her life. When I mentioned this to our GP recently he said it might be the first signs of Alzheimer's disease or one of the other forms of dementia. But it is too soon to tell and may be slow-moving, anyway.

Monday 8 March 1993

Robert Ferguson, the Senior Chaplain of Winchester College, preached another of his appalling sermons at Evensong yesterday. He usually comes at the invitation of Roger Job and always uses the opportunity to give vent to his extremely reactionary views on the state of the Church of England. He is of course perfectly entitled to do this and it is important that the Cathedral pulpit should be open to a wide variety of beliefs and understandings. But what we are given is not a thoughtful consideration of the theological issues at stake; rather are we subjected to point-scoring invective, directed without much respect for the facts against liberals and delivered in the most patronizing tone of voice imaginable. I cannot believe that he would be allowed to get away with this in the College chapel, and the Vicar of Twyford, who was present at Evensong, left in a state of anger such as I have never before encountered in any place of worship.

If I could ban Robert from the Cathedral pulpit I would certainly do so, but I cannot, and the Canons are free to invite whomever they wish. I have therefore sent them a letter expressing my concern about yesterday's sermon and also my hope that the pulpit will not be offered to intolerant preachers of any persuasion. It concludes:

> I am not, let me emphasize as strongly as I can, pleading for mealy-mouthed utterances with which no one could possibly disagree. But I do believe that the Christian pulpit is the place from which the central mysteries of the faith are to be proclaimed and that those who undertake this ministry should themselves be explorers of these mysteries and sensitive to the varied needs and understandings of those to whom they are privileged to speak. A cathedral should have a special concern for the depth of its preaching and also the breadth of the reception of its preaching. This means that care needs to be taken over the choice and the briefing of visiting preachers and that we ourselves need to set a good example.

I don't know if this will do any good, but I think it needs to be said.

Wednesday 10 March 1993

Shortly before leaving for London this morning I was telephoned by the BBC with a request that I should go to their Winchester studio for an 'on the line' interview about our forthcoming 'Rave in the Nave' – an adverse article about this having appeared in today's *Daily Mail*. I replied that I had a train to catch and had not seen the article; they had better contact Canon Keith Walker, the chairman of the committee responsible for the event.

I bought a copy of the *Daily Mail* at the station and was astonished and horrified by a full-page article written by Paul Johnson. Headed DESECRATION, it has a picture of the High Altar of the Cathedral, upon which is superimposed a half-naked figure of a raver – obviously from a photograph taken at one of the secular 'raves' which are causing concern because of their association with drugs and disorder. 'What kind of society lets the young trample on its hallowed heritage?', screams the sub-heading.

There follows an extraordinary piece which consists mainly of a potted history of the Cathedral, emphasizing its glorious past and contrasting this with its allegedly dissolute present: 'Here is a natural amphitheatre for sacred music, from mediaeval plainsong to Benjamin Britten's *War Requiem*. To belch out grotesquely amplified pop music here is to insult the very stones themselves, let alone the kings and bishops who erected them. The spirits of these benefactors are still there, to register disapproval of the coming saturnalia.'

Earlier in the article Paul Johnson, who never bothered to speak to me about the event, says, 'The Very Reverend Trevor Beeson, Dean of Winchester, has decreed, "The main thing is that the young people have a good time." It does not seem to have occurred to the Dean that "having a good time" is not the purpose for which cathedrals exist.' It concludes with a reference to Jane Austen and others buried in the Cathedral and says, 'Many others who are not yet safely in their graves and can make their indignation felt, will want to prevent one of England's most precious cathedrals being handed over to the rock-crazed and the clown-priests.'

What Paul Johnson does not recognize, or has chosen not to acknowledge, is that the rock bands constitute only one part of a four-hour programme that includes Bible study, prayer groups, a youth choir, incense and icons. The 'Rave' is in fact no more than an up-dated version of the old diocesan youth rally. Rarely have I seen a newspaper distort the truth so comprehensively, but of course the tabloids are in the business of providing entertainment rather than accurate information.

Back in the 1960s when Paul Johnson was editor of the *New Statesman* I was one of his admirers, but his conversion to a reactionary form of Conservatism accompanied by the revival of his Roman Catholicism in an equally reactionary form has done neither him nor his readers any good at all. He now writes, as in today's article, like someone who is deranged, and combines arrogance with intolerance and scant regard for facts. The circulation of this kind of stuff in a mass circulation newspaper can cause a deal of trouble, as I am sure I shall shortly discover.

Thursday 11 March 1993

Trouble indeed over the 'Rave in the Nave'. More than fifty letters of protest arrived this morning, some expressing acute distress over what they read in yesterday's *Daily Mail*, many couched in abusive terms. The Friends of the Cathedral office has received anxious telephone calls from members, two of whom have resigned. The media are now descending upon us in a big way and I am doing everything possible to give accurate information about the event and its context. Much of the difficulty has arisen over the implication of Paul Johnson's article that our 'Rave' will have affinities with those of the secular kind and be associated with drugs and sex. It is amazing what people will believe.

I now discover that Jonathan Sewell, the Diocesan Youth Officer who has been largely responsible for the organizing of the event, issued a press release last week. This placed considerable emphasis on the presence of the rock bands, all of which are actually Christian groups, and although the other items in the programme were mentioned, they were played down somewhat. Hence the skewed reporting and the excuse for Paul Johnson to distort the whole thing. Jonathan was well exceeding his authority in issuing a press release about a Cathedral event without reference to me, but he could not have foreseen all the fuss it has created, and I am not sure that I would have significantly changed the release had I seen it. There have been similar events in other cathedrals which have gone unnoticed by the media.

Wednesday 17 March 1993

The furore over the 'Rave in the Nave' continues unabated, and I and Esmé my secretary are occupied more or less full time with its ramifications. I have now received about 200 letters on the subject, mostly against but a few in support. It is curious how many of the objectors use vitriolic language, some of it quite violent. One from Bristol advised me, among other things, to get my hair cut, which means I suppose that a picture of me has appeared in some West Country newspaper. Letters of complaint from Holland, Germany and Nova Scotia indicate that the news is spreading. But a delightful letter from an elderly lady in Andover expressed whole-hearted approval and she enclosed a cheque to 'pay for the young people to have refreshments'. I have been driven to use a photocopied letter of acknowledgment and explanation for most of my replies.

A very tiresome element in the fuss is that it is being extended by other newspapers which have picked up the story from the *Daily Mail* and, without checking the facts, put their own gloss on it. Last Wednesday, for example, *The Daily Telegraph* carried a thoughtful article by their columnist Lesley Garner about the dangers inherent in some of the American-based religious cults. This led her to suggest that there is a tendency for mainstream religion to adopt some of the lures of the cult in order to attract the trade. Thus,

> The proposed 'Rave in the Nave' at Winchester Cathedral is simply one sign that the church is desperate to associate God with good times. Cults and established church alike are using the feel-good factor to draw people in. The crucial question to ask is: what does a religious organization do with people once it has made them feel good?

A telephone call to me could have avoided this erroneous interpretation of our event, and the *Telegraph* has published a letter from me putting the record straight, but of course the truth would have robbed Lesley Garner's piece of its topicality and probably her main point.

Winchester is a remarkable place and the Cathedral people always respond when the right note is struck. Brother Geoffrey, a Franciscan friar and one of our Honorary Canons, has for many years been working in Zimbabwe. He was over here last summer and attended the St Swithun's Day celebrations, at the end of which he mentioned to me the serious situation created by a long drought in Zimbabwe. I remembered this when we were allocating money from our emergencies fund in December and we sent him £500.

In last month's Newsletter I quoted from Geoffrey's grateful reply and added:

> I think a cathedral which has just received £7 million for its own needs here in England had better do more than spend a mere £500 for a member of its community's ministry among the poor in Africa. If forty-nine readers of this letter will send me £10 we can let Brother Geoffrey have another £500 quickly and I invite you to do this.

The response to this was remarkable. Gifts poured in, and we have just sent Geoffrey a cheque for almost £2,000. No doubt he will be astonished, and although it is still only a small amount he will be able to do quite a lot of useful things with it in his desperate situation.

Monday 29 March 1993

The fuss over the 'Rave in the Nave' raised in my mind, and in the minds of some Cathedral people, the question of whether or not Paul Johnson's article in the *Daily Mail* might be libellous. The suggestion that I am causing the Cathedral to be desecrated is certainly not very complementary, nor is that statement that I am organizing saturnalia. The whole gist of the article is that the Dean is quite oblivious to what a cathedral is really for and is therefore turning Winchester into a place of entertainment. If, as seems to be the case from all the letters, anyone believes all this nonsense to be true, it can only be damaging to my reputation. Have I any protection against such damage?

I raised this point with Jeremy de Souza, a member of the Cathedral congregation who is a partner in Farrer & Co – the Queen's solicitors – and he kindly arranged for one of his colleagues, who is a libel specialist, to examine the evidence and give me a preliminary opinion. This is now to hand and I am not really surprised to learn that 'a libel claim would be difficult'. The opinion goes on:

A jury may well find the word 'desecration' to be used subjectively in the sense of violation of the sanctity of the Cathedral, and 'saturnalia' to be no more than noisy revelry.

The law allows a considerable latitude for people to hold obstinate and prejudiced views without liability. In my view Paul Johnson may well have a successful defence of fair comment. This defence is rather a misnomer since the comment does not need to be fair in the usual sense of the word bur rather in the sense of honestly held.

It is not possible to separate the headline from the balance of the text, since readers are presumed to read the word in context and to suspend judgment on a headline until they form a view based on the subject matter of the text.

It might be possible to defeat the defence of fair comment if you were able to show that the *Daily Mail* published the article with an improper motive of injuring you. This kind of evidence is quite difficult to amass and the burden of proof would be on you. The fact that the *Daily Mail* were prepared to publish your reply to the article, albeit in a very abbreviated form, would tend to work against any suggestion of malice on their part.

The possibility of my becoming involved in a libel action against the *Daily Mail*, with its huge financial risk, was always remote, but I now at least know that I have taken all possible steps to protect the Cathedral and, for what it is worth, my own reputation.

Tuesday 30 March 1993

The unveiling of Antony Gormley's striking sculpture 'Sound II' by Sir Alan Bowness at the end of January was a notable occasion attended by many leading figures in the art world. Sir Alan, who was Director of the Tate Gallery in the 1980s went so far as to say that the placing of this sculpture in our Crypt could turn out to be as significant an event as was the placing of Henry Moore's famous Madonna and Child in St Matthew's Church, Northampton fifty years ago.

But now a tricky problem has arisen over its setting. Framed by a fine eleventh-century arch and reflected in the water in the Crypt, it looks superb, but the unity of the composition is disturbed by the presence of a stub wall which is about two feet high and protrudes from the aisle wall by nearly five feet. It is apparently the remains of a much larger wall that was demolished sometime between the early fourteenth century and 1886, and it is quite ugly and intrusive.

The obvious solution is to have it removed and store the constituent stones elsewhere in the Crypt. But this proposal has brought us into conflict with the archaeologists and other conservation-minded members of the Fabric Advisory Committee. They argue that the wall is of archaeological significance and should therefore remain in its present position. John Crook, our Consultant Archaeologist, takes the line that if this section of the Crypt were required for liturgical use, he would be ready to see the wall carefully removed, but he cannot support its removal for aesthetic reasons alone.

We had a full discussion of this matter at the FAC meeting this afternoon and Keith Walker and I spoke strongly in favour of removal. But the committee, admirably chaired as always by Colin Badcock, divided equally, and a report of the discussion is to be sent to the Cathedrals' Fabric Commission for England which will for sure demand retention of the wall. When conservation fashions change it will no doubt be removed.

Easter Day 11 April 1993

Today's Easter services were especially significant and splendid, coming as they did at the opening of our 900th anniversary year. This was particularly true at Mattins where, as usual, we were packed to the doors. Seeking something dramatic to add to the normal festive service, I lighted on the idea of having some of the Cathedral treasures and symbols of its history carried in procession. We settled on:

A volume of the Winchester Bible	twelfth century
The Winchester Madonna sculpture	fifteenth century
The Letters Patent granted by Henry VIII to the new Dean and Chapter	sixteenth century
The Prayer Book presented to the Cathedral by Charles II	seventeenth century
A history of the Cathedral written by a Roman Catholic priest	nineteenth century
A diver's helmet of the kind worn by William Walker when underpinning the foundations	early twentieth century
Christus – sculpture figure	late twentieth century

These were carried to different parts of the building, immediately after the Bishop's sermon and with considerable effect, the only problem being with the large and heavy Christus, which even the tall and powerful Keith Walker found almost too much to bear. At one point I thought we were to have a re-enactment of the drama of Christ falling beneath the Cross, but Keith, glistening with perspiration, managed to recover his balance and complete the course.

Tuesday 20 April 1993

I should really be at the annual Deans and Provosts Conference now being held in a Roman Catholic girls' school near Chelmsford, but an alarming experience at about three o'clock this morning led me to abandon the conference and return home for medical advice.

I was feeling rather tired when I drove around the M25 and through the Dartford Tunnel yesterday afternoon on the way to Essex, but the evening went well enough. After the usual welcomes, John Holroyd, the new Secretary for Appointments at 10 Downing Street, introduced himself and we had some talk about appointments, prefaced by an over-lengthy speech from Peter Berry, the Provost of Birmingham. I enquired if the lack of cathedral canons among those now being appointed as deans or provosts pointed to an absence of talent in the chapters, but no one seemed inclined to pick this up. There was more interest in Peter Berry's suggestion that black priests should be appointed to chapters, and I thought to mention the disastrous appointment of Sebastian Charles to the Westminster Chapter, but in the end decided that I had better not. At dinner I had an interesting conversation with Mgr Peter Cookson, of Liverpool Roman Catholic Cathedral, who is an able man. Then to bed in one of the small and somewhat claustrophic rooms normally occupied by a schoolgirl.

I awoke at about 3 a.m. feeling breathless and threw open a window to gain more air. Returning to bed, my heart began to thump and I was filled with a deep sense of fear, which speedily led to the conclusion that I was unlikely to survive until the morning. Not wishing to disturb anyone or call for medical aid, I walked up and down a corridor for a time, noting the location of the loos in case I was about to be assailed by the consequences of eating and drinking too much. But the feelings of breathlessness, weakness and fear remained. Sinking back into bed, I thought, 'This is going to be a strange place in which to die.'

Eventually I fell asleep, woke again at about six o'clock, breathing more freely but feeling exhausted. I thereupon decided to return to Winchester, so I left a message for John Moses, the Provost of Chelmsford, who was hosting the conference, and somehow or other managed to navigate a very busy M25 and reach the Deanery at about 9.30 a.m.

A telephone call to the doctor secured me a late morning appointment and an electro-cardiogram which indicated no cardiac disturbance. The doctor concluded that I am simply exhausted and in need of a good rest, but Harry Haysom, our Head Sidesman and a retired surgeon, told me this afternoon in the Close that the incident almost certainly had a cardio-vascular cause and must be treated as a warning to ease up. Easier said than done at the beginning of the 900th anniversary celebrations, but I must obviously try to get some rest and keep things ticking over until we take a post-Easter break at Sandwich the week after next.

Monday 26 April 1993

I did not attend the 'Rave in the Nave' on Saturday, as the Chapter laid down the law on Thursday about the need for me to rest and to avoid the strains and stresses involved in that particular event. Apparently it was a huge success. About 1,000 attended, the feared invasion by secular 'ravers' did not materialize, the Lord Lieutenant came to show his support, and the whole evening expressed the combination of fun and serious purpose intended by the programme. Already there is strong pressure for a repeat performance next year. The afternoon programme in which Jonathon Porritt and Sir James Lovelock debated environmental issues also attracted a good crowd, but there have been protests from some evangelical groups in the Diocese on the alleged grounds that the two speakers are pantheists, not Christians. What next?

A letter from Lambeth Palace indicates that the Archbishop of Canterbury has received a lot of protest letters about the 'Rave' and that he is responding robustly. After informing his correspondents that he is unable to intervene in matters outside his own diocese, he goes on:

> I am confident that the Dean and Chapter of Winchester fully appreciate the veneration people have for consecrated buildings and also that they are acting from the best of Christian motives. So often the church is condemned for being out of touch and archaic. Here we see it reaching out to the young in terms which they understand – as the press, politicians and the public have clamoured for it to do in the light of recent tragic events – so that the Christian message and Christian moral values can be engendered.

This response contrasts favourably with the statement put out by our own Bishop. When the controversy was at its height I appealed to Colin for help, pointing out (a) that the 'Rave' was a Diocesan event, master-minded by his own Youth Officer; (b) that I was feeling very isolated in my defence of its nature and purpose; and (c) that we would all be grateful if the leadership of the Diocese was to 'own' the event and give it strong public support. But the statement he issued was so wishy-washy that not even our local papers bothered to publish it.

The *Daily Mail*, possibly repenting of Paul Johnson's sins, has printed a sympathetic report under the heading 'The Rave in the Nave – No sex, No drugs, just Rock 'n' Roll'. And the *Daily Telegraph*, under two coloured photographs, has given a fair picture, reporting the view of one allegedly angry participant: 'It wasn't anything like a rave. It was just full of born-again Christians. We'd have had more fun at McDonalds.' The reporter adds: 'There was one absentee from the Rave. The Very Revd Trevor Beeson, Dean of Winchester, had retreated to the Trollopian calm of the Deanery. He must be delighted that the evening went off successfully.'

Thursday 13 May 1993

Dogs and drugs in the Close occupied us at the Chapter Meeting this morning. Our prominently displayed regulations require dogs to be kept on leads, but many are allowed to run loose and it is proving difficult to enforce this discipline because some of the offenders are Close residents or members of the Cathedral congregation. We have asked for the dogs to be controlled, irrespective of their owners.

Drugs are an altogether more serious issue and the Close has become the local centre for drug dealing. The large open space between the Cathedral and the High Street provides ample freedom for transactions between the dealers and their customers, and the ground-staff now have to be very careful when collecting rubbish since there are often hypodermic needles among it. The police are not being very helpful, as the Close is officially private territory, which they will not enter unless called upon to deal with specific offences. The security firm we employ, at considerable expense, has now informed us that they are finding it very difficult to recruit staff for patrolling the Close, so unpleasant and unmanageable has the work become. Unless we are prepared to pay higher rates they will withdraw from the contract.

We asked the Treasurer and the Receiver General to discuss the matter, once again, with the police and the City Council. It is after all a problem for the whole community, not simply for the Cathedral, but neither seems willing to become involved. There are limits to the amount of money we can spend on law enforcement and on protecting the public from unpleasant behaviour by people under the influence of drugs or alcohol.

Friday 14 May 1993

Miraculously, I feel perfectly fit again. A week at Sandwich and generally taking things easy did nothing to restore either my energy or my spirits, so I suggested to David Shedden, our GP, that perhaps I should have a full medical check-up, of the kind that bishops are required to have every two years. I am, after all, now sixty-seven, and if I am to carry on as Dean for another three years it is important to know if this is likely to be feasible.

David asked if I had any medical insurance to meet the cost of an extensive check-up, to which I replied, 'No, I will pay the bill myself.' So I was seen this morning by a consultant physician, Dr Powell-Jackson, who as it happens has a boy at The Pilgrims' School. He gave me a very good once-over, aided by machinery of various kinds, and ended with a quite long, and I thought sensitive and perceptive, interrogation about my work and life-style.

His verdict was that I am very fit 'for a man of your age' and that my disorder is almost certainly emotional, rather than physical. He advised a two-week holiday and refused to accept payment for the consultation. As I drove back to the Deanery I began to feel my old self again and couldn't help recalling the Gospel miracle story of the man who 'took up his bed and walked'.

Reflecting on my discussion with Dr Powell-Jackson, it is certainly the case that trying to run the domestic life of the Deanery (because of Jo's increasing incapacity) in addition to the heavy responsibilities of the Cathedral has put me under considerable strain. I suspect also that the Rave in the Nave furore took far more out of me than I recognized at the time. And the incident at the Deans and Provosts Conference, diagnosed as a 'panic attack', left me fearful of something sinister and life-threatening.

Now I feel reassured and not really in need of the prescribed holiday, but I suppose I had better obey orders and go away now, rather than wait for our planned Autumn holiday in the Alps. I am also going to take seriously the suggestion of our daughters Jean and Catherine that I should employ more help in the house.

Monday 7 June 1993

Al Gordon, our delightful and most generous American benefactor, came for lunch one Saturday in March and subsequently telephoned me from

New York with an offer of £100,000 to enable us to complete the Visitors Centre by building the Education Wing. This was a marvellous offer, but it turned out that, because the building of the Centre is now so far advanced, the cost of the Education WIng has risen from about £150,000 to £285,000, so Al Gordon's kindness leaves us no better off than we were when the original tenders came in last summer.

The Chapter considered the situation when I was at Sandwich on sick leave last week and agreed with my own view, conveyed to them before I left Winchester, that there would be no justification for spending as much as £285,000 on the Education Wing, even if we could lay our hands on all the money, which we cannot. It would be better to ask Al Gordon to give us a reduced figure of about £50,000 to enable us to turn the old Pastoral/ Refreshment rooms into an Education Centre.

Keith Walker, our education man, is opposed to this, even though he has no idea where the additional £185,000 might come from, but the more I think about the alternative proposal the more I like it. The adaptation of the old building will actually give us a much more useful range of accommodation, and although the main hall will seat only 70, rather than 100, the Prior's Hall in the Deanery can continue to be used for the relatively small number of large-scale events.

Thursday 8 July 1993

At today's Chapter we returned once again to the question of imposing a charge for admission to the Cathedral. In spite of the wonderful success of the appeal, our financial position in regard to day-to-day running costs is precarious. Keith Walker is also frustrated because there is no money available to spend on the visual arts.

In preparation for our discussion, Keith Walker, Richard Alexander (the Chapter Clerk) and I prepared papers expressing our personal points of view. Keith's paper was a curious document in which he attempted to argue theologically for admission charges and concluded that it is necessary for visitors to do something generous, like giving money at the Cathedral door, before they can be open to receive God's grace mediated through their experience of the building. I took the completely opposite line that, since God's grace is always freely offered and can never be earned, it is vitally important that cathedrals and churches should always be open without hindrance in order that these buildings may exert their influence on those who enter their doors. I added that in the present missionary situation in Britain it would be 'sheer folly' to restrict entrance to those willing and able to pay, and that in any case it is possible to raise money by other means. Richard thought the imposition of charges would be taken badly by lay people in the Diocese and County and impede the church's mssion.

We had a good discussion in which the Treasurer strongly supported my line, but the Precentor and Archdeacon supported Keith Walker in wanting to have the possibility of admission charges further explored. So it was 3-2 in favour, but as I am strongly opposed, it was recognized that there is no way forward in this direction. The matter was therefore deferred until 1996, by which time there will be a new Dean, the memory of the Appeal will be fading and the financial benefits of the Visitors Centre will be known.

Monday 12 July 1993

Monday morning is not normally a popular time for a church service, but the Cathedral was packed this morning for the Sung Eucharist in commemoration of St Benedict. Yesterday was actually his feast day, but Sunday was not convenient for the kind of celebration we planned, nor could the Benedictine monks and nuns who were to be our guests be away from their own communities.

The fact that Cardinal Basil Hume was the preacher was undoubtedly a great draw and brought in a lot of Hampshire Roman Catholics as well as Anglicans who wanted to hear him. The presence of about fifty Benedictines also made it special and I was deeply moved as the procession passed through the nave – the Bishop walking with the Cardinal and I with the Abbot of Fleury.

The Cardinal preached an unusual sermon in which he imagined St Benedict visiting Winchester in 963, then in 1093 and again today. On the first occasion he engaged in conversation with St Ethelwold, the activist, reforming Bishop who was planning a great meeting to devise a code for all monks. He reminded them that 'the monk must have one over-riding pre-occupation – God'. In 1093, at the dedication of the present Cathedral, Benedict, while admiring the grandeur of the building, warned the monks, 'Churches are not just buildings, but communities of persons who acknowledge Christ and his Gospel.'

On his visit today Benedict is bemused to find no monks but glad to realize that worship and praise still have pride of place in the life of the Cathedral. He is astonished to find that the church is now divided into many separate communities and he is saddened by the discovery that many people no longer seek God and think the praise of him to be unnecessary. As he leaves he says, 'You have many problems in your day, but then we had our problems in ours, many much worse than yours. Just remember this: I have spoken about seeking God, of exploring who he is and what he is like. In fact it is God who seeks us in the first place, and does so because he loves us.' The Cardinal concluded, 'These final words are not the product of anyone's imagination. It is the simple truth.'

It was a curious sermon, but I think it came off, not least because Basil Hume has such an impressive, godly presence that virtually anything he says seems right and true. After the Eucharist we had a splendid lunch in a marquee in the Close. This was generously provided by Graeme Jameson, the landlord of the Wykeham Arms, and was flawed in only one way – a member of his staff put salt instead of sugar on the strawberries and cream. But everyone was in good humour and many believed it to be a special Benedictine dish revived for the occasion.

This evening the Dean and Chapter entertained the Abbot of Fleury and one of his lay brothers to dinner and, since their English was better than our French, it proved to be a most convivial occasion. Altogether a memorable day.

Friday 26 July 1993

Sir John Wilson, who was chairman of the Friends Standing Committee until the end of last year, died today after a long battle against cancer. He was a very good friend to me from the moment I arrived here in 1987. At that time there was conflict between the Friends and the Trust, created by jealousy over publicity – who was being credited with what. John, trusted by both camps, was the chief agent of reconciliation. Indeed, he managed to turn conflict into close collaboration and it was through his strong leadership that the Friends raised £175,000 during the £7 million appeal.

He was superbly equipped for a reconciling role and, since he served in the Cabinet Office during the Suez crisis, the conflict here must have seemed no more than a minor diplomatic incident. For the last three years of his civil service career he was the Second Permanent Secretary at the Ministry of Defence, and such was his skill that under his chairmanship no Friends meeting ever lasted more than one hour. It has to be said, however, that the recent expansion of Friends' activities has inevitably involved longer meetings.

Beneath a somewhat dour exterior was a warm and most generous heart and, as a covert Labour supporter, a strong concern for the disadvantaged. Penny, his widow, is an absolute delight – quite without pretensions, plain-speaking and full of warmth.

The new Cathedral Shop has now been open for ten days and during this time the takings have totalled £25,000. The staff, a few salaried, the others volunteers, have been rushed off their feet and the whole enterprise is obviously going to be hugely successful. There will be much quieter periods of trading during the winter months when there are fewer visitors; on the other hand, when the Refectory is open this will draw the attention of its customers to the shop.

I am very pleased with the style and general ambience of the shop, which is similar to that of the National Trust shops and a long way removed from the somewhat amateurish style of our previous shop and of most other cathedral shops. My only worry concerns the sale of religious books, of which there are at the moment just a few, these of the popular, superficial sort that are sold in W.H.Smith and other booksellers whose only concern is to maximize profits.

Here is our problem. The Visitors Centre is costing a great deal of money and the Dean and Chapter has had to borrow about £400,000 to help pay for it. The Board of the Company we have set up to manage the Centre is, rightly, very profit-conscious and has appointed an excellent manager who has been set financial targets and offered incentives to exceed them. Naturally he will only wish to stock fast-moving, profitable items and therefore order only religious books that have popular appeal cultivated by television exposure. Some of these propagate views on the Christian faith which run contrary to what the Cathedral, under my leadership anyway, is all about. The more thoughtful volumes I favour will not sell so readily, which means a reduction in profitabilitiy.

My position is difficult inasmuch as the Board has been entrusted with the running of the Centre and will not welcome interference. I think therefore that I had better let the shop get well established and the fruits of its success to hand before I try to influence what is offered on its religious books shelves.

Thursday 9 September 1993

A number of extraordinary things have happened since I came here six years ago, but the latest is I think the most astonishing. On the day of my departure to France last month Esmé Parker, my secretary, chanced to see in the Cathedral Office a printer's proof of a fine brochure appealing for almost £500,000 for the building of the Education Wing of the Visitors Centre, for various educational aids and for a mural to be painted on an interior wall of the soon-to-be-completed Refectory. It turned out that copies of this brochure had been despatched to fifty American trusts.

All of which took place on the initiative of Keith Walker and the Visitors Centre architects, without reference to me or to the Chapter and in complete disregard of the fact that we had decided not to proceed with the building of the Education Wing and had accepted a gift of £50,000 from Al Gordon to enable us to convert the former Pastoral/Refreshments rooms into an Education Centre. This is really unbelieveable, but it has actually happened, and the only explanation I have been able to get from Keith Walker is that he thought I had agreed to something of this sort back in February. What happened then was that the architects said they might be able to put us in touch with some American trusts for the funding of additional art work, but of course there was no suggestion of funding the Education Wing in this way, and in any event we subsequently decided not to go ahead with the Wing and to solve the problem in a quite different way.

The generous side of me likes to believe it was merely a coincidence that the appeal brochures were sent on the day I left the country, but I have the suspicion that it was hoped to get a quick and favourable response from America and thus present the Dean and Chapter with a *fait accompli*: here is £500,000 for the Education Wing, for Robert Natkin's mural and other artistic items; let's get on and use it. Neither Keith nor the architects know anything about fund-raising, and it is of course naive in the extreme to suppose that brochures sent to fifty trusts in August, or any other month for that matter, will bring in £0.5 million just like that.

The immediate problem is threefold: (1) The Trustees responsible for the £7 million Appeal are still raising money to offset the Diocesan shortfall and are bound to wonder what on earth we are doing launching a new appeal in America without consulting them; (2) our American committee is also bound to feel puzzled, and possibly annoyed, if they learn of new approaches to American trusts, some of which may already have donated to our Appeal; (3) Al Gordon, who may hear of the initiative on the New York grapevine, will wonder why we have apparently rejected his generous gift and gone back on what was agreed with him about the substitute Education Centre.

We had a full and somewhat acrimonious discussion of all this at the Chapter Meeting this morning. It was eventually decided that I should write to the American trusts, apologizing for a 'misunderstanding' and asking them to ignore the appeal addressed to them. I am also to explain the situation to Jim Butler and the other Trustees and to consider with them how we are to explain matters to Al Gordon. The architects, who designed the brochure, are to be asked to pay for it, though they may feel that Keith Walker was acting for the Dean and Chapter in agreeing to its production and despatch. We shall see.

Most worrying of all, however, is the fact that a member of the Chapter felt free to launch a substantial appeal without reference to any of his colleagues, including the Dean, and in blatant disregard of a policy decision made in his presence. And even now he is unable, or unwilling, to acknowledge that this was a serious error of judgment. How can any institution be effectively run when such breaches of corporate responsiblity are possible? We must in fact keep very quiet about the incident lest it become a public scandal.

Wednesday 20 October 1993

The appointment of Geoffrey Rowell as Bishop of Basingstoke is an odd business, for several reasons. Colin James, the Diocesan Bishop, will almost certainly retire early in 1995, which means that by the time Geoffrey is consecrated and installed there will be only twelve months for them to work together. The next Bishop of Winchester will inherit a recently appointed suffragan in whose choice he has not been involved and, notoriously in the Church of England, this makes for trouble. The relationship between diocesan and suffragan bishops is always a delicate one and requires men who are capable of working together. Admittedly, Colin was thrown somewhat by Michael Manktelow's unexpected retirement from Basingstoke this year, but in the circumstances he would I think have done well to leave the post vacant and thus allow his successor to make the choice. The honorary assistant bishops could have been roped in to help with confirmations, institutions of vicars and other episcopal jobs.

Geoffrey Rowell is a very good church historian, but he has had no experience of running parishes and dioceses. He was ordained to a chaplaincy at New College, Oxford in 1968 and four years later moved to Keble College as Fellow, Chaplain and Tutor. He has been there ever since. When Colin James consulted me about the kind of man needed for Basingstoke I said that, given the gifts of the other members of his senior staff, it wouldn't do any harm to have someone with professional theological skill, but I did not mean someone entirely lacking in practical church experience. Fifty years ago the appointment of academics to senior church posts was more acceptable than it is today, and indeed some of them found time to continue writing, but the current needs of the parochial clergy, the demands of synodical government, and ever increasing financial problems require bishops who have had first-hand experience of the present pastoral situation.

Then there is the problem that Geoffrey was one of the leading lights – probably the most intellectually able – among those opposed to the ordination of women to the priesthood. It is surprising that he feels able to hold a bishopric in a church which, in his view, has so far departed from apostolic order, but leaving this to one side we may be sure that he will be unwilling to ordain any women to the priesthood or institute women as vicars of parishes. This means that the Northern half of the Diocese will have a bishop who is unwilling to carry out the full range of episcopal functions, which at best will be highly anomalous and at worst cause a great deal of difficulty.

It is unlike Colin James, who is a wise man, to make an appointment of this sort at this stage in the life of the Diocese, and I can only think that his judgment has been skewed by his dismay at the General Synod's decision to permit the ordination of women.

Wednesday 10 November 1993

The sudden, and totally unexpected, death last week of Jim Scott, the Lord Lieutenant, is a devastating blow, the pain of which has been felt throughout Hampshire. Today's funeral in the Cathedral was the County's equivalent of a State occasion and deeply moving. The only oddity was the absence of a Royal representative, but I dare say this was following some sort of precedent.

Apparently Jim had been out hunting and on his return to Rotherfield Park complained of feeling unwell. He went to bed but by the time Anne had made him a cup of tea he was dead – aged seventy-two. He was quite the best Lord Lieutenant of Hampshire, or indeed any other county, that could ever be imagined, combining dignity and strong leadership with a captivating warmth and friendliness that made him greatly loved by people in all walks of life.

Yet he was a reluctant Lord Lieutenant in the sense that the unexpected death of his Baronet father in 1965 required him to abandon a distinguished military career – he was at that time CO of the Household Cavalry Mounted Regiment – in order to take over the family estate at Rotherfield Park. When he became the Queen's representative in Hampshire, however, he immediately threw himself into public life with great enthusiasm and was unwilling to confine himself to the big occasion. The opening of a new Scout hut or a Christmas party for the blind people of a village had equal claim on his presence and support. I suspect that it was his inability to say No that ultimately claimed his life.

My own indebtedness to Jim is incalculable. He was one of the first people to send me a letter (handwritten) of welcome when my appointment as Dean was announced and he soon became one of my strongest supporters. The way in which he picked up the bits after the Trust débacle at the end of 1988 was remarkable and his leadership of our £7 million appeal was inspired. He was so widely admired that no one could refuse him, and this enabled him to recruit outstanding people to chair the various committees that were essential to the success of the enterprise. It is sadly ironic that he died only a fortnight before he was due to accompany the Queen to our 900th anniversary service and the official opening of the Visitors Centre, of which he was always an enthusiastic advocate.

Friday 12 November 1993

The Eric Gill roundel of the Lamb and Flag, installed in the Epiphany Chapel last Spring, is a very good acquisition and, I think, an excellent example of what religious art in cathedrals is about. It is a work of beauty which is not only aesthetically pleasing but also enhances the devotional environment of the chapel in which it has been placed. The position is just right, and to untutored eyes the sculpture might have been there since mediaeval times. In fact, Eric Gill created it for a wall of his workshop at Ditchling, and he would doubtless be astonished to learn that it has finished up in Winchester Cathedral, having been sold to us by a London gallery at a reduced price of £14,000 and paid for by a number of arts trusts.

Now the same gallery has offered us another Eric Gill piece – a holy water stoup – but we have decided to say No. For one thing, it is not a particularly notable example of the sculptor's art and, for another, holy water stoups at the entrance to cathedrals and churches are not part of the Church of England's tradition. To acquire this simply because it is the work of Eric Gill is not a good enough reason for spending £2,250, which we haven't got anyway.

Friday 19 November 1993

Today has been a most glorious finale to our 900th anniversary celebrations and I could not have hoped for anything better. November is a chancy month for an event that includes some outdoor activity, but although the day started with fog, this had dispersed by nine o'clock and left us with unbroken sunshine.

The Queen wore a coat and hat of striking purple which seemed just right for the Cathedral and the occasion, and throughout the visit both she and the Duke of Edinburgh were very relaxed and apparently enjoying the entire programme. They are obviously very well briefed and do their homework before these kind of events, for during a short pause at the beginning of the service the Queen talked to me about my time at Westminster Abbey as well as about the anniversary celebrations here.

I was intrigued to know why she had chosen to make the short journey from London to Winchester by train, rather than by car, and she explained that when they last came to the Cathedral, for the Maundy Service in 1979, it had been a very wet day and congestion on the roads had delayed their arrival by half an hour. Since they did not wish to risk this again, a royal carriage had been attached to one of the normal Waterloo-Winchester trains and the royal car, which had been brought down last evening, awaited them at the station.

The service, with its strong emphasis on the future as well as thanksgiving for the past, came off and was memorable. This in spite of the fact that earlier this week the Choristers were afflicted by a throat infection which made it impossible for them to sing. Yesterday we recruited women members of the Waynflete Singers to provide the soprano line, but at the end of a long rehearsal last evening David Hill was not satisfied with the result and sent out an emergency call for three professionals to come down from London early this morning to provide reinforcement. This paid off, and the music was superb. Naturally, the Choristers and their parents were very disappointed but all but one of the boys were well enough to robe and take part in the procession. The Queen and the Duke offered them a word of sympathy at the end.

I preached on the theme of Awe and Affection, suggesting that Winchester Cathedral evokes this response from all who are associated with its life and that this same response is evoked by our encounter with God. It is therefore the task of the Cathedral community, in common with the rest of the church, to help its many visitors to become more aware of the greatness and wonder of God and also of the fact that the awesome God so loved the world that he gave his only Son to redeem the world.

In this context I spoke of the significance of the new Visitors Centre, the primary purpose of which is not money-raising – though this will be important – but to be a place where those who come from all parts of the world may experience friendship. I also took the opportunity to mention our former Lord Lieutenant, Jim Scott, 'who combined in his own life the elements of Awe and Affection. He graced his high office with a singular dignity and at the same time breathed warmth and friendship wherever he went.'

After the service we went in procession to the Visitors Centre where Rachel, our youngest grand-daughter, presented the Queen with a posy. We then had the official opening and dedication of the Centre, followed by a reception. The Queen and the Duke stayed much longer than planned talking to members of the Cathedral community; she insisted on seeing the Refectory kitchen, while he compared notes with me on the stocking of the Gift Shop and the recently installed shop at Buckingham Palace, in which he is obviously interested. He was amused to find us selling boxer shorts and apricots in brandy, and ordered some jars of the latter.

The lunch party at Wolvesey was a pleasant, unstuffy occasion. The catering was carried out by Graeme Jameson of the Wykeham Arms and there are, I suppose, few places in England where a Bishop entertaining the Queen can invite the local pub to provide the meal. I sat between a Lady in Waiting and General Sir David Fraser, the Vice-Lord Lieutenant, and we spent some time discussing his recently published and widely acclaimed biography of Rommel. The Queen was talking animatedly when the Duke signalled to her that it was time for them to be on the move, so she hurriedly renewed her lipstick and they departed, to the cheers of schoolchildren who lined the Wolvesey drive.

Hugely successful in every way – and enjoyable.

Friday 26 November 1993

John Holroyd, the Prime Minister's Secretary for Appointments, came to see me this afternoon to discuss possible names for appointment as Lord Lieutenant, following the death of Jim Scott. It is interesting that the procedure for the appointment of Lords Lieutenant is much the same as that for Deans – widespread local consultation followed by a Prime Ministerial nomination to the Queen.

John Holroyd is an affable, likeable man, and much more open than any of his predecessors, though he came from the same civil service stable. We talked for a short time about Jim Scott being a hard act to follow and the need for his successor to make more use of the Deputy Lieutenants, even though this would disappoint those hoping for the top man.

My use of the word 'man' immediately led John Holroyd to ask why the appointment should not go to a woman. It soon became apparent that he, or most likely the Prime Minister, was determined that Hampshire should have a woman Lord Lieutenant as part of a broader policy to have more women in this important county office. There is, I believe, only one at the moment.

In my mind, the strongest candidates are Mary Fagan and Gilly Drummond, both of whom combine dynamism, elegance and great charm, and both of whom are great supporters of the Cathedral – and of me, personally. The only problems I foresee is their lack of a title, and in Hampshire where titles are two a penny this may not go down well with the County set; and both have such forceful personalities that it will be surprising if they haven't crossed swords with a number of people. But I hope one of them will get it.

Saturday 4 December 1993

The secretary of the Christ Church, Winchester, Parochial Church Council has sent me a resolution passed by his Council deploring the fact that our Visitors Centre is open on Sundays. The gist of the complaint is that we are desecrating the Lord's day in the cause of money-making. As might be expected from such an orthodox Evangelical assembly, there are a number of biblical texts which are alleged to support their unease.

One of the alarming aspects of the growth of Evangelicalism is the confidence it is now inspiring in its adherents. They believe that it is part of their Christian duty to seek out and correct evil, but unfortunately their concept of evil is very narrow; restricted, in fact, to the traditional bogies of Puritanism – Sunday observance, gambling and any manifestations of religious belief that do not accord with their own.

I will tell them that there is not a single word against Sunday trading in the Bible and that the Visitors Centre is, as I pointed out in my sermon when the Queen came last month, not primarily a money-making enterprise but rather a development of the Cathedral's mission to its many visitors. How much more sensible, and Christian, it would have been if the Christ Church people had sought a discussion of the issue, rather than passing a condemnatory resolution, but like most of their kind they are exceedingly insular and appear to be afraid of contamination by contact with those who do not share all their views.

Sunday 26 December 1993

Although the 900th anniversary celebrations officially finished with the visit of the Queen and the Duke of Edinburgh on the 19th of last month, they refused to die until Christmas. Both the BBC and ITV decided to televise Christmas programmes associated with the anniversary, and we were happy to extend our calendar to include the two broadcasts.

ITV recorded a programme of Christmas music given by the Cathedral Choir and the Waynflete Singers and transmitted on Christmas Eve. I contributed a brief welcome and introduction. The BBC chose to broadcast the Christmas Midnight Eucharist live, so this was an altogether more demanding operation. The Bishop presided – impressively, I thought – at the Eucharist and I preached the sermon, fairly brief, on love as the essential centre of family life. The producer and his team were pleased with the broadcast, and the one possible problem, that of drunks in the congregation causing a disturbance, did not materialize.

Two major television broadcasts within a fortnight is, however, a taxing experience, especially at this time of the year when there are so many Carol Services and of course the usual preparations for the Christmas worship. The Midnight Eucharist required endless rehearsals to get all the detail right, and the main participants must have heard my sermon about half a dozen times before we came to the actual service.

By the end of Christmas Day many of us were feeling pretty well exhausted, but it was, as always, a splendid festival and the opportunity to share it with millions of people all over Britain and Western Europe was worth all the effort.

1994

The ordination of women priests in the Cathedral, now planned for 28 April, has a number of implications for those members of our staff who have problems on conscience over this matter. Obviously the Precentor cannot be expected to organize a great act of worship, the central purpose of which he believes to be contrary to the will of God. The Archdeacon has, therefore, agreed to take over responsibility for all the liturgical arrangements on this occasion, and I am sure he will do it well.

Others likely to be involved are members of the Choir, one or two of whom may have problems, the Virgers, nearly all of whom are against women priests, and possibly some of the Sidesmen. It has been agreed that I should write to the heads of these departments explaining that any member of our community must be entirely free to exercise his conscience over this issue, but also seeking assurance that the departments will be able to make adequate arrangements for the service. I don't think it is going to be much of a problem, but a little improvisation may be needed.

At yesterday's Chapter Meeting we also discussed our policy about women priests presiding at the Eucharist in the Cathedral. This is rather more tricky. Cathy Milford, who is already a Cathedral Chaplain, will not expect her ministry to be restricted because she is a woman, nor should it be, and there are bound to be an increasing number of occasions when it will be appropriate for other women priests to preside. But Virgers are inevitably involved in all acts of worship and some – I do not know how many – members of the Cathedral congregation may have scruples about sharing in a Eucharist presided over by a woman priest.

We had a good discussion about this in the course of which Paul Britton, of all people, proposed that we acknowledge the existence of women priests and simply invite a number of them to preside at the Eucharist regularly, including Sundays. After I had recovered from the shock of such a proposal coming from such a quarter, I felt driven, reluctantly, to point out that this would not do (a) because the Sunday presidents are normally members of the Chapter, and (b) because what would be seen by some as an aggressive step on the part of the Cathedral might not be helpful to diocesan unity.

We decided in the end that Cathy Milford be invited from time to time to preside at weekday Eucharists and in due course on Sundays. Any visiting group that desires the ministry of a woman priest will be quite free to employ one. The question of whether or not the presence of a woman priest should be advertised in advance of services troubles me greatly. To do so is, in my view, just as offensive as it would be to advertise the presence of black priests. But it seems that we shall, for the time being anyway, have to provide some means of indicating whenever a woman priest is presiding simply to avoid unfortunate scenes when those opposed to them might be taken by surprise.

Thursday 13 January 1994

The meetings of the Cathedral congregation which should have been held last autumn were delayed, because of 900th anniversary pressures, until this week. Once again the number attending was up to the 400 mark and this year, instead of the Dean and the Treasurer holding the floor for most of the time with lengthy reports, each member of the Chapter gave a report on the work of his department.

This proved to be an altogether better arrangement, and certainly it saved me a lot of preparatory work, but I was quite unsuccessful in persuading the Canons to confine their reports to the agreed seven minutes each. Still, the overall picture was one of vigorous development and everyone seemed to be in good heart.

The revised format of these annual gatherings will be worth repeating, though it is very difficult to deal with the affairs of so large and so busy a cathedral in a meeting lasting little more than one hour.

Tuesday 25 January 1994

This evening we said goodbye to Paul Britton who, after a long rehearsal for retirement, is vacating his Canonry at the end of the month. This is a moment to which both he and I have been looking eagerly forward for some time. The busy life of the Cathedral today is a long way removed from that which attracted him to membership of the Chapter in 1980 and he undoubtedly believes me to be leading the community in an undesirable direction. He has opposed many of my ideas and has often been a negative force in our affairs. It is ironic that the Farewell party, after

Evensong for the Feast of the Conversion of St Paul, was held in the Visitors Centre Refectory which he moved heaven and earth to stop us from building.

None of this I mentioned, of course, in my farewell speech, concentrating instead on the positive elements in his contribution to the Cathedral's life – diligent attendance at the daily services, which after my Westminster experience I value above all else; the creation of the Triforium Gallery museum; careful nursing of our financial assets through investment in well-chosen equities; attention to the Close houses, leaving them in a better state of repair than for many years past. It is a great pity that all this hasn't been accompanied by a more ready collaboration in our generally developing life.

His response to my speech was, I thought, singularly ungracious and ended with a curious warning about pride coming before a fall. I am at a loss to interpret this unless he feels that the pleasure many people are expressing about the growth of the Cathedral's life is dangerous and likely to lead to some catastrophe. But there was no hint as to what form this might take and it was hardly in the spirit of a party to pursue such a matter.

Monday 7 February 1994

It is now seven years since I came to Winchester and this is stocktaking day for me. The last year, being occupied almost entirely by the 900th anniversary celebrations, including the opening of the Visitors Centre by the Queen, has been memorable. And, in terms of our engaging with the Hampshire community, pretty successful.

The celebrations were on a much larger scale than originally envisaged. When the planning began in 1991 there were some on the Chapter and on the staff who had vivid memories of what they regarded as a punishing programme of events in 1979. For some curious reason, the 900th anniversary of the starting of the building was commemorated in that year. It was decided therefore that this time there would be a much more modest programme – perhaps a dozen good events, including the Southern Cathedrals Festival, during the summer.

With a cavalier disregard for what had been decided, Keith Walker and his committee produced a programme on even more ambitious lines than that of 1979 and bludgeoned the Dean and Chapter into accepting it, at a cost far exceeding the original provision. And they were right to do so. The Cathedral community proved to be quite capable of sustaining the events, there was massive support from the wider community, new ground was broken with the Diocese and the world of the arts, and the whole thing was hugely enjoyable. I wonder how the millennial anniversary will be celebrated in 2093? Just as differently, I am sure, as ours has been from that of 1893.

Looking ahead, the report of the Cathedrals Commission is obviously going to be important, though I expect it will be several years before any significant proposals for change are implemented. Meanwhile Paul Britton's retirement will lead to a change in the balance of power in the Chapter. For the first time since I came the majority of the Canons will belong to my era as Dean and, I trust, be ready to support proposals for change. Which isn't to say that the pace of change will necessarily accelerate – institutions of this sort can cope only with so much disturbance – but at least changes should not involve the kind of struggle I have experienced during these last seven years.

I think, as a matter of fact, that there is now quite a lot of consolidation to be done. Several of our projects are unfinished and our administrative arrangements are a long way from satisfactory. There is no point in our starting new ventures before we can cope with them properly and, in any case, we must find ways of balancing the books, otherwise we shall be obliged to reduce, rather than increase, activity.

In spite of the scare over my health last spring, I seem to be quite fit and not lacking in energy. I only wish that I could say the same of Jo: the Alzheimer's continues on its relentless course and, although the day by day deterioration is imperceptible, one can see that over the last six months, and certainly over the last year, there has been a marked decline in her ability to cope with the demands of normal living. She now needs help with dressing and undressing. Fortunately, she is blissfully unaware of the problem and, as far as I can tell, remains happy. Quite a lot of Cathedral people drop into the Deanery to see her and almost all go away without discerning any sign of the illness. Which is, I am told, quite normal at this stage.

Sunday 13 March 1994

A sombre day in the Cathedral following the Vice-Dean's announcement this morning that he is resigning from his Canonry at the end of August over the issue of women priests. He made a simple statement at Mattins in which he said that, for a traditional high churchman of the Oxford Movement school such as himself, the admission of women to the priesthood is a breach of church order. If the Church of England is a true part of the Catholic Church its priesthood must, he said, remain male until a greater body than the General Synod determines otherwise. I responded with an expression of regret that he had felt driven to such a decision, with its heavy cost for one who had for so long been deeply immersed in the church's choral tradition, and I assured him of our continuing affection and prayers.

This step by Roger Job was, I suppose, inevitable, though I hoped it might have been averted. The General Synod's decision in November 1992 took him completely by surprise. He never dreamt the vote would go that way and was deeply shocked when the result came through. After it had become clear that the decision would not be overturned by Parliament or any legal device he preached three Evensong sermons on the subject which revealed someone seriously wounded and crying out in pain. As Precentor, as well as Vice-Dean, his responsibility for the organizing of ordinations and other services involving women priests would have made his position specially tricky.

Roger and I had a number of talks about the issue before today's announcement, but I could not really help him, since my own view of women priests is diametrically opposed to his own. The main thing, which I hope may not be insignificant in the long run, has been to accept the integrity of his decision and help him to see that it will not lead to any breach of a personal friendship, which began nearly twenty years ago when we were both at Westminster Abbey; nor will it reduce the high regard in which he is held by the entire Cathedral community.

There are, I suspect, several factors involved in his decision. He is, both ecclesiastically and politically, deeply conservative and distrustful of change. He converted to the Anglican Church from Methodism and was doubtless attracted by an understanding of church order which he believes us now to be casting aside. To him it must seem a betrayal. Like many talented musicians, he is an emotional rather than an intellectual thinker, and theological arguments tend to leave him quite cold. There is also the fact that he became stuck here in Winchester. Two years ago, after completing thirteen years as Precentor, he recognized that the time had come for him to move on, but nothing suitable came his way. It is a great pity that the Anglican chaplaincy in Rome fell through because of a housing problem; this might have saved the day.

However, the deed is done and we must do everything we can to make his remaining time here as happy as may be. And I must try to ensure that his decision does not become a divisive issue in our community. No doubt the media will try to make something of it: 'Vice-Dean of Winchester Cathedral resigns, etc.'

Thursday 14 April 1994

I have a bee in my bonnet about our failure to offer our thousands of visitors the opportunity to purchase intelligent books about the Christian faith. This seems hardly an unreasonable thing for a cathedral to do but, apart from the Receiver General, I can gain little support from the Chapter.

Our fine new Gift/Book Shop must, for the time being anyway, seek to maximize its profits and this means, apparently, that only a relatively small amount of space can be allocated to religious books, and these must be of the kind made popular by television programmes and the like, thus guaranteeing large sales.

Very well, then, why not sell some thought-provoking books on the Bible, prayer, Christian belief, worship, Christian ethics and so on within the Cathedral itself? A new Information Desk is, for about the fourth different time, being re-designed and it would be quite easy to incorporate into this a couple of racks to display ten to twelve paperbacks. The sales would not be huge, but they could be significant.

Curiously, Keith Walker, who is in charge of our educational work and mission and ministry to visitors, is most strongly opposed to this. He argues that the Cathedral is 'sacred space', which ought not to be profaned by the selling of books. But of course guide books are being sold all the time and money is changing hands at the entrance to the Triforium Gallery and the Crypt, so it seems odd to draw the line at the selling of a few books about the faith on which the whole of the Cathedral's life is based.

A not unrelated problem has arisen over the new signs which are soon to be placed at all the key points in the building. It has always been my hope that these might indicate not only location and particular objects but also tell visitors about their current liturgical and devotional use. But this has been ruled out on allegedly artistic grounds, i.e. the signs would not look elegant.

I am as keen as anyone about the imaginative use of the visual arts in cathedrals, but I am increasingly led to wonder how developments in this area can be related to the Christian mission.

Thursday 28 April 1994

The ordination of four women to the priesthood this evening was an historic event and memorable for several reasons. A total of nineteen women have become priests in this Diocese over the last three weeks and the other fifteen, who were ordained in various parish churches, came to this evening's service and turned it into a great celebration of the break-though in the Church of England's understanding of the place of women in its ministry.

The Cathedral was crammed to capacity, and the combination of solemnity and joy produced an atmosphere of such intensity as I had not previously experienced anywhere. It was undoubtedly a great occasion and felt absolutely right. One could only wonder what all the fuss has been about and why it needed so long and so bitter a struggle to get women accepted for the priesthood.

A sad note was struck, however, by the absence of the Diocesan Bishop, Colin James, who consistently opposed the women priests proposal, agreed that women might be ordained in this Diocese but said that he would not himself ordain any. The suffragan Bishop of South-ampton, John Perry, was therefore authorized by the Archbishop of Canterbury to act as his Commissary for the purpose. Which solved the practical problem and displayed proper regard for the integrity of all concerned. But the absence of the Diocesan Bishop from so important and so moving an occasion felt altogether wrong. It was rather like a father absenting himself from his daughter's wedding, and the thought that Colin was at home in Wolvesey while we were so significantly engaged in bestowing the sacrament of Orders on four women was well nigh unbearable.

John Baker, the former Bishop of Salisbury, alluded to the sadness of this in his sermon and made the point that the admission of women to the priesthood is now part of the official doctrine and order of the Church of England. It is not to be regarded as a concession to an eccentric minority; rather, the woman priest is as integral to the church's life as is her male counterpart.

This being so, I think that Colin's position, while understandable, is now untenable, as is that of those other Diocesan Bishops who will not ordain women. It cannot be that the Bishop of a Diocese has conscient-ious scruples which preclude him from ordaining *any* duly qualified candidates. I am sure Colin must recognize this and, since he is in any case now past his sixty-seventh birthday and feeling the burden of the responsibilities he carries, I believe he will announce his retirement before the end of this year.

Friday 13 May 1994

The Cecil Collins painting of Christ before the Judge, now installed in the Gardiner Chantry and visible from the Presbytery North Aisle, is very powerful and, I think, a considerable acquisition. It is on loan from a private collection in Hampshire for an initial three years, with a hint that it may be allowed to stay for much longer.

The painting portrays Christ as defenceless, but by no means cowed, before a grotesque figure, which has claw-like hands, bared teeth, goggles and a curious head-dress, with downward pointing feathers – a representation of evil. A spare white light touches Christ and sustains him in his struggle on behalf of God against evil. Evidently Cecil Collins believed that the essential battle in the universe is between good and evil, God and the Devil, being and non-being, and he has certainly captured the magnitude and intensity of this struggle.

The fact that the painting is viewed through the iron bars of the chantry seems to increase its power, as well as provide some necessary security, and I am sure it is more at home in this setting than it could ever be in a country-house drawing room.

Wednesday 18 May 1994

An exhibition of wire mesh sculpture by Sophie Ryder in the Inner Close is giving enormous pleasure to the many passers by. Titled *Animus*, it consists of a number of lively animals – a group of dancing hares, a splendid horse rolling on its back, a leaping dog, a hare sitting up on its hind legs, and a marvellous flock of sheep, so realistic that dogs have been observed barking at them. All created out of wire mesh and pieces of scrap metal, and bringing a real sense of *joie de vivre* to the Close. A large display of birds created of out sheet metal and looking somewhat rusty is, I think, less successful, though some people like it.

But even an exhibition of this sort is not without its controversial element. When it was first mooted some months ago. Keith Walker brought me a catalogue of Sophie Ryder's work, so that I might know what to expect and give approval on behalf of the Chapter. We went through the various items, not all of which were destined for our exhibition, and when we reached a huge Minotaur, with genitals to scale, I suggested that this would not be appropriate for the Close. I thought no more about this, but now the exhibition is here it turns out that the artist and various other people in the sculpture world believe the Dean to have been prudish, and they have told the Press so.

It makes an amusing story for the papers, but I shan't lose any sleep over this.

Today, being Whitsunday, was an appropriate moment for the dedication of the new Touch and Hearing Centre that will enable visitors with sight problems to understand something of the Cathedral's architecture and history. The ingeniously designed model, placed at the West end of the Nave, makes it possible to feel the layout of the building, while audio-tapes and books in Braille provide additional detail.

The large congregation at Evensong included many from local organizations concerned with the welfare of the blind and partially-sighted, and we heard a remarkable sermon from John Hull, the Professor of Education at Birmingham University, who is himself blind. He spoke movingly of the experience of blindness with its permanent darkness and related this powerfully to the light of Christian faith.

The centre, which cost about £20,000, has been paid for entirely by donations made as a consequence of a television programme involving Dame Betty Ridley last December. Betty was invited to reflect on the significance for her of the daily Evensong in the Cathedral, which she often attends. The result was a programme of great sensitivity and beauty which attracted a lot of attention and much favourable comment from the TV critics.

Among the many letters she received was one from a blind couple in Sussex who lamented their inability to appreciate the beauty of Winchester Cathedral in ways possible to the sighted. Although well into her eighties, Betty, after consultation with me, undertook to raise enough money to provide Winchester with a Touch and Hearing Centre such as had been successfully installed in a number of other cathedrals. Those who had written to her about the TV programme were invited to contribute and in next to no time over £20,000 was raised, leaving some to spare for additional aids for the blind.

It never fails to astonish me what a little dedicated effort can achieve in Winchester.

Friday 10 June 1994

A useful meeting this morning of the small committee we have set up to make recommendations concerning the offer by the Jerusalem Trust of a major piece of sculpture to be commissioned for location either in the Cathedral or in the Close. Back in April, Tim and Susan Sainsbury, whose Trust this is, told us that they would like to make about £90,000 available for such a sculpture, which must be Christian and representational, not abstract. They appointed Edwina Sassoon, a voluble lady and an arts consultant, to represent them in the negotiations and commissioning.

This is of course a marvellous offer. I knew Tim and Susan well when I was Chaplain of the House of Commons, he being MP for Hove and she very active in the Parliamentary Wives Group. Both, she particularly, are zealous evangelicals. At the committee's first meeting last month we discussed possible sites for the sculpture and, although first thoughts favoured the Cloister Garth (now devoid of Cloisters) or the site of the former Chapter House, I made a strong plea for a statue of St Swithun to stand in the Retro-Quire where the saint's shrine was located until its destruction at the Reformation. Initially there was hesitation about this, but eventually it was agreed that this would be our first choice, provided we could find an artist capable of producing something suitable for so sensitive a site.

Today we have considered possible artists, Edwina Sassoon having produced catalogues and photographs of the work of the leading contenders. Quite a number of these were rejected because their work is largely abstract, but we settled on Antony Gormley, whose 'Sound II' is now happily settled in the Crypt, William Turnbull, unknown to me, and Stephen Cox, who has produced some remarkable sculpture for a church in North London.

The next step is for us to meet these artists and also to inspect examples of their work on different sites in London and the Home Counties. This will obviously take some time and the Sainsburys are anxious that we should get on with it, so it needs, and deserves, prioritiy. I am certainly going to keep in close touch with this project, lest it get out of hand, and I am thrilled at the prospect of our being able to place on the site of the shrine a new focus of devotion to St Swithun. I have always wanted to do this but could never believe it might happen during my time as Dean.

Wednesday 15 June 1994

Last evening Jo and I dined in Nelson's cabin on board HMS Victory at Portsmouth. We were the guests at an official dinner given by Admiral Sir Michael Layard who is Second Sea Lord and Commander-in-Chief of Naval Home Command. The other guests included three Admirals, the Adjutant General of the Army, Dame Elizabeth Butler-Sloss, who is a Lord Justice of Appeal, and the former Headmaster of the prep school attended by the Admiral's children.

Apparently only the Admiral is allowed to host dinners in Nelson's cabin and I was amazed at its size. Located in the stern, it appears to occupy almost half of its deck, but we were told that whenever the ship went into action cannon were rolled in and the cabin was transformed into a powerful action station. Today there is room for a dining table accommodating twenty-two, plus a Royal Marines orchestra, and plenty of space for armchairs. A fine portrait of the great man provides a fitting reminder of its most famous occupant.

In case I was asked to say Grace, I took the precaution of carrying with me one devised by Nelson:

> God save the Queen,
> Bless our dinners;
> Make us thankful.

Sure enough the Admiral called on me, and I was glad of the opportunity to use it in that place. In accordance with Naval custom we remained seated both for Grace and later for the Loyal Toast – the most plausible explanation for this being the low ceiling above us.

I was placed between the wife of the Adjutant General, who talked interestingly about her husband's work and her own involvement in army life, and the second wife of an elderly Admiral, Sir Fitzroy Talbot, who as a young officer had won two DSOs while leading a flotilla of Motor Gun Boats in the English Channel between 1940 and 1942. Unfortunately she turned out to be a rather disagreeable woman, full of complaints about Bishop David Jenkins and other features of contemporary church life. Our host gave a short but eloquent speech, mainly about Nelson.

The dinner, cooked ashore and carried on board – there being no galley – was appropriately splendid, and profiteroles with blue cheese was a savoury I had not previously encountered. The fact that I would have to drive home afterwards made me cautious with the wines and I envied those who had drivers or had accepted the offer of overnight hospitality.

Afterwards those of us who were agile enough were taken on a tour of the ship. In contrast with the Great Cabin, it provided extraordinarily cramped accommodation for some hundreds of sailors, not to mention the guns and the live animals carried for a fresh meat supply. We were shown the barrel in which Nelson's body was allegedly pickled in rum for his return to England and funeral at St Paul's. A macabre ending to the evening.

Monday 4 July 1994

After a great deal of discussion and consultation we have now produced a Mission Statement. It reads:

Winchester Cathedral exists for the Glory of God and its community is called to share in God's mission to the world and to advance his Kingdom.

Therefore, it:

1. Offers a regular round of daily worship and encourages other communities and groups to offer their life and work to God in the context of worship.

2. Provides a focus for the ministry of the Bishop and a centre of spiritual unity for the diocese and the wider community.

3. Seeks to share the Christian faith, in word and deed, with all who enter the building either as worshippers or visitors.

4. Endeavours to strengthen the faith and devotion of Christian believers and to relate the Gospel to the needs of individuals and communities.

5. Conserves, enhances and interprets the building and its environment, on behalf of the Church and the Nation, as a symbol of God's presence.

This is accompanied by a sixteen-point statement of corporate objectives covering virtually every aspect of the Cathedral's life. All of which goes back to the recommendation of the management consultants we employed in 1992.

Apparently all well-run institutions now have mission statements to indicate to outsiders what they are about and to remind management and staff of the ultimate objectives of their labours. Keith Bamber, our Receiver General, has been very keen on our pursuing this and it has, I think, been a quite useful exercise in concentrating our minds on the purpose of the Cathedral's existence and helping us to determine priorities. It will also be handy to give to new members of the Chapter and the staff, and I suppose it ought to be on the table at all Chapter Meetings to serve as a reference point for decision-making. But it is only too easy for documents of this sort to be left to gather dust once the impetus that led to their production has weakened.

Friday 8 July 1994

I have said No to a request that a new building at The Pilgrims' School should be named The Beeson Handicrafts Centre. I explained to the Headmaster and to the assembled company at today's annual Prizegiving that my record in the realm of handicrafts is far from illustrious.

During my schooldays, in 1940 to be precise, I was set the task of converting a block of wood into a lampstand. The handicrafts master, appropriately named Mr Ash, became so exasperated by my efforts that he exclaimed one day, 'Beeson, it is a shameful thing that sailors should be risking their lives bringing timber across the Atlantic for you to treat it in such a disgraceful manner. You had better move over to the metalwork where you will do less damage.'

Mr Ash has long since departed to a better place and it would be unkind to disturb his tranquility with the news that a fine preparatory school, located in the historic Close at Winchester, has a new handicrafts centre named after his erstwhile, unskilled pupil.

Thursday 14 July 1994

Back in Winchester after three stimulating days at Fleury – or Saint-Benoit-sur-Loire, as it is known geographically. The link between the Cathedral and this Benedictine Abbey, established by my predecessor, has proved to be a creative one and, besides the remembrance in daily prayer, there has been quite a lot of coming and going between our two communities. This was my first, long overdue, visit. I should really have gone quite soon after my arrival in Winchester, but decanal duties quickly took hold of me and, moving from one crisis to the next, there never seemed time enough to get away. Which means, I suppose, that I did not accord a visit high enough priority.

There was every reason to go this week, for Monday was the annual feast day commemorating the translation of Benedict's bones from Monte Cassino to Fleury in 655, and this year is the fiftieth anniversary of the return of the monks to the Abbey. At the time of the eighteenth-century French Revolution the monastery was suppressed and the conventual buildings destroyed. The church remained, simply as the parish church of the surrounding neighbourhood, but not long after D-Day in 1944 a community of Benedictine monks was re-established, and when the war ended they began to reconstruct the cloister and other buildings.

The church is a magnificent Romanesque edifice and quite the finest I have seen. It is not unlike Romsey Abbey, which was also built mainly in the late eleventh and early twelfth centuries, but it is infinitely richer in its carvings and altogether more grand. We were quite a large contingent – the Dean and Chapter, the Choir, the Receiver General, the Curator and a number of Chorister parents – the clergy being accommodated within the monastery, the rest either in the guest house across the road or in local hotels.

The Choir sang the Mass on the feast day and gave a very well attended recital in the Abbey on Tuesday evening. The Winchester Chapter robed for all the main services, read Lessons, and I shared with the Abbot in the giving of the Blessing at Vespers. We did not receive Communion at the Mass, but I celebrated the Eucharist for the Winchester party in the Crypt chapel where the remains of St Benedict lie in a large, heavily secured, case just above the altar. The Abbot attended and we all found it a very moving experience. I was also very taken by the simple, flowing vestments used in the Abbey and obtained details of their makers. Something like this would suit us well.

For the rest of the time there was much talk and generous hospitality. I spoke to the monks in the Chapter House for about twenty minutes, aided by John Crook, our Chorister Master, who acted as interpreter, and they asked questions afterwards, mainly about our Cathedral life and the issues facing the Church of England, e.g. the ordination of women. They seemed to find it interesting.

Etienne, the Abbot, combines intellectual distinction, efficiency and warmth in a most attractive way and I like him very much. The community is relatively large, though many of the monks are fairly old and, as everywhere, there is a dearth of novices. But this, of all the French Benedictine houses, will have to be maintained somehow.

At the celebratory lunch on Monday I sat next to the Archbishop of Sens, who had come as a special guest and presided at the Mass. Before he became a bishop he was Rector of the Catholic Institute in Lyons and is obviously a man of considerable calibre. He was very forthcoming in answering my questions about the life of the Catholic Church in France and confirmed my impression that its problems are, in many ways, even greater than those of the Church of England.

The shortage of priests is acute and the Archbishop told me that in one of his parishes it is possible to have only one funeral/requiem a month. The bodies of the deceased are stored by funeral directors until a visiting priest arrives to conduct a service. Efforts to recruit more priests for the Diocese of Sens have been of no avail, since local ordinands attend seminaries in distant towns and never return to the rural areas of central France. He also told me that the Archbishopric of Lyons has been vacant for over a year as the Vatican has failed to persuade any of the suitable candidates to accept this important post. Evidently Rome does not compel acceptance of bishoprics, though those who decline are expected to offer convincing explanations of their decisions.

After lunch, coffee was served in the garden, where the Archbishop sat under a tree, surrounded by the monks and the members of a community of Benedictine nuns who had been given a dispensation to leave their enclosed convent in Orleans for the day. He spoke about the development of lay ministries in the church, then answered their questions. It was like a scene from the Middle Ages.

On Tuesday I managed a short walk on the banks of the Loire, which is especially wide at this point, and on the way home yesterday we had an hour in Chartres Cathedral, which never fails to enthral.

Tuesday 19 July 1994

This afternoon's annual cricket match between the Choristers and the Dean and Chapter XI was, as usual, great fun but ended unusually. The Choristers went in first and, after losing their best batsman first ball and some other early wickets, recovered to make a respectable score of 118. The Dean and Chapter XI struggled for a time until the middle-order batsmen, led by David Dunnett the Sub-Organist, added about sixty runs, but then came a collapse, and when I went in as last man ten runs were still needed for victory. A series of singles reduced the target to four, whereupon young Nathaniel Lippiatt delivered me a fast full-toss which, by some freak action, I struck to the boundary.

That the Dean, in his sixty-ninth year, had won the match for his side by hitting a four in the last-wicket stand caused great hilarity. But not on the part of the Headmaster who seemed to regret that the age-old tradition of the Choristers being allowed to win the match had been broken. Obviously, this must not happen again, and that will surely be the last boundary I shall ever hit on a cricket ground, but maybe the Choristers will value their future victories all the more because of this reminder that they are not unbeatable.

Monday 19 September 1994

Alec Knight and I went across to Wolvesey this morning to have a talk with the Bishop about my idea that the office of Vice-Dean should for the next year or two be held by the Canon-in-Residence on a rotating basis. This is allowed by the Statutes and will enable our new team to settle down and also give my successor in 1996 freedom to make his own nomination.

Colin thought this a good idea and went on to tell us that tomorrow he will announce his intention to retire at the end of next March. We assured him that this news will be received with great regret in the Diocese and the County, where he is a highly regarded figure, but we acknowledged the heavy burden of work and responsibility he has been carrying for a long time. The recent portrait painted by Andrew Festing depicts him looking exceedingly tired, which is how he must often feel, but I certainly would not like this mood to be captured quite so accurately and as permanently as oil on canvas makes it.

Friday 14 October 1994

The Cathedral Guides and some others are up in arms about the change to the sign on a twelfth-century tomb in the Quire. Traditionally this has been regarded as the tomb of King William Rufus who was killed by an arrow in the New Forest in 1100 and, despite the protests of the monks, buried in the Cathedral. Tradition asserts also that the collapse of the central tower soon after his burial was a sign of divine displeasure at the admission to the Cathedral of so wicked a king.

Recent research suggests, however, that the tomb is more likely to be that of Henry de Blois, the great twelfth-century Bishop of Winchester, and in fact the name of Rufus is recorded on one of the mortuary chests on the Presbytery screen, which suggests that his bones may now be there.

On the strength of all this, Keith Walker's signing committee has replaced the Rufus tomb sign with a new one that indicates it to be the resting place of Henry de Blois, thus spoiling the story the Guides delight in relating to visitors. The Dean and Chapter were not consulted about this change, which was an unfortunate, even if predictable, omission, and we have now decreed that the sign shall include a reference to the William Rufus tradition. Matters of this sort cannot be swept aside at the whim of a committee.

Saturday 15 October 1994

The installation of Philip Morgan as Canon Residentiary this evening completes the renewal of the Chapter and brings us back to full strength after several months when we were two members short. Charles Stewart was installed as Precentor during the early part of last month.

Both are, I think, notable acquisitions. Good Precentors do not grow on trees and it is fortunate that, within days of Roger Job announcing his resignation last March, David Hill chanced to meet Charles Stewart, who had been a Choral Scholar at St John's College, Cambridge when David was the Organ Scholar. It turned out that Charles was due to leave his post as Precentor of Bath Abbey, so I moved very quickly and secured him for Winchester. Although he has a slight stammer, he has a wonderfully rich singing voice and all kinds of ideas about the ordering of worship.

Philip Morgan has the advantage of previous cathedral experience – he was at Norwich for a time as Sacrist and at St Albans as Sub-Dean – and also a first-class pastoral reputation. The fact that he is now fifty-nine is not without significance, because it means that, pending the hoped-for changes about freehold offices, he will at most be able to serve for no more than about ten years. I don't think he is very keen to be our Treasurer, but most of this work ought to be handled by our lay staff, anyway, and our greatest need is for a pastoral Canon.

It is ironic, and surely quite absurd, that it has taken eight years to reach the point at which I have a team of colleagues in whose appointments I have had a hand and with whom I have some expectation of being able to work closely, yet I myself have only just over one year to go before retirement. This should be a good team to hand on to my successor, but he may not think so and it will be a very long time before he can do anything about it.

Tuesday 18 October 1994

We announced today to the Press and to the first of the annual meetings of the Cathedral congregation our plan for increasing revenue by means of greater pressure on visitors to make a donation when entering the building. We have been working on this for several weeks and Richard Alexander, the Chapter Clerk, has done an excellent job studying the method employed at Salisbury and applying it to our situation.

In my Installation sermon in February 1987 I vowed that during my time as Dean there would be no charge for admission to the Cathedral. I have re-affirmed this on a number of occasions since then and I intend to stick by it. But the deficit on our day-to-day running costs was £88,000 last year, it is likely to be about £115,000 this year, and £155,000 next year, which means a reduction of our capital funds by over £350,000 in three years. There is nothing unusual about this inasmuch as three-quarters of the English cathedrals now have annual deficits. On our annual expenditure of £825,000 inflation alone adds a susbstantial amount, the Church Commissioners' grant is to be reduced by £20,000 this year and more next year, and increased activity has required the strengthening of the administrative staff and a consequent higher salaries bill.

During the last four years, however, donations by our 400,000 visitors have remained on a plateau of about £225,000, i.e. an average of 50p per head. We suggest £2 but most give nothing. In the present situation we have just two options: we can make drastic cuts in the Cathedral's life or we can try to persuade our visitors to give more. Having rejected the first as defeatist, we are left with the second, and here there are three possible methods:

1. Impose admission charges, as at Ely and St Paul's.

2. Strengthen our present invitation to visitors to make a donation. This is, on past experience, unlikely to be successful and we cannot take the risk any longer.

3. Indicate to visitors that we expect them to make a contribution on a particular scale, ranging from £2 for adults to 50p for children, and so organize the entrance arrangements at the West door that they have to opt out of giving, rather than opt in.

The third method is the one we shall employ from the beginning of next March and if we can increase the average donation from 50p to £1, our overall income should increase by about £200,000.

It will be necessary to have an entrance desk manned by carefully trained staff who will take the money but at the same time encourage waverers who are unable or unwilling to make a donation to enter the building all the same. We have to emphasize that visitors are still free to enter without parting with money, and 'supporters' cards will be issued on request to the Cathedral congregation, citizens of Winchester and churchpeople in the Diocese who may feel embarrassed if they pass the entrance desk without making a donation. Charges for photography, entrance to the Crypt, and for the lighting of the Holy Sepulchre Chapel will be abolished. The desk will not be manned on Sundays or for a period of forty-five minutes before weekday services.

I am very sorry that we have been driven to this, and I shall be even more sorry if it discourages anyone from entering the Cathedral, but unless we are to reduce our activities there is really no choice. It is, I suppose, hardly unreasonable to expect visitors to a great building such as Winchester Cathedral to give an average of £1 towards its preservation and ongoing life.

The overwhelming majority of those who attended the congregational meeting this afternoon agreed with the steps we are proposing to take. In fact, the only opposition came from a small number who believed we should impose an admission charge.

I gave the Press a very careful briefing and did a few local radio interviews, so I hope we can get our plan across clearly to the general public. The last thing we want is a headline screaming 'Charges for Cathedral entry' or 'Pay up, says the Dean'.

Wednesday 19 October 1994

The Secretaries for Appointments to the Prime Minister and the Archbishops have spent the last two days in Winchester canvassing opinions about the choice of the next Diocesan Bishop. They have cast their net very widely, consulting all manner of people both individually and in groups, in order to build up a picture of the kind of man required, though there is a tradition, broken only once during the last six centuries, that Winchester, because of its seniority, is filled by the translation of one of the other diocesan bishops. This tradition, if continued, is bound to limit the choice, since a high proportion of the bishops are now in their sixties, and therefore too old to be considered, or have only recently been appointed to dioceses and cannot be moved next year.

Yesterday the Secretaries met the Bishop's Council at which the discussion followed predictable lines – a good pastor, proven record of strong leadership, able to communicate the faith, experience of parish ministry, and so on. The Evangelicals, ever fearful of liberalism, pleaded for someone who would uphold biblical faith and the historic creeds, while the Archdeacons spoke about the need for 'collaborative ministry'. I made the point that, since Hampshire is packed with people who commute to London and hold positions of considerable responsibility in public life, the new Bishop had better be someone of intellectual distinction who would be respected by them. And, since the diocese will be faced by considerable financial problems, he will need to be interested enough in money to give a strong lead on the fund-raising front. Four members of the Council were elected to serve on the Crown Appointments Commission that will meet quite soon to choose two names for submission to the Prime Minister.

This morning I had a personal meeting with the Secretaries at which I expressed the hope that the new bishop would continue in the good relationship the Cathedral had enjoyed with his predecessor. It is evident, however, that the cupboard of candidates is pretty bare. Stephen Sykes, the scholar Bishop of Ely, would be ideal, but he ought to succeed John Habgood at York. Mark Santer of Birmingham would also be an excellent choice, but he is still recovering from the sad death of his wife, Henrietta, and I gather that he would not be ready to move to Winchester on his own. Richard Harries is the only other serious contender among the diocesan bishops but I don't know whether a move from Oxford to Winchester would make much sense and the area scheme in Oxford diocese gives him a lot of freedom for writing and broadcasting that he may not wish to relinquish.

I said that if, in this situation, the CAC is prepared to look beyond the Diocesan Bishops, it might do well to examine the credentials of some of the deans, among whom there is a fair amount of talent. In particular, Wesley Carr of Bristol has an outstanding intellect and a wide vision of the direction in which the Church of England ought to be moving. His appointment as Bishop of Winchester would cause more than a few eyebrows to be raised but it would be a bold move and one that in the circumstances I would welcome. The Secretaries seemed by no means shocked by this suggestion but they are highly skilled in not revealing their views or reacting to opinions.

Wednesday 2 November 1994

Today, being All Souls Day, was an appropriate moment to inter in the Crypt the very large quantity of human remains that have been stored in cardboard boxes in the chamber above the Guardian Angels Chapel since the archaeological excavations in the Outer Close in the 1960s.

Martin Biddle, who led those excavations, was very much against our action this evening, but he and his colleagues were given ample opportunity to carry out any further examination of the bones that might be thought useful, and it is really improper for human remains to await the convenience of archaeologists before being returned to their permanent resting place.

The ceremony of interment – they were placed within a specially created sepulchre – proved to be a very moving occasion. After the singing of the Requiem for All Souls Day in the Quire, the clergy, the choir, the architect and the clerk of the works went in procession to the Crypt. Earlier this week we wondered if the rising water level might prevent us from going ahead with the ceremony this evening, but with the aid of stepping stones in the water we just managed it.

In candlelight the choir sang two beautiful mediaeval items in remembrance of the Departed and I said some commendatory prayers. All very simple and occupying no more than five minutes, but a hugely satisfying action.

Friday 11 November 1994

A tricky problem has arisen over the possible involvement of girl choristers in the Southern Cathedrals Festival. Salisbury started a girls' choir, to work alongside its boy choristers, about three years ago, and this is now deemed to be of a standard high enough for it to be able to sing choral services.

The girls are treated as an integral part of their choral foundation and, understandably enough, Salisbury believe they should take part in the annual SCF. But Chichester will have none of this. Alan Thurlow, their organist, says that the introduction of girls into cathedral choirs is undesirable and likely to make the recruiting of boys more difficult. He has the support of his lay clerks and also his chapter, though I believe that John Treadgold, the dean, would be happy to have the girls involved in the Festival if his musicians would agree.

For Salisbury, and especially for Hugh Dickinson, the introduction of girl choristers has become something of a crusade. They believe that all cathedral choirs should be moving in this direction in the interests of plain justice and, although they are not calling for immediate action by the SCF, the crunch will come in 1997 when the Festival is due to be held in Salisbury again.

The Winchester line is that we recognize the Salisbury position and are ready to share in a festival in which their girls are fully involved. But there are some logistical and financial problems associated with such a development and, it seems, a real risk that Chichester may withdraw if the girls are allowed to share in SCF's liturgical element. How far all this is tied up with the widespread antipathy to women priests in Chichester diocese is impossible to tell.

A rather tiresome Winchester woman is pressing us, with the aid of the media, to admit her daughter to our choir and she will not accept David Hill's judgment that boys' and girls' voices are different and should not normally be mixed. It would be good if we could start a girls' choir, but this would involve major changes at The Pilgrims' School, which at the moment is for boys only, and like Salisbury we would have to raise a lot of money to put the girls on an equal footing with the boys over scholarships.

Once the new Precentor is settled in we shall have to look at this very seriously.

Monday 14 November 1994

The Deans and Provosts meeting held today at the Church Commissioners was devoted to the report of the Archbishops' Commission on Cathedrals. Many, in fact most, of the deans have become very steamed up about this report and expressed their opposition strongly.

Alex Wedderspoon, of Guildford, set the ball rolling by asserting that historic institutions such as cathedrals should not be tampered with and that the radical proposals of the report were both unnecessary and undesirable. John Arnold, of Durham, followed with a long speech in which he expounded the romantic notion that the dean is the successor of the mediaeval prior and should rule his cathedral in the manner of a Benedictine monastery. And so the discussion continued – anxiety about accountability to a Greater Council, fear of untutored laity being appointed to chapters, disquiet about the abolition of the freehold – revealing a body of men apparently afflicted with paranoia.

At which point I got to my feet and reminded my colleagues that the report was not being imposed upon the cathedrals by hostile forces: the Commission was set up at the request of the deans and provosts, some of our number had served on it, cathedrals had all been visited, we had financed the Commission's work. We had asked for a commission because we were aware of a number of serious problems in some cathedrals that were arousing a great deal of unfavourable publicity, and some of us, at least, were conscious that crises of a similar sort were waiting to erupt in our own communities. In asking for a Commission we were of course aware that unless we took the initiative the General Synod soon would, because there is considerable anxiety in the church as a whole about recent events at Hereford, Lincoln, Exeter and St Paul's.

I suggested therefore that we should continue to collaborate with the Commission and try to discover how its proposals might best serve our cathedrals' interests. The Greater Council need not be a threat; on the contrary it could become a most useful asset in strengthening the link between the cathedrals and the wider community. The laity now had an assured place in all the councils of the church, except for the cathedrals, and I, for one, would welcome the skilled contribution they might make to the work of the chapter. The limiting of the tenure of cathedral appointments to, say, ten years could hardly be regarded as oppressive and a hardworking dean or canon could achieve a great deal in that time.

This seemed to change the course of the discussion somewhat and a number of others then spoke up in support of my line, though I suspect that those who represent the deans and provosts in the General Synod will still try to mount some kind of rearguard action when the Commission's recommendations come before the Synod. It is, I suppose, the case that few people are ready to relinquish power willingly – always it has to be seized from their grasp – and I suspect that most of the deans and provosts did not realize what a risk they were taking when they agreed to ask the Archbishops to appoint a Commission.

Tuesday 6 December 1994

The Jerusalem Trust sculpture project has ended disappointingly. During July Edwina Sassoon signalled to us that the Trustees seemed to be back-tracking on their original offer and that Tim and Susan Sainsbury proposed to visit Winchester at the beginning of August to discuss the matter and inspect possible sites. Unfortunately, I was on holiday when they came, but Keith Walker, who chaired a meeting with them, reported that everything had been 'sweetness and light' and much enthusiasm had been shown. A statue of St Swithun had not immediately appealed to the Evangelical convictions of Tim and Susan, but they were happy for this to be considered.

Unfortunately, our benefactors had gone on from Winchester to visit a sculpture park between Stockbridge and Salisbury where their eyes had lighted on four pieces of sculpture representing the evangelists. These they would like to present to the Dean and Chapter for display on the Cloister Garth. They are the work of an elderly sculptor, Mary Spencer Watson, who is by no means of the first rank, and Keith Walker and some other people from the Hampshire Sculpture Trust were horrified that we might accept them.

So this afternoon we went, as a Chapter, to the sculpture park to see them for ourselves. They are certainly far removed from the specially commissioned item we had in mind, but they are not all that bad. Indeed, I would quite like to have them. They would be much too small for locating on the Cloister Garth, where they would have the appearance of carvings rescued from the exterior of the Cathedral, but they might go in the new Dean Garnier Garden when it is finished or possibly the Chapter House site. I don't like the idea of rejecting £28,000-worth of sculpture simply because it is not of the very highest class.

But the rest of the Chapter are unanimous that we should decline the offer, so I must send a very tactful letter of explanation to Tim and Susan Sainsbury. No doubt some other cathedral will find the evangelists a home and the money saved on our £90,000 project will enable the Trust to make offers elsewhere. But it has been a strange affair and I still don't understand why the original offer, with all its exciting possibilities, was so radically modified.

1995

The dedication last evening of a Memorial to Lancelot Andrewes was an immensely satisfying event. This was very much Colin James's baby because he has for some years lamented the fact that Winchester lacked a memorial to its most notable Bishop after Swithun and one who, like Swithun, now has a place in the church's calendar of commemorations.

The explanation of Andrewes's absence is simple. He was an important figure in the court of King Charles I and when he died in 1626 he was residing at Winchester House – the London home of the Bishops of Winchester at that time. Consequently he was buried in the nearby collegiate church of St Saviour and St Mary Overie which in 1905 became Southwark Cathedral. There the great bishop has a magnificent tomb, which includes a splendid effigy of him, and at that particular period in history I do not think the Cathedral had the central place in the life of the Diocese that would have required him to be transported to Winchester and buried alongside Edington, Wykeham, Waynflete and Fox.

Still, with his life and work still greatly admired – more so, perhaps, than at any other time since his death – Winchester should have some visible memorial to his presence here, and this is what we now have. Colin James's attempt to raise money for a memorial from the institutions with which Andrewes was associated met with a disappointing response, so the Friends of the Cathedral came to the rescue with a £5,000 grant, and fortunately Simon Verity, a leading sculptor and letterer, was prepared to design and execute the work at what must, I think, have been well below the price he would normally command.

The memorial is not huge, but it includes a bust of Andrewes taken from a contemporary engraving and is a rich variety of symbols expressive of his virtues and his work. Beneath the bust is, in beautifully flowing letters reminiscent of the seventeenth-century style, one of his prayers which will be a real aid to devotion for anyone who inspects the memorial:

Lord, lift thou up the light of thy countenance upon us,
That in thy light we may see light:
The light of thy grace today, and
The light of thy glory hereafter.

The placing of the memorial was a tricky business. A small group led by Keith Walker searched the building for a suitable site and eventually recommended a location in the South aisle of the Retro-Quire, opposite the site of the former shrine of St Swithun. This seemed reasonable, but shortly before Christmas, while on one of my daily walkabouts, it came to me that the proposed position, in company with two somewhat undistinguished eighteenth-century Prebendaries of the Cathedral, was altogether wrong. So, very late in the day, the question of the site went back into the melting pot and Colin James himself came up with the bright idea that the memorial should go on the wall alongside the episcopal throne in the Quire. This seems absolutely right and it is astonishing that we did not think of it in the first place.

The service of dedication was memorable. The Bishops of Ely and Chichester, two sees held by Andrewes before he came to Winchester, were there along with representatives of Westminster Abbey, where he was Dean; Pembroke College, Cambridge, where he was Master; and the Merchant Taylors' Company, whose school he attended. Kenneth Stevenson gave an appropriately learned sermon on the significance of Andrewes for today.

Tuesday 7 February 1995

I thought that after the heavy programme of last year's 900th anniversary celebrations my eighth year in Winchester, completed today, would be more relaxed and provide some opportunities for reflection. But this is not the way it turned out, which is a pity, because cathedrals should be havens of peace as well as centres of mission, and it is not good for their deans to be always frenetically busy.

The truth is, however, that the cathedrals have reached a point in their history when they are facing unprecedented challenges and opportunities that simply cannot be neglected. It is to be hoped that the proposals contained in the report of the Archbishops' Commission may help us to adjust our administrative arrangements so that we can cope with the administrative burden more efficiently and with less stress.

The renewal of the Chapter through the arrival of two new members has been the most significant development of the past year and already there is a different, more collaborative, feel about our life. The great success of the Visitors Centre is also gratifying and the verdict of a customer survey that it is 'a friendly place' is a clear indication that the success is not only financial.

Yet there is no escaping the need for increased revenue. Last year we had a deficit of £88,000 on the Cathedral's income-and-expenditure account and the projected deficit for 1995 is £140,000. Obviously deficits of this magnitude cannot be tolerated, and the new cash desk, which is to be installed at the main door next month, should bring about a dramatic reduction in our losses. Indeed, I am hopeful that it will bring us into surplus and thus remove what has been a constant source of anxiety for most of my time here.

Wednesday 15 March 1995

The new entrance desk installed at the main door on 1 March has so far been an unqualified success. The aim is not to impose an admission charge but rather to require visitors to opt out of making a donation, instead of opting in.

A high proportion of the visitors, as I have myself observed, seem perfectly happy to make a donation on the suggested scale, while those who do not are very cordially invited to enter the building by the carefully selected and trained women who staff the desk. Quite a number of those who fail to give at the door put gifts in other boxes later. The Guides are providing extra free tours, and we have abolished the charges for photography permits and for entry to the Crypt. Already the level of income received from visitors has increased significantly, and all being well this should solve our main financial problem.

What we do not know, however, and must soon seek to discover, is how many visitors have been deterred from entering the Cathedral by this new arrangement. Although the notices emphasize the element of welcome and state that the suggested donations are voluntary, there is obviously a risk that some visitors will interpret them otherwise and turn away. I hope there may not be many of these because it is, I believe, a matter of great seriousness if anyone is deterred from entering a place of worship by financial pressure.

Saturday 25 March 1995

Colin James was given a very good retirement send-off in the Cathedral this morning. A Sung Eucharist for the Feast of the Visitation of the Blessed

Virgin Mary appealed to the high churchman he is, and there was a very large congregation drawn from all parts of the Diocese. It was slightly embarrassing to us that the Cathedral choir was absent, because of a long-standing commitment to an American tour, but this opened the door to a composite choir enlisted from Romsey Abbey, Christchurch Priory and other churches with good music. In some ways this was more appropriate to the occasion.

Characteristically, Colin chose to preach simply on Mary and made virtually no reference to his own personal ministry or to the life of the Diocese during his ten years as its Bishop. He has, I think, been a very good Bishop – of the pastoral sort, which in these days requires high administrative competence as well as wisdom and compassion. Although conservative in some matters, most notably over women priests, and not an innovator, he was generally open to experiment and change, and displayed great discernment in evaluating people and policies. I never heard him preach a bad sermon, which is quite an episcopal achievement, but on the other hand I rarely heard from him anything that might be regarded as prophetic or highly stimulating. He is that kind of man.

Relations between the Bishop and his Cathedral could not have been better. He and I have had a good relationship; we have been aware of boundaries but tried to be sensitive and generous both in observing and in disregarding them. He has played a large and welcome part in our worship, supported us in matters great and small, and had a very significant role in the £7 million appeal. My only complaint concerns the long hours I spent in his monthly senior staff meetings when I had hardly anything to contribute. Maybe he thought I must be a useful ally if the going ever got rough, but it never did.

Attendance at these meetings did, however, enlighten me about the heavy burden of responsibility that diocesan bishops now carry and the slogging hard work from which they cannot escape. Most of this seems to be created by the endless meetings and consultations ushered in by synodical government and by lack of confidence on the part of the parish clergy who now need their hands holding to assure them that they are all right.

Winchester is by no means a difficult diocese; in fact it is among the relatively easy ones to run, but the work is relentless and it is small wonder that Colin has in recent years seemed tired. Sally is also looking exhausted and this is not surprising, for she has been the perfect bishop's wife – greatly admired and deservedly so.

The opening of our new Education Centre this afternoon was a significant occasion. The fact that we were unable, for financial reasons, to build an Education wing on to the new Visitors Centre in 1993 has turned out to be a blessing. The refurbishment of the former Pastoral Centre/Tea Room has given us more useful space than would have been available in the projected new building.

What we now have is owed entirely to the generosity of Al Gordon of New York, who has given us £60,000 to meet the cost. Aged ninety-four, and as sprightly as ever, he came over to perform the official opening ceremony, which gave both him and us enormous pleasure. In some ways he is like a caricature of an old-style American, but beneath the bonhomie and vivid turn of phrase is immense wisdom and a genuine desire to use his wealth for the advancement of Christianity.

The annual Conference of Deans and Provosts, which started here on Monday evening and concluded this morning, is deemed to have been hugely successful, and I think it was. It is the first time the conference has been held in Winchester, though there was a gathering of deans here in 1919.

The main reason why it has not come here before is, I suspect, related to the problem of accommodation and general facilities. The hotels are much too expensive, and even if King Alfred's College were to be available, it would not be much fun commuting between the College and the Cathedral. So we took the risk of trying to secure about eighty beds in houses within or very near to the Close; the new Visitors Centre offered a facility for meals; and the Deanery a venue for meetings and general sociability. And it came off, even though the Chairman and Secretary of the Conference had early misgivings about the proposal to billet members in the homes of Cathedral people.

We were lucky to have so many beds available to us within such easy reach and to have Anthea Fortescue, formerly a professional conference organizer, to run the whole thing. Everything went like clockwork and the change of style seems to have been found refreshing. A lot of local people now need my personal thanks.

The meeting at Lambeth with the Archbishops of Canterbury and York on Monday afternoon, before everyone came down to Winchester, was, however, somewhat disappointing. George Carey delivered a speech of unexceptional content but in general terms, and I suspect that it was one he produces for all sorts of gatherings. It could equally easily have been given to a conference of archdeacons or diocesan secretaries or churchwardens. There is obviously a problem when archbishops are called upon to address so many different bodies and lack the time to produce something that is both distinctive and substantial. Bob Runcie used to cope with this, very sensibly I thought, by asking someone to provide him with a good draft, which he then knocked into final shape and made personal. Maybe George Carey does the same, in which case the drafts are not being produced at the right intellectual level – at least, not for a meeting with deans and provosts. John Habgood of York, who took the chair, would have done better.

The prepared responses by the Dean of Durham and the Provost of Chelmsford on deans and provosts in the life of the church and the wider community were also, I thought, missed opportunities. In a mixture of triumphalism and defensiveness, both spoke of the many opportunities now facing cathedrals and the marvellous way in which these are being seized. It all sounded far too good to be true and had I been one of the archbishops I would certainly have asked why, if everything in the cathedral world was sweetness and light, the deans and provosts had asked for the appointment of a Commission to investigate their many problems.

In the course of a wide-ranging discussion of the church's mission I asked the archbishops if they felt that the Church of England's traditional parochial system, with its wide dispersal of resources, was compatible with the need to create fewer but stronger bases for mission. Neither of them attempted an answer, prefering to flannel their way on to the next question.

The conference itself at Winchester was the usual mixture of Bible study, worship, lectures, discussion and business. A candlelit dinner in the magnificent hall of Winchester College was specially memorable and, with Geoffrey and Elspeth Howe as guests, opportunity was taken to thank her ladyship for her chairmanship of the Archbishops' Commission. A fine lunch provided by the City Council was also a happy occasion and the Cathedral Choir won universal praise, which is praise indeed, since most deans and provosts are normally convinced that their own choirs are the best in the country.

Monday 8 May 1995

Yesterday's service to mark the fiftieth anniversary of the ending of the war in Europe, VE Day, was a great County event – one of several held over the weekend. As anticipated, the Cathedral was absolutely packed and Robert

Runcie, the former Archbishop of Canterbury, gave a fine sermon. It may perhaps have been a little on the long side, but this was due, in part, to the immense trouble he took to relate the war to Hampshire's history and traditions. The Abbot of Fleury, who chanced to be spending the weekend with us, read one of the lessons in French, which was a happy touch, but it was a pity that we could not manage to involve also someone from Germany.

The only real misfortune, however, involved the seating arrangements – always a tricky business. The British Legion were given responsibility for this and, faithful to the hierarchical principle, they allocated all the 'best' seats to the County VIPs – Deputy Lieutenants, senior military people and the like. Thus most of the ex-servicemen who fought in the war, and were wearing rows of medals to prove it, were relegated to seats often far-removed from the central action of the service.

Not surprisingly, I am getting complaints about this – 'Same old story: officers in the best places, other ranks pushed anywhere' – and I am sorry that we did not foresee this possibility and insist on priority for the heroes of the occasion.

Friday 26 May 1995

The long delay over the appointment of the next Bishop of Winchester is, not surprisingly, causing a good deal of concern and some rumour and speculation. *The Times* has now suggested that the bishopric has been offered to four or five other bishops, all of whom have turned it down. This implies that Winchester is a poisoned chalice. All of which is quite untrue, for the simple reason that, given the Crown Appointments Commission's schedule of meetings and work, there has not been time enough for as many as five offers to be made and declined.

I have no inside information on this matter but my reading of the situation is as follows. After Colin James's announcement at the end of last September of his intention to retire at the end of March, the Appointments Secretaries got to work quickly in the hope that a successor might be secured before they had to turn their attention to the appointment of a new Archbishop of York.

Thus the necessary consultations were carried out in the Diocese and County in mid-October, and the Crown Appointments Commission met in early December. But they were unable to make nominations, either because they disagreed about the candidates or, more probably, because the most eligible of the candidates had to be left available for consideration for York.

This opportunity missed, the CAC was obliged at its February meeting to deal with the appointment to York and, since the Commission meets only at two-monthly intervals, Winchester could not be reconsidered until April. At this meeting it was agreed to retain the tradition of translating to Winchester one of the other diocesan bishops and, from a very small field, two names were chosen. After careful consideration both declined, so we have reached May with no new Bishop in sight and, as far as one can tell, no possibility of getting someone appointed and enthroned before the end of the year, this being fifteen months after the outgoing Bishop gave notice of his impending retirement.

Clearly the system of appointment is not working well. In these days of acute financial and manpower problems, no diocese ought to be left so long without leadership. John Perry, the Bishop of Southampton, is doing well as the acting-Bishop but all the important decisions must await the arrival of the new man. The long delay is sending out all the wrong signals and the uncertainty is not good for clergy morale.

The initial difficulty seems to have been caused by the entanglement of the appointments to Winchester and York. These should, as a matter of good organization, be clearly separated, though of course no one can dictate to Bishops about the announcement of their retirement dates. A gentleman's agreement on this point would surely help. Problems and consequent delays could also be avoided if, without any breach of confidentiality, it were ascertained in advance of CAC meetings whether or not particular bishops might be prepared to consider the possibility of translation elsewhere. The archbishops could do this informally in the same way that bishops do with their diocesan clergy. In this way the CAC would not waste time considering the nomination of men who had no intention of leaving their present posts.

This raises a broader issue in relation to Winchester. Until fairly recently this diocese, being fifth in episcopal seniority and replete with historical prestige, was one to which most other diocesan bishops would have accepted appointment with alacrity. But things have changed. Personal prestige counts for less than it used to do, all bishoprics carry less *cachet*, and the stipend of Winchester is no longer different from that of any other diocese. Why, then, should any other diocesan bishop, heavily engaged in the challenges of his present responsibilities, up sticks and move to Winchester?

To talk in these terms is undoubtedly an affront to Winchester's *amour propre*, but this is the reality of the situation, and if delays such as we are now experiencing are to be avoided, the choice of a Bishop of Winchester must be made from the widest possible field and not confined, even initially, to the existing diocesan bishops. This might well lead to better appointments, too.

Sunday 4 June 1995

Today being Whitsunday, when we are celebrating the dynamic element in the church's life and the flexibility demanded by the Holy Spirit, seemed a good moment to preach about change in the church and, in this context, announce my retirement from the Deanery on 29 February next year.

This is in fact rather long notice, though anyone aware of my birthday and the rule about clergy retiring at seventy will have been aware that 2 March 1996 is my *terminus ad quem* at Winchester. The Prime Minister's Secretary for Appointments was rather keen for me to make an earlier, rather than a later, announcement, not – as he assured me – through any desire to hustle me off the scene, but rather to assist him the the planning of his diary over the next few months. Hopefully, this will lead to a shorter interregnum at Winchester – an important factor is our particular circumstances.

In view of the inordinate delay in appointing a new Bishop of Winchester, I wondered at one stage whether to offer to stay on a little longer beyond my seventieth birthday until the new Bishop had settled in and become equipped to make a useful contribution to the discussion about the kind of new Dean required. But it turned out that the law requires retirement to start no later than the seventieth birthday and, in any case, Jo's health has deteriorated to a level at which it is becoming increasingly difficult to care both for her and for the Cathedral.

The reaction to my announcement has been kind and generous, though one elderly member of this morning's congregation said after the service that she was 'very happy' to know that I am to retire. I think she meant that she was happy I am to be released from responsibility to what she hopes will be an enjoyable retirement.

Wednesday 7 June 1995

The consultation on liturgy we held at Alton Abbey yesterday was useful, I think, but in some ways disturbing. The Dean and Chapter were accompanied by the Organist, the Head Virger and five members of the congregation. The Director of Training from Bath and Wells Diocese acted as chairman/facilitator and Dr Kenneth Stevenson of Guildford as our professional liturgist.

The purpose of the exercise was to review the Cathedral's pattern of Sunday morning worship. Here is a difficult problem. With the exception of Durham, Winchester is the only cathedral in England that has Mattins, rather than a Sung Eucharist, as its chief Sunday morning act of worship. It is held at 10.30 am and attracts about twice as many people as attend the Sung Eucharist at 11.30 am.

The changes brought about in the Church of England over the last fifty years by the liturgical movement have passed Winchester by and there is a certain irony in this inasmuch as Winchester's present Dean was General Secretary of the Parish and People movement which during the 1950s and 1960s spearheaded these changes. The Canons all find Sunday morning in the Cathedral theologically unsound and devotionally unhelpful, and they are anxious for change. So also are the Organist, the Head Virger, and those members of the congregation who were nurtured in parishes where the Eucharist was the main Sunday morning service.

Yet our Mattins still attracts large numbers, and the Cathedral is just about the only church in central Hampshire where it is offered to a high choral standard. No doubt many of those who attend do so for conservative reasons. Some are retired military people or from public school backgrounds where Mattins reigned unchallenged. Others are of the Low Church tradition and would agree with a former Bishop of Southampton, John Cavell, that a proper Sunday morning requires 'A good Mattins, a good sermon and a good lunch'. But there is another group, for whom I have a particular concern, who are on the edge of Christian faith – seriously interested but not ready to enter into the commitment implied by participation in the central act of the church's sacramental life. Mattins suits them well.

There was strong pressure at the consultation for us to reverse our Sunday morning order, bringing the Sung Eucharist forward to 10.30 a.m. and putting Mattins back to 11.30 a.m., but I resisted this and in the end had to say quite frankly that there is no possibility of such a change taking place during my remaining time as Dean. Instead, I offered to use whatever influence I still have to promote a change to 10.00 a.m. Mattins and 11.00 a.m. Sung Eucharist, each with a sermon, but this was not accepted. It was decided to enhance the content of the present Sung Eucharist and to reflect more on the theological and pastoral need, pending the arrival of a new Dean.

I find myself in a curious position. This is the only occasion during my time at Winchester when I have resisted the Chapter on a matter of change. The boot has always been on the other foot. This may be interpreted as a sign of my advancing years or of unreadiness as I approach retirement to face the upheaval and inevitable controversy of major liturgical change.

But I do not think either of these possibilities to be the explanation. Rather is it that my time at Westminster and Winchester, now extending over twenty years, has brought me to believe that the vocation of great churches such as these is to provide open, unfenced spaces of spirituality in which a great variety of people can worship and pray more or less on their own terms. This conviction makes me increasingly uneasy about the sacerdotalism reflected in much of the current liturgical development. 'Liturgy and Society' – the theme of the Parish and People movement in its pioneering days – has been replaced by something best described as 'Liturgy and the Sanctuary', this reflecting an unhealthy regard for what is believed to be liturgically correct, rather than what actually works as an appropriate act of worship in a particular place. This is widening the gulf between the church and the secular world.

Because of this I think that the present arrangement at Winchester, although created and to some extent sustained by conservative forces, is actually more advanced and more useful than that which obtains in most other cathedrals. We can of course improve our pattern, and what I proposed would I feel sure go a long way towards redressing the balance between word and sacrament, uncommitted and committed. But once a Dean has announced the date of his retirement his influence declines rapidly.

Tuesday 27 June 1995

At last the new Bishop has been appointed – Michael Scott-Joynt, the present Suffragan Bishop of Stafford. I was given advance notice by 10 Downing Street yesterday, the official announcement was made to the media in Church House, here in the Close, at 11.00 this morning, and I and other members of the Senior Staff met the Bishop and his wife at Wolvesey early this afternoon.

He is not a man I know, and until today I had met him only once before, and that very briefly last January when, after my son-in-law's installation as a Canon of Lichfield, he spoke to me from his car as we were all leaving the reception. But towards the end of last year, when the quest for a new Bishop of Winchester was just beginning, Ronnie Bowlby, the former Bishop of Southwark now living in retirement in Shrewsbury, said to me over the telephone, 'Michael Scott-Joynt is your man'. I have the greatest respect for Ronnie's judgment, but, since I did not know the man he was talking about, I failed to pursue the matter. In any event it seemed highly improbable that a suffragan bishop would ever come under consideration.

Yet, after an inordinately long delay and doubtless much tortuous negotiation, this is precisely what has happened. Having failed to gain acceptances from any of the diocesan bishops who were approached, the Crown Appointments Commission turned, hopefully in not too much desperation, to Stafford.

Certainly he is an impressive looking bishop, standing some 6 foot 4 inches tall I should say, and with a very warm, friendly personality. The same goes for his wife, Lou, though she is nothing like so tall. What kind of ideas he has remains to be seen. He is naturally cagey about expressing any of them at this stage. But, interestingly, both he and his wife are excited at the prospect of living in Wolvesey.

During recent months we have heard a great deal from senior people in the Diocese about the impossibility, even the undesirability, of the Bishop of Winchester continuing to occupy the historic episcopal palace. Enquiries have been made about the possibilities of finding him a house in the Close. My response to this has always been; (a) there is no house available now, nor likely to be within the forseeable future; and (b) if a bishop is not prepared to accept the challenge of making something of Wolvesey and exploiting its historic links with Hampshire's community life, he ought not to become the Bishop of Winchester. I am therefore very pleased, in fact mightily relieved, to find that Michael Scott-Joynt is rising to the challenge and sees the point of it. This is a good start, and it looks as if he may be able to come either just before or just after Christmas – shortly before my own departure.

Monday 1 July 1995

In his weekly page in the London *Evening Standard* last Friday, A.N.Wilson had a snide comment, intended to be humorous but in fact very nasty, on Michael Scott-Joynt's appointment as Bishop of Winchester. It appeared under the heading 'Holy Hamburgers!' and after saying, falsely, that half a dozen others were approached before they persuaded Scott-Joynt, he went on:

The poor old Church of England is in a parlous state financially. The mismanagement of its portfolio by the financiers of Church House has created a crisis which cannot be solved by bring-and-buy sales and garden fêtes. The Dean and Chapter of Winchester hit on the vulgar idea not long ago of amalgamating with a hamburger shop and offering a Big Mac and Choral Evensong in exchange for a few pounds.

There is of course not a shred of truth in this allegation and, as I have pointed out in a letter to the editor of the *Evening Standard*, had such a proposal ever been put to us it would have been immediately rejected. What is the origin of A.N.Wilson's lie? I suspect that he confused Winchester with Salisbury which, for a brief period, entered into some sort of arrangement with McDonald's hamburger chain, but I am not going to do his research for him and he must find out this for himself.

Will the editor print my letter? I doubt it, for no newspaper will willingly admit to its readers that it prints lies.

Wednesday 5 July 1995

Keith Walker is very keen for us to exhibit in the North Transept, possibly for quite a long time, an extraordinary painting by Paul Storey entitled 'The Virgin in Glory'. It is about ten feet square and at the moment hangs in a London gallery awaiting a purchaser. Keith has supplied me with a catalogue illustration.

Paul Storey is obviously a hugely talented painter who uses acrylic and, apparently, paints his elaborate pictures directly on to canvas without any preliminary sketches. But this offering, though purporting to be religious, seems to me to be entirely devoid of authentic religious content and therefore quite unsuitable for exhibition in any church.

The 'glorified Virgin' is portrayed as a seated figure, naked apart from a curious green hat, with her body split from top to bottom and revealing certain internal organs. Her face expresses intense fear, which is hardly surprising since she is surrounded by a frightening multitude of emaciated bodies and separated human limbs reminiscent of the first photographs of the Auschwitz death camp. The painting seems to owe something to the work of Hieronymus Bosch.

I am prepared to believe that it is a work of considerable distinction and could well find a home in a secular art gallery, where it would be judged on its own merits as a painting. But if any painting is to be hung in a cathedral it must, in my view, illuminate, edify or challenge its viewers in the context of the Christian faith which the building exists to express.

Paul Storey is probably concerned to highlight the chaotic element in modern Western civilization, including its religious dimension, yet I cannot believe this to be something we exist to promote. I have expressed this opinion to Keith, who is sure to be disappointed, but he is free to raise the matter in Chapter and cause certain consternation there.

Now we know why it took so long to find a new Bishop. The secret was disclosed in an anonymous letter I received this morning; postmarked Oxford.

> Perhaps if the Dean had been tactful and informed the world of *his* coming retirement a little earlier, it might have been easier to find a new Bishop – one, for instance, who knew he'd not have to suffer the present incumbent of the Deanery who seems to think it is *his* job to settle in any new Bishop. After all, the Diocese has two very good Suffragans whose first job it is to welcome their new boss.
>
> We might have been blessed with Stephen Sykes had the Dean said he too was going.
>
> We now have the answer to our prayers and hopefully will get a new Dean who is less interested in cordon bleu meals in the Refectory, Bridge and other leisure pursuits, and making money, and rather forgetful that his job is to bring people into the church and tell them the Gospel story, rather than sell them souvenirs.
>
> What of the SERIOUS jobs has the Cathedral tackled and solved – not just welcoming the tourists but evangelizing his own flock into a band of holy men and women?
>
> WORSHIPPER IN THE CATHEDRAL

Well I never! I must incorporate this into my speech at the General Chapter lunch on St Swithun's Day. It should increase the hilarity of the occasion.

We have discussed today the possibility of re-locating the Winchester Bible – our greatest treasure and almost certainly the finest example of Romanesque illuminated manuscript in Europe. At the moment its four volumes are housed in a glass-topped exhibition case in a small room adjacent to Bishop Morley's attractive seventeenth-century library.

At various times we have talked about displaying the Bible in a more dramatic and accessible form in a specially created setting in the wing of the Triforium Gallery now occupied by the Cathedral library and archives. This is perfectly feasible, the only obstacle being the cost, and Tim and Anthea Fortescue have drawn our attention to the commercial advantages of better display and to the new National Lottery as a possible source of funding. Certainly it seems to be the kind of project that might well attract a substantial Lottery grant.

We have therefore asked a small group, meeting under the chairmanship of Keith Walker, to discuss the possibilities with the exhibition designers who created the prize-winning Triforium Gallery, and to produce a costed scheme. There is, however, some resistance to my idea that the scheme should not be simply historic and artistic but also indicate the religious significance of the Bible, in any form, in today's world.

I am sure we must insist on this.

Wednesday 23 August 1995

Jo was rushed into hospital this morning because of a pulmonary embolism which obviously developed, without our realizing it, last evening. She had one of these soon after a knee replacement operation in 1992 and then, as now, the diagnosis was made in good time by the ever-helpful Harry Haysom, a retired surgeon and the Cathedral's Head Sidesman, who lives conveniently in the Close.

Pulmonary embolisms can, apparently, be highly dangerous and, as before, Jo will need to be on anti-coagulant treatment for a long time, perhaps for the rest of her life, to ensure no recurrence. Now she is in a large old-style, medical ward in the Royal County Hospital, which is by no means an ideal location for someone who is also an Alzheimer's victim. She is thoroughly confused by the change of environment and the nursing staff, always hectically busy, are having some difficulty in getting her to keep the anti-coagulent drip in place, for she has no comprehension of what it is for. There is also a problem about her meals, with which she needs some assistance.

If all goes well she will be in hospital for about twelve days, and when she returns home she is bound to be even more disorientated than she was when we came back from France in August.

Wednesday 7 September 1995

Jo is now home again and the Social Services are arranging for her to have nursing care every morning. An excellent District Nurse persuaded me this morning that the amount of care now needed is beyond my capacity to give while I am fully employed as Dean, and in any case it requires a degree of experience. I will, however, continue to get Jo to bed in the evening, as the carers are available only at a very early hour, and Susan and Joan will continue to help with the general housekeeping on two half-days a week. Both are invaluable.

As predicted, Jo will now be on the anti-coagulant Warfarin for the remainder of her life, and I see in this decision the beginning of one of those moral problems that have become common in modern medicine. What steps is it appropriate to take to protect the life of someone in the severe stage of Alzheimer's whose future holds out the absolute certainty of decline into an appalling state of dehumanization? At the moment this difficult question does not have to be faced because Jo is generally happy and still finds some – not much, but some – meaning and purpose in life. But I can see the day coming when the question will be less easily avoided.

Monday 25 September 1995

This morning the General Chapter elected Michael Scott-Joynt as the next Bishop of Winchester. It was a quaint, and in some ways absurd, ceremony, but it has a long history and an attempt by the General Synod to abolish it was overturned by the House of Commons.

We assembled in the Lady Chapel, wearing our cassocks, at 10.30 am and the Chapter Clerk called the names of members of the Chapter to ascertain who was present, or rather who was absent. There were two absentees – Brother Geoffrey, engaged on missionary work in Zimbabwe, and Tony Wilds, the Vicar of Andover, whose mother-in-law died earlier this morning. According to the law, I should, by means of a ferocious statement, have declared both to be contumacious, but I obtained from the Chapter permission to send Tony Wilds a letter of sympathy instead.

I then said a few words about the election, pointing out that it remained an historical anomaly inasmuch as there was only one nomination, made by the Queen, and although the penalties for refusing to elect the nominee had been removed it was in no sense an election in the common understanding of that process. Nonetheless, while the ceremony remained, it provided the senior clergy of the Diocese with an opportunity to express their acceptance of the new Bishop and, if by chance it was felt that a serious mistake had been made over the choice, the Chapter could record publicly its unhappiness. That might be influential.

I then asked the Chapter Clerk to read the *congé d'elire* – a licence granted by the Queen under the Great Seal authorizing the Chapter to hold the election. Next came the Letter Missive indicating the Crown's nomination of Michael Scott-Joynt – expressed again in flowery legalese – and signed by Virginia Bottomley, the Heritage Minister. At this point I felt constrained to ask those present to note that the apostolic ministry of the One, Holy, Catholic and Apostolic Church in this land has now been relegated to the responsibility of the Department for the National Heritage.

Sunday 8 October 1996

Today's annual Law Sunday service, always a fine pageant, was special for two reasons. First, because we had David Jenkins, recently retired from the Bishopric of Durham, as the preacher. His sermon was, as anticipated, about twice as long (thirty-one minutes) as the service would carry and packed full of subordinate clauses demanding the closest attention. In order to cram everything in he delivered the sermon at breakneck speed, which the pulpit microphone simply could not cope with. So a high proportion of the congregation heard only a whirr of words. However, those – mainly in the front rows – who were able to pick up his message were treated to some sparkling stuff, concentrated mainly on an examination and denunciation of the Home Secretary's latest proposals for the toughening of prison policy. I am a great admirer of David and it was a wonderful thing that he was able (by Prime Ministerial mistake, I suspect) to spend the final phase of his ministry as Bishop of Durham, but I just wonder if his quest for audience response, whether this be shock or laughter, has not become a little self-indulgent.

The other unusual factor today was the involvement of one of the resident judges, Charles Mantell, in the frightful trial of Rosemary West now taking place in our Crown Court. The television people wanted to film him reading a lesson during the service, but I consulted him about this and we agreed that he should be filmed only while processing from the Judges' Lodgings to the Cathedral.

At the lunch held in the Lodgings afterwards there was much talk about what has come to be called 'The Trial of the Century', and great sympathy was expressed for Charles Mantell on account of the sordid evidence he is being required to hear – a lot of which even the tabloid newspapers are sparing their readers from reading. Lord Nolan, Lord Ackner and other senior judges who were at the lunch agreed that it was a unique case inasmuch as never before has a woman been charged with murdering her own children after sexually abusing them. The nearest to it was, they thought, Myra Hindley and the 'Moors murders', but the children were not her own and the scale of the tragedy was not quite so horrific. Out of his wig and robes, Charles Mantell is an unpretentious sort of man, but he combines a fine brain with a warm personality and he has been joining us for weekday Evensongs – doubtless to cleanse his mind of some of things he has already heard in the court.

John Holroyd, the Prime Minister's Secretary for Appointments, is spending a couple of days in Winchester gathering information and opinions about the appointment of my successor. He has already done a certain amount of preliminary work, but the fact that the new Bishop has not yet arrived, and in any case knows next to nothing about the Cathedral's needs, is making things complicated, and speedy action is going to be needed if a lengthy interregnum is to be avoided. This was the whole point of announcing my retirement early.

I wasn't at all sure that John Holroyd would wish to see me, but I received a last-minute summons to a meeting with him this afternoon. He began by kindly saying how much everyone seemed to have appreciated my ministry here and all were asking for 'more of the same'. Did I have anyone in mind?

I emphasized the need for the new Dean to be someone with strong cathedral experience, possibly the Dean or Provost of another cathedral. Winchester has developed so rapidly in recent years, and become such a very big organization, that it is not a place where a new Dean might cut his teeth. Strong, experienced leadership is essential.

That said, who is there to meet this requirement? I had trawled the *Church of England Yearbook* and my own memory and found only Wesley Carr, Dean of Bristol, and John Moses, Provost of Chelmsford, to be suitable and likely to be available. Michael Till, Archdeacon of Canterbury and a Canon Residentiary of Canterbury, might fill the bill, but I don't really know him and he may be thought a little too old for this job.

We talked about these people, and John Holroyd wondered if a suffragan bishop might make an interesting and useful appointment. I advised against this, pointing out that the role, and therefore the experience, of a bishop is very different from that of a dean and also that the precedents of translating bishops to deaneries had rarely turned out to be happy ones. I did not express my fear that Winchester might be landed with a problem suffragan bishop who needed to be moved from his present post.

The truth is that the cupboard of candidates for major deaneries is pretty bare, and it is quite likely that St Paul's and Westminster will also have to be filled during the next twelve to eighteen months.

I have had some complaints about the televised version of Ruth Rendell's thriller *Heartstones* which was filmed in and around the Cathedral. The concern, which I share, is not so much about the story itself but rather with the fact that we allowed the programme to be made here.

The ingredients were a supposed Canon, recently widowed, his two daughters, the deceased wife (possibly poisoned), the Cathedral Architect (with whom she had been having an affair), and a number of other Cathedral figures in minor roles. A complicated medley of vision, nightmare, adultery and conflict leads to the 'mystery' of whether one of the Canon's daughters fell accidentally, or was pushed, from the scaffolding high on the Cathedral's West end. The whole thing was a very long way from edifying, indeed it was exceedingly sordid, and not what we are in the business of encouraging.

I was sent part of the script just before the filming in order to vet the content of a sermon to be preached from the Cathedral pulpit. This was unexceptionable and, knowing Ruth Rendell to be a distinguished writer of thrillers, I did not ask for the rest. I think now that I should have done so, but had I vetoed the project the Cathedral's hard-pressed funds would have lost the £25,000 facilities fee.

A number of incidents during the filming were memorable. One morning I was saddened by the sight of a funeral hearse standing outside the Organist's house and of a flower-decked coffin being carried through his front door. Before I could convey my sympathy to the Organist on the unexpected death of a relative I was informed that I had witnessed no more than a scene from *Heartstones*.

The arrangements for the dramatic fall from the Cathedral that led to this 'funeral' were interesting, and at one point alarming. The actress playing the part of the unfortunate daughter fell no more than two or three feet without risk, but a stunt actress fell the whole distance on to a large inflated mattress of the bouncey castle sort. An ambulance, standing by in case of accident, was fortunately not needed.

Then there was an amusing coincidence. The Dean, digging in his garden, stubbed his foot on the spade and uttered an expletive. His wife, standing by, rebuked him: 'You must not say that, Trevor.' Whereupon a local resident with a walk-on part informed the Director of the Christian name of the real Dean. Consternation and the hurried change of the fictitious Dean's name to Charles.

This afternoon I carried out the opening ceremony of the new Cathedral garden named after Thomas Garnier – the nineteenth-century Dean who was also a distinguished horticulturalist. It has been a perfect October day, with a clear blue sky and unbroken sunshine.

There were, I suppose, upwards of 150 at the opening, and clearly the project has aroused a lot of interest and enthusiasm. The layout of the rectangular space reflects the Nave, Quire and Lady Chapel of the Cathedral, and each has been furnished with an appropriate collection of trees, plants and shrubs.

Expert designers and gardeners have had a hand in all this and the total cost of about £40,000 has been met entirely from grants and gifts. Obviously, it will be some years before the garden reaches maturity, but even now it has the capacity to give pleasure, and the views of the Cathedral from the garden are spectacular. It should be an asset to both the Cathedral and the City for many yearts to come and, provided a regular supply of volunteer gardeners can be maintained, ought to be self-financing.

Thursday 9 November 1995

At this week's annual meetings of the congregation, again very well attended and obviously meeting a need, we were able to revert to the arrangement by which every member of the Chapter reports on the work of his department and its future plans. Predictably, the Canons found it difficult to stick to the agreed seven minutes allocated to them, for there is much to report, and the time available for questions from the floor and discussion was again too short.

I dealt with more general items of overall policy, but pointed out that, since I would shortly he handing over the reins of leadership to a new Dean (not yet named), it was not for me to plan or even speculate about the Cathedral's future. I confined myself to saying at the end of the meetings:

> During the last nine years the Dean and Chapter and the large body of people associated with this Cathedral have accomplished quite a lot. But even more remains to be done, because cathedrals are dynamic communities, faced with tremendous opportunities for worship and mission. This is why the prospect of new, more youthful leadership is to be welcomed. The new Dean will be a busy man.
>
> When I came here nine years ago I found a warm, open, welcoming community and this is something we have tried to develop and extend. It

is I believe of the utmost importance that all cathedrals should be warm, open, welcoming communities and that they should fiercely resist any temptation to become exclusive, judgmental or forbidding. Winchester Cathedral is a very large building; it needs, and must always have, a large-hearted community so that others may, through their encounter with the Cathedral, come to experience something of the largeness of God's love. There is your agenda.

Tuesday 12 December 1995

Downing Street has announced the name of my successor – Michael Till, the Archdeacon of Canterbury. The possibility of this became known to me at the end of November when John Holroyd, the Appointments Secretary, telephoned to ask if the Archdeacon and his wife might view the Deanery. This is a new, and surely sensible, development because in the old days there was no possibility of seeing the house until one had actually accepted the appointment. There was, I think, a fear that news of an appointment, or at least the possibility of an appointment, might leak and thus undermine the intense secrecy in which the Crown operates.

Michael Till I barely know. We met once when he came to take a wedding in the Cathedral, and we have spoken a couple of times on the telephone during the last fortnight. On paper he seems all right. Fourteen years at King's College, Cambridge, and nine years as Archdeacon of Canterbury, with a spell as Vicar of Fulham in between, should have given him the right kind of experience, and he ought to be sympathetic towards the Winchester regime. Whether or not he has the creativity necessary for moving the Cathedral into the next phase of its life remains to be seen. I hope so.

Tessa, his wife, who came alone to inspect the Deanery, certainly looks as if she might. I like her and, having enjoyed a large, historic house at Canterbury, the Deanery here is an attraction, not a problem for her. She belongs to Hampshire, having been brought up at South Warnborough where her father, Stephen Roskill, the distinguished naval historian, lived. She is also a niece of Eustace Roskill, the Law Lord, who lives in North Hampshire, so she is in a sense coming home.

They hope to move in next May.

Wednesday 20 December 1995

Last evening I attended my last Turkey Feast – always a special occasion in the calendar when the Dean and Chapter entertain the Choristers. It goes

223

back to the early 1930s and was initiated by the then Dean, Gordon Selwyn, who, I believe, copied it from King's College, Cambridge.

The Christmas meal is served in the festively decorated Prior's Hall, in the Deanery, and the Choristers sing a Latin Grace which I always find unusually moving. Everyone then tucks in, the Dean makes a short speech thanking the boys for their contribution to the Cathedral's life and wishing them a happy Christmas. The 'fishing game' follows and involves cardboard cut-out fishes, with rings attached, which are strewn about the floor of the Deanery entrance hall. The boys, equipped with hooks on long strings, endeavour from the lofty first-floor landing to catch and haul up the numbered fish. The one with the best catch wins the prize.

Meanwhile the Prior's Hall has been cleared of tables to allow a conjuror to perform and after the tricks comes the 'Waterloo Cup' – a coin-passing game which arouses intense rivalry between the Decani and Cantoris section of the Choir. The evening ends with the Head Chorister making a speech of thanks to the Dean and Chapter.

Simple, now a tradition, and something that former Choristers, some in their seventies, always recall vividly and nostalgically.

1996

Today's Enthronement of Michael Scott-Joynt as Bishop of Winchester was, as intended, a spectacular occasion and, thanks to the Precentor's diligent preparations and careful rehearsal yesterday, went without a hitch. Michael's great height makes him an impressive figure and he has a friendly smile that suggests a caring pastor.

Fortunately, the 'Gay Rights' demonstration for which we had been warned to be prepared did not materialize, and the problems with a few Chorister parents, who objected to our recalling the boys from their Christmas holiday, were ironed out. It is interesting that involvement in the Enthronement of a Bishop of Winchester, which would at one time have seemed an honour and a privilege, is now regarded by some as a tiresome intrusion on a ski-ing holiday.

The Dean has a large part in an Enthronement and I am glad that I had the opportunity – only just – of playing it during my time here. An unusual, probably unique, coincidence was created by the fact that the Archdeacon of Canterbury, who actually installed the new Bishop, is to be the next Dean of Winchester. I recognized this by greeting him officially at the beginning of the service as 'Mr Archdeacon and Mr Dean-designate' and later there was the sight of the present and future Deans conducting the Bishop to the Throne. When last did an Archdeacon of Canterbury become the Dean of a cathedral in which he had previously installed its new Bishop?

There is great relief that the new Bishop is now here and also some confidence that a very good appointment has been made.

Thursday 1 February 1996

At today's Chapter Meeting there was excellent news on the financial front, which is very satisfying for someone who is about to leave office. The forecast surplus of £33,000 has turned out at £72,000. This is due partly to increased investment income and also to legacies which, in the nature of things, cannot be accurately forecast. Donations at the Cathedral entrance have increased by 40%, rather than the 50% hoped for when we installed the desk. This is disappointing, but without the 40% increase our financial position would have been precarious and the income from this source will become increasingly important.

Overall, the present position is much healthier than it has been for several years, but vigilance will always be necessary in a cathedral that attempts so much but has only limited, and often uncertain, resources.

Sunday 11 February 1996

The Cathedral was crowded for my official Farewell this afternoon. I hate events of this sort when the focus of attention is so personal and would have much preferred to slip away quietly after a normal weekday Evensong. But of course this isn't possible, partly because there needs to be a clear and decisive end to a leadership ministry, and partly because a community needs a special occasion for the severing of the personal link.

Choral Evensong, which I suppose I am going to miss most, was as lovely as ever, and I preached on the text 'Remember Jesus Christ, born of the seed of David, risen from the dead according to my gospel' (II Timothy 2.8). Having made the point that today is for me inevitably a day of memories, marking as it does not only the end of my ministry in Winchester but also the end of my ministry in the full-time service of the church extending over almost forty-five years, I went on to assert that the primary demand on the Christian memory is not on priests and people and places, but on Jesus Christ, the pioneer and perfecter of our faith.

So the rest of the sermon consisted of an exposition of the faith that has informed my ministry, and I ended by saying that the Christian remembrance of Jesus is a dynamic, contemporary remembrance, not merely an historical remembrance, and that our remembrance of him is also a subversive remembrance inasmuch as it constitutes a most powerful challenge to the way things are both in our personal lives and in the communities to which we belong.

Then came the speeches and presentation. Mary Fagan, the Lord Lieutenant, who has been one of my strongest and most understanding supporters, spoke warmly of my work in the County and Diocese, and Keith Walker, in what seemed to me to be a somewhat curious speech, referred to my close attention to detail in every aspect of the Cathedral's life. The envelope he handed over contained a cheque for an embarrassingly large amount contributed by the Cathedral communitiy.

In my response I said that I was grateful, not only for what had been said and for the gift, but for many other things – for the opportunity to have been Dean of Winchester, for all that I inherited when I came here, for the regular round of worship offered in the Cathedral day by day to the very highest standard, for the great army of people who express their love for the Cathedral by serving its life either on the staff or in a multitude of volunteer tasks, and 'for your support, your friendship, your love, your generosity and in recent years your sensitive understanding of Jo's health problems and your great kindness in helping her, and me, to cope with them. We owe you more than we can say.'

Afterwards wine was served and another hour passed before I shook the last hand and said the last Goodbye. The process of departing, with its many parties, dinners, lunches and presentations, has been like one of those sevenfold Amens that goes on and on and seems as if it will never end. But eventually it does, and so has my ministry at Winchester, though there are a few clearing up matters to attend to, including a final Chapter Meeting, before I actually depart.

Thursday 29 February 1996

Presiding over a Chapter Meeting is not quite the most exciting way of spending the morning of one's final day as Dean, but I was very happy that the diary fell this way, mainly I suppose because I was not keen to have a blank day with time for meditation on my imminent departure, but also because it seems important to emphasize the 'business as usual' aspect of my going.

We learned with some surprise that Salisbury is no longer pressing its claim that its girls' choir should participate fully in the Southern Cathedrals' Festival, and we discussed the proper place of the Prime Minister's Appointments Secretary at the installation of my successor. It has, it seems, become customary for this official to attend installations and present new deans on behalf of the Crown. No one can pretend that this is the most important problem now facing the English cathedrals, but it raised a nice constitutional point of whether the Crown is appropriately represented by a member of the Prime Minister's staff. One problem I shall not have to deal with.

At the end of the meeting Richard Alexander, the Chapter Clerk, who has been wonderfully supportive throughout my nine years here, spoke generously of my ministry and, after drinking some rather good champagne, we departed.

During the next fortnight I must complete the gargantuan task of reducing the furnishings of this vast Deanery to a size suitable for a small, three-bedroomed house in Romsey. It will be a relief to see the back of most of the stuff.

Index